TAKING SEX .

CARLETON CONTEMPORARIES

A series of books designed to stimulate informed discussion of current and controversial issues in Canada, and to improve the two-way flow of ideas between people and government.

TAKING
SEX INTO
ACCOUNT:

The Policy Consequences
of Sexist Research

EDITED BY

JILL McCALLA VICKERS

CARLETON UNIVERSITY PRESS
OTTAWA, CANADA

"Women, The Forgotten Housing Consumers"
by Cassie Doyle and Janet McClain © Authors

ISBN 0-88629-020-1 (paperback)

Cover/Design: Gallant Graphiste, Ottawa

ACKNOWLEDGEMENTS

Carleton University Press gratefully acknowledges the support extended to its publishing program by the Canada Council and the Ontario Arts Council.

This book has been published with the help of a grant from the Canadian Research Institute for the Advancement of Women (CRIAW), using funds provided by the Social Sciences and Humanities Research Council of Canada and the Women's Program of the Secretary of State.

Canadian Cataloguing in Publication Data

Main entry under title:
  Taking sex into account

(A Carleton contemporary)
Includes index.
ISBN 0-88629-020-1

1. Social sciences—Research.   2. Sexism.
3. Public policy.   I. Vickers, Jill, 1942-
II. Series.

HQ1233.T34   1984   300'.7'2   C84-090213-1

Distributed by:

Oxford University Press Canada
70 Wynford Drive
DON MILLS, Ontario, Canada, M3C 1J9
(416) 441-2941

Printed and bound in Canada.

Table of Contents

PREFACE

The Canadian Research Institute for the Advancement of Women/Institut canadien de recherches pour l'avancement de la femme is happy to present this collection of papers on "Sexism in Research and its Policy Implications", the theme of our 1982 annual conference, held November 19-21 in Ottawa.

CRIAW/ICRAF was founded in 1976 with a very specific mandate: to encourage, co-ordinate and communicate research into women's experience, and thus promote the advancement of women. Much of our effort has focussed on the consolidation of organizational structures, the development of research tools and the establishment of programs and projects such as the annual conference. We have always considered the conferences to be an important means of communicating feminist research results.

Now, it is true that many women's conferences are held each year. Women scholars meet within their own fields of research to share their findings, forcing their own disciplines to begin the integration of women's experience into the web of their theories and general outlook. Unfortunately, scholars meet mainly during the Learned Societies, independently at different times, and thus opportunities to share our knowledge and encourage each other in our work are accessible primarily to those working in any particular discipline.

We think that CRIAW/ICRAF, through its conference, can play a useful role in offering an interdisciplinary platform, not only to scholars but also to women's groups and non-academic researchers. Also, in treating themes such as "Sexism in Research and its Policy Implications", we feel CRIAW/ICRAF can reach all disciplines, for sexism is rampant in research of all kinds, whether it be conducted in government, in business or in academic halls.

It is therefore gratifying to CRIAW/ICRAF that, with the help of Carleton University Press, we are able to diffuse these papers to a wider public, and hence further promote the welfare of women.

Corinne Gallant
President, CRIAW/ICRAF
1982-83

ACKNOWLEDGEMENTS

Many people contributed in various ways to the production of this volume, and I would like to express my thanks for their support, services and assistance.

The conference would not have been the success that it was — indeed, it would not have been possible — without the members of the conference co-ordinating committee, most of whom belong to the CRIAW Ottawa chapter: Caroline Andrew, Katie Cooke, Ann Denis, Hélène Doyon, Barb Freeman, Pat Finn, Gabrielle Goliger, Deborah Gorham, Johanna Hickey, Jean Higginson, Pat Masters, Andrea Nugent, Diana Pederson, Marion Porter, Denise Roberge, Patricia Smart, Elizabeth Thomas and Judith Wouk. Thanks are also due to the many volunteers who worked both in front of and behind the scenes to ensure that all went well.

After the conference drew to a close, the CRIAW Publications Committee undertook responsibility for ensuring that the proceedings achieved printed form. Committee members Micheline Dumont, Margrit Eichler, Corinne Gallant, June Gow, Anne Hart, Lyse Huot, Willadean Leo, Thelma McCormack and Gerry McPherson have worked consistently towards their goal, and can feel a sense of achievement and satisfaction on viewing the fruit of their efforts.

Willadean Leo copy-edited the papers and proof-read the word processed version of the text. She also kept track of picky details, and was responsible for most of the liaison and co-ordination with the authors, the Publications Committee and Carleton University Press. The other members of the CRIAW national office staff — Anne Carter, Lyse Huot, Thérèse Saintonge and Aisla Thomson — provided valuable support services and assistance.

Donna Jowett developed the index, and Louise Gallant created the cover design.

For the Carleton University Press, Michael Gnarowski, Naomi Griffiths and Sandy Nolan have been particularly involved in the publication of the volume.

Finally, I would like to acknowledge the role of the Social Sciences and Humanities Research Council of Canada, which provided financial assistance both to the conference and to the production of this volume; and the Women's Program, Department of the Secretary of State, which also gave financial support.

— Jill McCalla Vickers

Taking Sex into Account:
The Policy Consequences of Sexist
Research

Introduction

JILL McCALLA VICKERS

The papers contained in this volume represent part of the proceedings of the Conference "Sexism in Research and its Policy Implications" sponsored by the Canadian Research Institute for the Advancement of Women and held in Ottawa, November, 1982.

The Problem Outlined

The aim of this collection of papers is to present to the Canadian academic community a "state of the art" survey of a problem which, until recently, was invisible to most and had no name. Certainly "sexism" in the world at large has been a named problem visible to the women's movement and, increasingly, to the male domain of agenda-setters and policy makers for the past two decades. Its roots in our tools of thinking have, however, been mostly hidden and unexplored. The academic community, therefore, has been surprisingly untouched by the challenges presented by feminist scholarship and methodology. And yet, to borrow Helen Robert's beautiful opening salvo in **Doing Feminist Research,** "It must be clear to even the most traditional of male scholars that we can no longer follow Evans Pritchard's advice to 'behave like a gentleman, keep off the women, take quinine daily and play it by ear'." [1] The terms "gentleman" and "scholar" no longer march together in quite the same game of "snap" as salt and pepper or bacon and eggs.

And yet, with the best will in the world, most male scholars (and some female scholars as well) remain bemused about just what sexism in research is, why it is troublesome, and what they can reasonably be expected to do about it.

Recent works such as Dale Spender (ed.) **Men's Studies Modified**[2] and Miles and Finn (eds.) **Feminism in Canada**[3] have illustrated the growing volume and strength of feminist research in many disciplines. They also document, however, the sadly slight impact that this new body of knowledge has had on what Spender calls "men's studies" — the dominant, male, respectable academic disciplines. And yet the question of how best to achieve an impact to the end of creating a truly human knowledge which transcends sexism has only begun to be explored. As Chaviva Hosek has argued about the new knowledge, "You don't just say 'we've left out a section, let's stick it on with crazy glue'."[4] Nonetheless, although it is clear that a "crazy glue" approach is inadequate, the development of ways of taking sex into account involves rather more than consciousness of the problem and good will, important though each of these ingredients is.

Eradicating sexism in research and the policy consequences which ensue from such research involves learning how and when to take sex "into account" as a variable. This process, however, is not as straightforward as it may appear initially. Partly, this reflects a lack of clarity in our understanding of the meaning of "equality" and "equal treatment".[5] To many people, equality means treating all people in the same way, regardless of differences in such things as sex or race. In this context, therefore, women have demanded, for example, sex-blind hiring policies, and have considered policies which take a prospective employee's sex "into account" to be sexist. By contrast, we have *at the same time* demanded maternity leave, child-care facilities, protection from sexual harassment, etc., all of which reflect our special needs as female workers. That is, we consider it "sexist" in many circumstances when our sex is *not* taken into account. A similar problem prevails in research. As a number of the papers in this volume illustrate, knowing when and how to take sex into account is the key to developing a truly human knowledge on which to rest our understanding and from which to gain our policy insights.

The problem of taking sex into account, however, strikes rather more deeply at the established ways of the academic venture than any of us initially imagined.[6] For example, although the largely anglophone group represented in this volume addressed the issue of sexism in the languages we use to express our research questions and findings, we were made aware of the infinitely greater complexity of this aspect of the problem in the French language. Nor are "tried and true" methodologies immune to scrutiny and challenge. In fact, as Margrit Eichler puts it in her chapter, it is now apparent that *really* taking sex into account would amount, in effect, "to a Copernican revolution in scholarship." This volume represents the first serious attempt to outline the nature of sexism in research in the Canadian context and its implications in terms of wasteful and misguided policies. It is a first step in that "Copernican revolution in scholarship" so crucial to women and men alike.

The Design of This Volume

The papers which follow trace the development of concern about sexism in research in Canada from an early preoccupation with the fact that women were being ignored or were invisible in much research, to a focus on the biased assumptions and conclusions about women evident in much male-stream research employed to guide policy decisions. This development illustrates the growing strength and confidence of the feminist research community in Canada; the connections drawn by feminist activists between biased research and unsuccessful policies of social intervention; and the shift in orientation among feminist researchers from short-term research objectives (the documenting of specific examples of discrimination) to the long-term objective of revealing the structures which perpetuate male dominance.

Eichler, in the lead chapter "Sexism in Research and Its Policy Implications" (the text of the conference's opening address), outlines four points in which sexism may enter the research process: (1) who can participate and in what capacity; (2) the conditions under which research is conducted; (3) the research process itself; and (4) how results get reported and published (or not published) and how they are received. Her main focus (and the main focus of this volume), is however, on the ways in which sexism can enter the research process itself.

Eichler identifies five ways:
1. through the use of sexist language;
2. through the use of sexist concepts;
3. by taking an androcentric perspective;
4. through the use of a sexist methodology;
5. through a sexist interpretation of results.

The articles which follow Eichler's state-of-the-art survey are organized in three sections:
1. Sexism in Language;
2. What is Sexism in Research?
3. The Policy Consequences of Sexism in Research.

While not all of the issues raised by Eichler are pursued, the major elements are developed in depth.

Sexism in Language: Does it Matter?

Perhaps no area of feminist activity has been as controversial as the attempt to deal with language which we think (or suspect or know) structures our experience and knowledge of the world in a sexist way. Responses to our efforts to change language bring derision as often as comprehension. "My dear, you're far too sensible to care if you're called 'Chairman'." Symptomatically, the chief press reaction to the Conference at which these papers were presented was to pick up on the suggestion that the NAME of the Museum of MAN be changed. "Thought-police", the editorial writers cried. And yet, if, as the "gentlemen" of the press suggested, the issue is so trivial, then why the storm of protest about changing one small name which makes even some women feel uncomfortable and excluded?

The papers in this section deal with the issue at two quite different levels. The first "Naming the World: Consciousness in a Patriarchal Iceberg" is by a team of two women from the University of Alberta. Angéline Martel and Linda Peterat write about the sexism embodied in both the French and English languages which are "evident through the lexicon, morphology and syntax", and show how it perpetuates the dominant patriarchal ideology. They argue that "Language shapes our consciousness and lets live through us a particular view of the world." Not content with analysis, however, they insist that "For feminists, the question is what do we do about the power which language commands of our lives?" In a paper filled with poetic and inventive language, they examine "the essential aspects of making language our own, of listening to the primordial silence and the language of our daughters." The paper does not just "tell us"; it shows us how to create transformative language and consciousness.

The second paper in this section deals with the issues from the point of view of educational policy. By Donald Power, Marlene Stewart and Viola Nikkila from Lakehead University, "Sexism in Language in the Curriculum of Ontario Schools: The Case of 'Man in Society' " presents the results of their survey designed to investigate the question "Do people consider the title of the Ministry guideline 'Man in Society' to be sexist?" The paper presents the sorts of argument given by those who felt that the guideline was sexist (178) and those who felt that it was not (51). By an analysis of these perceptions, the authors illustrate the nature of the debate concerning the perceived impact of language on consciousness in learning and research.

Whereas in the paper by Martel and Peterat the assumption is made that language is fundamental to the issues raised by sexism, many of the survey's respondents failed to perceive the issue as important at all. In particular, their results suggest that many younger women may be avoiding the issues raised by sexism in language because they fear that exposing their concerns will provoke conflict and derision. In short, this paper illustrates in detail how fiercely political the "trivial" issues of sexist language are.

Certainly, this is an area in which debate will continue along the lines outlined by the two papers. Demands now being made on the national granting councils, for example, to encourage the use of non-sexist language in the research that they fund have provoked reactions out of proportion to the "trivial" nature many presume the issue to have.

What is Sexism in Research?

A fundamental problem we face is identifying what we mean by "sexism" in research. As some of Eichler's illustrations demonstrate, it is sometimes "sexist" NOT to take sex into account. There is no single, simple test which can be applied and provide a clear warning that we have erred, like litmus paper changing colour.

The first paper deals with the very difficult nature/nurture, biology/socialization debate by examining one aspect of the question of what is biologically caused in sex/gender and what is not. This paper deals with biosocial explanations of female athleticism in an effort to clarify the question: When is it "sexist" (and when is it not) to take sex into account because it is a biological category? The paper "Females, Sport, and Biosocial Explanations" by M. Ann Hall from the University of Alberta, examines "the possibilities for a biosocial explanation of female athleticism because, in arguing for sex equality in sport, we simply cannot ignore biology." The author first examines "the evidence for a hormonal basis to sexually dimorphic behaviour arguing that this evidence is not nearly as unequivocal as it might initially appear to be and that there are alternative explanations for some of the findings." She then goes on to show "that despite these problems insightful research in behavioral endocrinology and neuroendocrinology cannot be dismissed in the same way that it is possible to discredit the biological determinism of sociobiology." While arguing that we should not posit "some form of biological essentialism in our attempts to overcome cultural determinism", the author concludes that "biological processes influence and interact with our social situation, and to recognize this in no way concedes the case to . . . biological essentialism."

The second paper in this section deals with the issues from a distinctly different perspective. By Mary O'Brien, from the Ontario Institute for Studies in Education in Toronto, "Hegemony and Superstructure: A Feminist Critique of Neo-Marxism" takes the issue of how to "take sex into account" into the lions' den of neo-marxist thought and scholarship. O'Brien argues that, within neo-marxism, which she understands as "The attempt to rescue Marxist understanding of the state from the crude pincers of economism and reductionism. . .", sexism persists in the sense that it does not know how to "take sex into account". In an examination of hegemony theory developed out of Gramsci's thought, she concludes that it fails because "Gramsci has no notion of patriarchal hegemony and the reality of gender conflict." From the basis of her original theoretical position which sees "Patriarchy [as] a set of social relations . . . grounded in the process of reproduction", she demonstrates the sort of major revision of neo-marxist theory required to ground it in the human facts of sexuality and reproduction.

The third paper in this section, "Sexism in Research: Anthropological Perspectives", by Annamma Joy of Concordia University in Montreal, raises the complex issue of the meaning and impact of "male bias" in the discipline of anthropology. Using Eichler's characterization of the nature of sexist science, Joy discusses the waves of the debate concerning male bias within anthropology and reveals the complexity of the issues of theory, methodology and language raised by the controversy. Joy argues that a major value of the debate concerning male bias in anthropology has been the stimulation of fresh perspectives: "What is most impressive about this literature is the overwhelming number of specific testable questions it has produced."

The final paper in this section, "Sexism in Psychological

Research'' by Cheryl Malmo, explores in detail the themes outlined by Eichler in the key discipline of psychology. Using examples primarily drawn from behavioral psychology, Malmo shows how ''The *description* of the images and roles [about women] becomes a *prescription* for behaviour.'' Deeply concerned with the effects of sexist bias in her discipline, Malmo argues that ''. . . we must find ways to bridge the gap between researchers and the people being researched, so that the power of our knowledge can be shared by all.''

The Policy Consequences of Sexist Research

A series of papers is presented in this section which take the debate into substantive policy areas of importance both to women's lives and to society in general. Each paper illustrates the connection between sexist research and policy initiatives which either fail or are counterproductive. In addition, most of the authors suggest positive ways in which research could be re-oriented to guide policy formulation more effectively.

The first paper, ''Labour Market Discrimination and Policy Options'' by Barbara Cameron of York University, deals with the varied literature which attempts to explain sex discrimination in the labour market and which proposes conflicting views of the policies which would eliminate it. As Cameron states, ''How one evaluates affirmative action programmes and other policies directed at eliminating sex discrimination in the labour market depends on one's analysis of the causes of that discrimination.'' In the development of her theme, Cameron outlines the biases evident in the approach of the Fraser Institute to the issues. She shows that ''The neo-classical economic explanations of labour market discrimination . . . do not address seriously the problem of the sex-typing of occupations, the female job ghettos.'' She then examines feminist attempts to explain sex discrimination in the labour market, although she is also critical of the overdependence on affirmative action as a policy remedy, seeing it as more effective in some economic sectors than in others. In general, she concludes that the policy options presented by the

Fraser Institute *et al.* will fail to eliminate sex discrimination in the labour force because their explanations for its causes do not "take sex into account" in an effective way.

The second paper in this section, "Research on Child Abuse in Liberal Patriarchy", by Kathleen Lahey, Professor of Law at the University of Windsor, examines research on child abuse from the perspective of radical feminism. In addition to exploring the status and condition of the child from both patriarchal and feminist perspectives, Lahey reviews legal attitudes towards child abuse. For example, she finds that "The traditional legal treatment of assault and battery of children reflects the belief that children are mere property and can be disciplined in any way necessary to conform their conduct to their parents' expectations or desires." She shows how the doctrine of intra-family tort immunity precludes a child from civil remedies against a battering parent, and how the law sanctions "discipline" of a child by anyone entrusted to care for her/him, including teachers, siblings and babysitters. In the final sections, she shows how "The existence of each type of child abuse can be traced back to the patriarchal organization of society." She also demonstrates the failure of the research on child abuse to make links between the abuse of women and the abuse of children — often by women. Finally, she demonstrates how the bias in both law and research render useless most policy initiatives to protect children from abuse.

In the third paper, "Sexism in Social Science Research on Aging" by Elinor Burwell of Carleton University, the author demonstrates that "Bias is present [in research on aging] in subject selection, in methodology, in interpretation of findings, and in the nature of topics investigated, or omitted from investigation." She finds that "The failure to acknowledge the fact that research on older women has been minimal, the callous disregard of the present poor quality of life of many older women, and the ignoring of the implications of the suggested funding priorities for the lives of older women in the future, all add up to sexism." While Burwell discovers that there has been some progress in the elimination of sexist language in the field, she finds little recognition of the fact that aging women have different experiences and needs than aging men, and that masculine models of the human experience obscure those experiences and needs.

The fourth paper, "Sexism in Policy Relating to Welfare Fraud" by Marion Porter and Joan Gullen of Ottawa, deals with the sexist notions which form the basis for the nature of welfare and welfare relationships in Ontario. In particular, the sexist assumptions underlying the administration of welfare policy are examined. The paper also explores the "criminality" of women who receive welfare and break the "man-in-the-house" rule. In this paper, perhaps more clearly than in any other, the tragic results of policies based on sexist research are shown.

The fifth paper, "Women, The Forgotten Housing Consumers" by Cassie Doyle and Janet McClain of the Canadian Council on Social Development, deals with the assumption in the research on housing needs that women are not primary consumers of housing. The authors point out the assumptions that men, not women, would continue to be the major housing consumers "were based on a static view of the position of women and sex bias which, to some extent, allowed the primarily male group of housing forecasters to overlook some fairly obvious facts and trends." Following a survey of the housing policy literature, the authors also take feminist research to task for ignoring housing as a "women's issue". They conclude that issues related to the secure access to good shelter and related to the use of space must become a major target for non-sexist research.

The final paper in this section, "Male-Dominated Criminology: Implications of Women in Correctional Institutions", by Maureen Baker of Scarborough College at the University of Toronto, deals with the policy effects of the fact that women are the "invisible actors and victims of crime". Baker shows that, in the case of criminology, sex has always been "taken into account" in the sense that "women's criminality has been perceived as fundamentally different from that of men." Baker shows how this assumption has affected policies — both legal and administrative — dealing with women criminals. In many ways, then, this paper is a mirror image of the sexism problem. In some of the fields explored, sexism involved women's invisibility or the assumption that male and female experience was the same. In criminology, Baker shows the reverse case and demonstrates how it has also led to policies which do not work because sex was not understood as an independent variable in the research process.

Footnotes

1. Helen Roberts (ed.), *Doing Feminist Research* (Routledge and Kegan Paul, London, 1981), p. 1.
2. Dale Spender (ed.), *Men's Studies Modified* (Permagon Press, Oxford, 1981).
3. Angela Miles and Geraldine Finn (eds.), *Feminism in Canada: From Pressure to Politics* (Black Rose Books, Montréal, 1982).
4. Quote in Sarah Murdoch, "We're not here for Rap Sessions", *Canadian Women's Studies/les cahiers de la femme*, Vol. 3, No. 1, 1981, p. 53.
5. See J.M. Vickers, "Major Equality Issues of the Eighties", *Canadian Human Rights Yearbook,* (Carswell, Toronto, 1983) pp. 47-72 for a full discussion of the issues involved.
6. See J.M. Vickers, "Memoirs of an Ontological Exile: The Methodological Rebellions of Feminist Research" in Miles and Finn, *Feminism in Canada*, pp. 27-46 for a fuller discussion.

Sexism in Research and Its Policy Implications

Sexism in Research and Its Policy Implications

MARGRIT EICHLER

Introduction

As an opener to our consideration of sexism in research and its policy consequences, I would like to start out by telling you a story about Beatrix Potter.

We probably all know Beatrix Potter as the creator of Peter Rabbit. Most of us, however, probably do not know that Beatrix Potter was a gifted natural scientist before she turned to writing and illustrating children's books. She has a passionate love for fungi, and at one point in her life desired nothing more than to observe and paint the approximately 40,000 species of fungi which were known at the time.

> During her teens and twenties, Beatrix Potter's search for fungi took her out of doors each day that weather permitted. Nothing discouraged her, not even the average of seventy insect bites ("suspect spiders" [she wrote in her diary]), that she received on each search. What mattered was climbing over a hedge, going into a wood, and finding a "paradise of funguses". Even danger of getting lost in the depth of a black fir forest did not deter her from plunging through the bracken until she found the yellow *Peziza* in the moss of the gigantic *Cortinarius* (Gilpatrick, 1972:41).

The area in which she broke new theoretical ground was with respect to lichens. Beatrix Potter was the first person in England to affirm "that the colorful patches growing on trees, fences, tombs, and rocks are actually a merging of two discrete plants —

17

an alga and a fungus — to make a third kind of plant, a lichen, which in function and longevity was different from either of the two originators'' (Gilpatrick, 1972:41).

After being consistently set down, in the most galling manner, while trying to attract the attention of the scientific noteworthies of her time, at least to such a degree that she could discuss her theory with them, she received some help and support from her uncle, Sir Henry E. Roscoe, a chemist who had been knighted for his scientific contributions. He encouraged her to write a paper on her theory for presentation at the most prestigious scientific society of the time, the Linnean Society. On April 1, 1897, the paper, entitled ''On the Germination of the Spores of Agaricineae'' was read at the Linnean Society — by a man, George Massee, not by Beatrix Potter, since only men were allowed to attend the meetings of the society. Indeed, for that same reason, Beatrix Potter was not even present when the paper was read (Gilpatrick, 1972:94-95).

The paper was never published, and two years after Potter had asked for its return she gave up the study of spores to write and illustrate children's books, which, after some initial set-backs, became an enormously successful endeavour.

Between that time and today some significant progress has been made. Today, women present papers at scientific association meetings and often their research results do get published. Nevertheless, we have barely started to address the problem of sexism in research, much less to correct it.

I started out with the example of Beatrix Potter to illustrate that there are several dimensions to the problem of sexism in research, and to place the focus of my own remarks into a wider context.

As a minimum, we can identify four entry points for sexism into the research process, namely:

(1) the issue of who can participate in the research process in what capacity;

(2) closely associated with (1), the conditions under which research is conducted;

(3) the research process itself; and

(4) how research results get reported and published (or not published) and how they are received.

Beatrix Potter's story provides a poignant example of how women used to be excluded from the research process. Had she been a man, a dedication such as hers, combined with her brilliant ability to observe and theorize, would almost certainly have led to public recognition and rewards in her field of study, and she (had she been a he) would very likely have been held up as a shining example to the next generation of scientists. As it was, she became famous for writing children's books.

While women today are participants in the research process (although in fewer numbers than men), the conditions under which we do participate are very often less than optimal. Even today, women are greatly underrepresented in the prestigious research organizations which conduct much of our research and, where they are represented, they tend to have junior rather than senior level appointments.

Nevertheless, women have very likely participated in the creation of knowledge to a much greater degree than we tend to realize. Consider, for instance, the many dedications and acknowledgements that husbands have written into the prefaces of their books, in which they thank their wives for what seem to be very substantial contributions to the final product. It is interesting to note that the number of books co-authored by husband-wife teams has increased in the 1970s. I suspect that this does not denote a real departure from previous practice, but merely a more appropriate reflection of what has been going on all the time. There is also the proverb ''Behind every great man there is a great women'', to which one of my male colleagues added, when giving credit to the contributions his wife had made to *his* career (at the expense of *hers*): ''And in front of every great woman there is a man — in her way.''

At this point, however, we will focus neither on who does the research, whether women or men, nor on the circumstances under which research is performed (for a few contemporary descriptions of examples, see Hanmer and Leonard, 1980, or Woodward and Chisholm, 1981), nor on the roadblocks inherent in publishing (see

Spender, 1981), but on the research process itself. There *are* a few men who manage to do non-sexist research, and there *are* women who do fall into the trap of doing sexist research, so that we are not talking about a straight sex balance issue. It is important to realize, however, that we can start to define the outlines of the gigantic task that remains to be done in order to rid the research process of sexism only because there has been already some slight advance in integrating women into the research endeavour. For as long as research remained an almost exclusively male activity, carried out by men in male-dominated institutions funded by male-dominated organizations for doing research on male-defined issues, we could not even perceive the need for what amounts, in effect, to a Copernican revolution in scholarship. Some of you may think that the historical description I just gave of the collective research endeavour is a pretty good description of research today. However, I would like to remind you that there are now organizations such as the Canadian Research Institute for the Advancement of Women, the Canadian Women's Studies Association, and others, as well as special conferences, courses, programmes, publications, etc. which are starting to make the point that research is (and should be) carried out by members of both sexes.

Sexism, then, can enter the research process in at least five ways.

   I. through the use of sexist language,
  II. through the use of sexist concepts,
 III. by taking an androcentric perspective,
  IV. through the use of a sexist methodology, and finally,
   V. through a sexist interpretation of results.

Often, all five types of sexism go together, but any one of them suffices to make a particular piece of research sexist. We will now look at these five ways in which sexism can enter the research process in more detail.

Sexist Language

Most research is carried out through the medium of language.

If the language used is inexact, the results will also be inexact. Both English and French are profoundly sexist languages, and to the degree that language utilized in scientific discourse is sexist, it constitutes an improper medium.

Sexism in language takes a variety of forms, the most easily identifiable one of which is the use of male terms as generic terms. (For a discussion of some of the other problems as well, see Spender, 1980.) For instance, "he" is utilized to mean "he and she" — but also sometimes only "he". "Man" is utilized to refer to "women and men", but also sometimes only to "men". Occupational and positional titles, such as chairman, policeman, salesman, fisherman, etc., are used to indicate males and females playing such roles — but also sometimes only males playing such roles.

There are, then, two issues which concern us here. The first one is that sexist language is highly confused and confusing. In itself, this should be a sufficient reason to rule out totally the use of any sexist language in scientific discourse. Let me give you, in non-sexual terms, an analogy to the use of sexist language which employs male terms to make sex specific as well as generic statements.

Let us assume that we live in a society which discriminates against left-handed people as well as against anything that is left, and that, therefore, we have evolved a language structure in which "right" is considered a generic directional term which subsumes in itself "left" as well as "right". When receiving traffic directions — for instance, to reach Main Street, you turn right at the second corner, then right at the third corner and right again at the next corner — we could never be sure whether we were supposed to turn right, right and right, or perhaps left, right and right, or right, left and left, etc. Obviously, there would be a number of difficulties in reaching a destination if we were confined to using such a confusing language. Yet that is exactly the situation in which we find ourselves with respect to research concerning humans and other animals, where we can never be sure whether statements are in fact applicable to all humans (or monkeys, or rats), or only to males.

The other issue in sexist language is that we have, by now, some empirical evidence that the use of so-called generic male terms does not evoke gender neutral images most of the time for most of the people, but, rather, sex specific images. In reviewing 14 empirical studies on this question, Silveira (1980:170) has noted that:

> In all 14 studies the GM [generic male] terms caused more male-biased responses than did the more neutral wording. Thus, pictures illustrating generic *man* contained more males than pictures illustrating *people*. Characters referred to as generic — *man, he,* or *his* were given a male identity more often than characters referred to as *persons, their, he or she* or *his or her*.

In one of these studies, for example, students were asked to select pictures they would use to represent chapters in an introductory sociology textbook. Depending on whether they had been told to illustrate "Social Man" or "Society", "Urban Man" or "Urban Life", etc., students tended to provide significantly more pictures of males in the cases in which male terms had been used than where non-sex specific terms had been used (Schneider and Hacker, 1973).

The fact that so-called generic male terms are not adequate for conveying generic meanings is illustrated by syllogisms in which the substitution of a sex specific term indicates that the statement was not generic to begin with.

For instance, there is the well-known syllogism:

All men are mortal.

Socrates is a man.

Therefore, Socrates is mortal.

It is usually regarded as a generic statement applying to all people. If we introduce a gender specific example, namely a particular man, there is no conflict. However, if we introduce another gender specific example, namely, a particular woman, the statement is perceived as non-sensical. Thus, we would not experience the following syllogism as making any sense:

All men are mortal.

Sophia is a man.

Therefore, Sophia is mortal.

Moulton (1981), from whose work this example is taken, provides a non-sexual analogy by creating another non-sensical syllogism using a term with a double meaning in two different contexts:

All banks are closed on Sundays.

The Outer Banks are banks.

Therefore, the Outer Banks are closed on Sundays.

(Moulton, 1981:110)

Equally, phrases such as ''the common man'', ''the man in the street'', etc., are not gender neutral. For instance, we do not regard it as a contradiction when we hear the following two statements in sequence:

The rich cannot possibly appreciate the impact of inflation on the average working man.

The average working man earns almost twice as much as the average working woman.

(Examples taken from Miller and Swift, 1980:14)

You realize that we have just switched the meaning of the term ''man''. Since both sentences strike us reasonable, we are obviously not reading the supposedly generic term as a gender neutral term, but as a gender specific term.

En français, les problèmes sont bien différents de l'anglais. Néanmoins, il y a des similarités. Le problème d'un double sens des mots masculins signifiant le genre masculin et le sens générique sont comparables dans les deux langues. Si ''. . . on dit *les grands hommes*, on ne pense généralement pas aux femmes, et quand on écrit: 'l'homme est le seul mammifère qui ait recours au viol', on y pense encore moins. Enfin, quand l'Eglise nous dit que Dieu a créé l'homme à son image, il nous est difficile de nous représenter que cela concerne aussi les femmes car Dieu est métaphoriquement mâle.'' (Yaguello, 1979:187)

Outre le fait que la langue française accorde un genre masculin ou féminin à presque toutes les choses, la question de l'attribution de signification sexuelle est beaucoup plus difficile à circonvenir en français qu'en anglais. ''. . . les locuteurs d'une langue sans genre grammatical sont d'autant plus libres de faire jouer la métaphore sexuelle, car les locuteurs d'une langue à genre sont obligés de faire cadrer les représentations symboliques avec des structures grammaticales préexistantes.'' (Yaguello, 1979:113)

Mais ''les dissymétries les plus criantes, en fin de compte, sont celles qui se cachent dans les sens de mots en apparence symétriques. Ces dissymétries *sémantiques* proviennent de la péjoration généralisée de tout ce qui sert à qualifier ou à désigner les femmes. Si nombre de mots masculins n'ont pas d'équivalent féminin, là où coexistent masculin et féminin, ils sont souvent connotés différemment.

Femme, dans un sens absolu, peut être équivalent de *femme de mauvaise vie* (aller chez les femmes, se ruiner pour les femmes), alors que *homme*, pris dans un sens absolu, ne peut être que laudatif: 'Sois un homme!' On ne dit pas: 'Sois une femme, ma fille!'. . .

Une *femme galante* est une femme de mauvaise vie, un *homme galant* est un homme bien élevé.

Une *honnête femme* est une femme vertueuse, *un honnête homme* est un homme cultivé. . . .

Une *femme légère*, l'est de moeurs. Un homme, s'il lui arrive d'être léger, ne peut l'être que d'esprit.

On dit une *fille* ou une *femme facile*, mais pas un *homme facile*, une *femme de petite vertu*, mais pas un *homme de petite vertu;* on dit une *femme de mauvaise vie*, mais on dit un *Don Juan*. On dit une *faible femme*, mais pas un *faible homme*. Un *homme faible* est un homme trop indulgent.

On aime les *petites femmes*, mais on admire les *grands hommes*. Les *petits hommes* n'existent que chez Gulliver et les *grandes femmes* on du mal à s'habiller en confection.'' (Yaguello, 1979:141-142)

Le but de la recherche est de décrire et d'expliquer. En utilisant un langage dont les mêmes mots sont employés parfois dans des énoncés faisant appel à un genre en particulier, et parfois dans des énoncés sans rapport au genre, autant en anglais qu'en français, nous utilisons un medium embrouillé et en désordre qui nous empêche de faire des énoncés précis et exacts.

De plus, il est impossible d'exprimer des idées non-sexistes avec un langage sexiste, ce qui signifie que nous devons porter une attention très particulière au langage que nous employons. Cependant, on ne peut pas, malheureusement, en dire autant de l'énoncé contraire. Il est tout à fait possible d'émettre des idées sexistes avec un langage non-sexiste; aussi, soigner notre langage n'est qu'un début, et pas plus. Ceci nous amène donc à la question des concepts sexistes dont le sens sexiste est exprimé dans un langage non-sexiste.

Sexist Concepts

I am suggesting that concepts are sexist if the meaning they convey is sexist. Let me give you a few examples of concepts which are non-sexist in their language but sexist in their meaning.

One concept of this type which has been widely criticized is that of the *"head of household"*. "Head of household" expresses an asymmetrical social relationship in which one adult — by definition the male if there is an adult male within the household — is seen as socially, legally, and economically responsible for other household members, such as women and children, who in turn are seen as his dependents. There were historical periods in which this was, indeed, an adequate description of the circumstances that prevailed. In such cases, it is not the concept that is sexist, since it merely provides an adequate description of the type of relationship that obtains, but the social structure. The concept simply expresses this fact. Today (as of 1978 and later), however, we have family laws in Canada which, by and large, stipulate that the responsibilities of husbands and wives concerning each other and their joint dependents are identical (see Eichler, 1983:273-78). In addition, the majority of Canadian wives today are in the labour force. Due to this fact, women are also to a lesser degree socially placed through their husbands, since most of them now have an independent income and an independent source of status. To use the concept of "head of household" under such circumstances is, therefore, sexist, i.e., incorrect, since it indicates a relationship that no longer exists. The Canadian census no longer uses this concept although a number of economic and statistical studies do continue to use the concept, which is clearly inappropriate.

Another sexist concept is the social science definition of "work", which often specifically excludes unpaid work (Jaffe, 1972:470), so that, for instance, for the purposes of computing measures of the overall productivity of a society, women's contributions in the form of unpaid labour are customarily ignored. One of the consequences of this definition was that housework was usually considered non-work. It is only since feminists have challenged this definition that there has been some grudging recognition that housework is, in fact, work (see, e.g., Adler and Hawrylyshyn, 1978).

Three other examples will, I believe, suffice. Psychologists have long used the concept of "*maternal deprivation*" to describe situations in which mothers do paid work that takes them out of the home and therefore away from their children during working hours. This concept is sexist because it is one-sided. When fathers take on paid work that takes them away from their children during working hours, this behaviour is *not* described as "paternal deprivation"; indeed, it is interpreted as good behaviour for a father! Mothers, therefore, are accused of "neglecting" their children, while fathers are lauded for "caring" for their children, when both of them do exactly the same thing! A non-sexist way of describing the absence of parents from their home for specified periods of time would, for instance, be the expression "parental absence".

At a more subtle level, psychologists some time ago developed a method which tests differences in the perception of a stimulus in a surrounding field. In the experiment that was devised, subjects could either separate the stimulus (an embedded figure) from the surrounding field, or they could see the whole; in other words, they could see the stimulus as part of the surrounding field. In general, it turns out that females are more likely to see the stimulus and surrounding field as a whole, while males are more likely to separate the stimulus from its context.

Witkin, who originated this experiment, labelled the male behaviour as "*field independence*" and the female behaviour as "*field dependence*". Since dependence is customarily regarded as a negative trait (and not so incidentally also as a female trait), while independence is usually regarded as a positive trait (and not so incidentally also as a masculine trait), two different capacities thus received labels which carry an intrinsic value judgement, with a higher value given to the male capacity. Spender (1980:164-65), who reports this matter, suggests that if one wanted to assign a higher value to the female trait, one might just as well call the female response "context awareness" and the male response "context blindness" — and the connotations of these two concepts are quite different from those used by Witkin!

The most drastic type of sexist concept, in my opinion, is displayed in the notion that conjugal violence (meaning wife battering) is a form of conflict resolution! The battering is hardly experienced by the woman as the *resolution* of a conflict, but instead as the problem that needs to be eliminated.

The concepts of "conjugal violence" or "spouse battering" show a form of sexism which is the reverse of the sexism found in the examples we have so far considered. In the vast majority of cases, conjugal violence takes the form of wife battering. A recent study revealed that, of all cases of conjugal violence which came before the family court in Toronto in 1979, 95% involved wife battering (cf. Kincaid, 1981). To describe this as "conjugal violence" rather than "wife battering" creates an image of symmetry which is uncalled-for, given the actual occurrence of this crime. Therefore, using sex neutral terms when there is, in fact, a sex specific statement to be made is simply the reverse form of sexism as it appears in concepts. Other examples include the use of the word "parents" in cases in which the discussion is, in fact, about mothers (or fathers) only, or the use of "spouses" when in fact only wives (or only husbands) are referred to, etc. In Piaget's work girls are so much of a rarity that the index omits the word "boys" altogether, since the "child" is identified with the male child (Gilligan, 1979:441).

Sexist concepts are one manifestation of an overall androcentric viewpoint. We will turn to this issue next.

An Androcentric Perspective

An androcentric perspective expresses itself in two major

ways. The most common manifestation of an androcentric perspective occurs when women (or females in general) are largely ignored in the research process. In other situations, we are also dealing with an androcentric perspective if women (or females in general) are considered but only insofar as they pertain to males, or when anything that is male is seen as establishing the norm and the female counterpart to it is seen as the exception, the deviation from the norm. This is incorporated in the notion of women as the "other" sex. An observation that women are "different" takes men as the reference point and compares women against men. One might just as well take women as the reference point and thereby argue that men are "different". That is, however, not commonly the case at present (and would constitute a gynocentric perspective, the reverse form of sexism). A non-sexist approach incorporates both the male and female perspectives.

When we deal with history, it is predominantly history as it pertains to men, and not to women. Let me tell you a personal story. A number of years ago, I did a little study, together with one of my students, on the way reform histories portray the suffragette movement. For this purpose we examined sixty-one general American history books, as well as twelve reform history books, with respect to their treatment of Suffragism. In order to have a point of comparison, we also examined their treatment of Populism, which, according to all objective indicators, was a social movement of less social and theoretical significance than Suffragism. We found that, by and large, Suffragism was ignored as a serious social movement of its time, and concluded that this seemed to be so because of sexist bias on the part of the historians concerned (see Eichler and Nelson, 1977).

After we had completed a draft of this paper, I spoke to one of my colleagues, one of the major experts on reform history in Canada. I asked him whether we (neither of us being a historian) had omitted any major text, done injustice to anybody in our interpretation of the results, or otherwise committed any errors. He had no substantive criticism to offer, but suggested that it would be a poor idea to submit the paper for publication. Pressed for a reason — since apparently there were no errors or omissions of which we should have been made aware — he finally said: "Well, it's like this. In the third edition of my book [a reform history] I had actually included three pages on the suffragist movement. When my publisher read that, he said to me, 'Are you actually throwing that sop to women's liberation?' And so I said, 'You are right', and threw it out again." Sadly, this attitude does not seem to be totally atypical of social scientists in general.

History as it pertains to women is customarily not regarded as general history, but specifically as the history of women, as a *subfield*! The same applies to the other social sciences. Why is it necessary to have special courses, programmes, publications, lecture series, etc. pertaining to women? Why do we need to have sub-specialties such as psychology of women, anthropology of women, sociology of women, etc.? Because these fields, as they are currently constituted, in general do *not* pertain to women but to men. To give just one example, a recent content analysis of two basic and widely used Canadian art history texts found that women were grossly underrepresented. Textual references averaged 8.4% female and 91.6% male, colour illustrations averaged 2.1% female to 95.7% male (the remainder were listed as anonymous), and black and white illustrations were 4% female and 94.5% male, the remainder again being anonymous (cf. Sasha McInnes-Hayman, 1981). A current research project demonstrates that such disparity is not due to any great numerical prevalence of male artists, but rather to a selective representation of artists (the Womanspirit Art Research and Resource Centre, in London, Ontario, and its project on "Canadian Women Artists Working Prior to 1930").

Ignoring females and taking a male viewpoint results in overgeneralizations concerning males and undergeneralizations concerning females. However, although the focus is on men in this process, they do *not* become visible as men. This is one of the unexpected consequences of an androcentric perspective: not only are women largely invisible, but men are also seen in a distorted manner. The British sociologist David Morgan, for instance, in a self-critical essay in which he reflects on his

Master's and Doctoral theses, observes that, by ignoring the sex of his subjects as a relevant factor in his study, he managed not to see a crucial factor explaining the behaviour of the clergy. Concerning Max Weber's famous study on the Protestant Ethic and the Spirit of Capitalism, for instance, he remarks: "In this study, as in many other studies, men were there all the time but we did not see them because we imagined that we were looking at mankind" (Morgan, 1981:93).

Thus, an androcentric viewpoint views females through masculine eyes, as in a distorting mirror. In addition, an androcentric perspective ignores, not only women, but men as well. "Thus taking gender into account is 'taking men into account' and not treating them — by ignoring the question of gender — as normal subjects of research" (Morgan, 1981:95). I hasten to add that the primary purpose in trying to get beyond an androcentric perspective is not only to understand men as men, but also to understand women as women, and eventually, perhaps after we have given considerable thought to this question, to understand people as people.

An androcentric perspective is fostered by sexist language, sexist concepts, and a sexist methodology. Next, let us examine how sexism may creep into the very methods we use.

Sexist Methodology

A common manner in which sexism enters the methods employed in the research is in the process of creating research instruments. For example, if a researcher creates some instrument with reference to one sex only, but subsequently treats it as if it were of universal validity, we are dealing with a blatant type of sexism. For instance, Kohlberg developed his famous stages of moral development on an all male sample, but treated the stages as if they were of human applicability. Using this method, it would appear that women usually attain a lower level of moral development than men do. However, if we had developed a system of stages of moral development on an all female sample, maybe men would normally appear to reach a lower level of moral development than women (Gilligan, 1979)! We are not concerned here with the question of whether men or women are generally more moral creatures, but merely with the fact that developing a research tool with reference to one sex, and then claiming validity for both sexes, is not an acceptable scholarly practise.

Similarly, survey research often asks different questions of the two sexes, as a consequence obtains different answers, and then interprets this as evidence that, indeed, women and men are fundamentally different. So, for instance, women have long been asked about conflicts between their paid work and their family involvement and, indeed, when researchers ask these questions, they tend to find a considerable amount of conflict. However, men have rarely been asked about conflicts between their paid work and their family involvement, so that the conflicts they experience are much less well documented (some recent studies *have* started to provide evidence that men also experience a considerable amount of conflict; for a summary of some of them see Eichler, 1983:75-78). The conclusion which is often drawn on the basis of such one-sided questions is that women experience role conflict between work and family roles, and that men do not — a conclusion which is patently absurd, since it is based, at best, on half knowledge. Sometimes it is better to know nothing and to be aware of that fact, than to ask the wrong questions and end up with the illusion that we do know something when, in fact, we do not — which is generally the case when we employ a sexist methodology.

A parallel case exists with respect to stratification studies, which customarily focus upon men, and therefore tell us — at best — about male stratification, but not about stratification in general. As a consequence, we do not, at present, have a comprehensive theory of social stratification.

As a last example of sexism employed in a method let me read you some questions from an article published in 1978 and entitled, "Do Adolescents Believe the Employment of Wives is a Threat to Marital Relationships?". Respondents in this little study were asked to express their feelings, ranging from "strongly agree" to "strongly disagree", to the following five statements:

1. A husband should feel like a failure if his wife works.
2. A husband should feel like a failure if his wife earns more than he does.
3. A working wife is likely to be less of a companion to her husband.
4. A working wife is likely to neglect her husband.
5. A working wife is likely to become too independent. (King, Abernathy and Chapman, 1978:232)

This is a rather blatant example of sexist research. The questions are premised on the notion of a natural differentiation of tasks based on sex. This idea results in one-sided questions: there are no corresponding items, for instance, that a wife should feel like a failure if her husband works, or if he earns more money than she does, that a working husband is likely to be less of a companion to his wife, is likely to neglect her, and is likely to become too independent. There is also no possibility of finding out if a husband feels like a failure if his wife does *not* work. Beyond that, there is no possibility of a positive reaction to a wife's working for pay; in other words, the questions allow for only half of a possible continuum of responses. All the questions are phrased in negative terms. The most a respondent can do is to reject the negativism, but there is no possibility of expressing a positive reaction to a wife's holding a paid job. This could, of course, be easily achieved by phrasing the questions differently. For instance, if the intent of a question was to explore the relationship between perceived companionship within a marriage and working status, a non-sexist way of addressing this issue could be: "A couple in which both spouses have a paying job is likely to share more (less, the same amount of) companionship than a couple in which one spouse only has a paying job".

Another reason why the above represents an example of an androcentric bias is that the wife's job is seen only in relation to her husband, not to herself. Ostensibly, the intent of the article, as expressed in the title, is to see whether adolescents perceive a wife's employment as a threat to a marital *relationship*, but, in fact, the questions address themselves to the reaction of the *husband* only. What if the wife's job had a positive effect on her but a negative effect on the husband? In fact, there are some Canadian data which suggest the opposite: the wife's job increases the husband's marital happiness significantly (cf. Lupri and Frideres, 1981). Here, however, we are only concerned with the phrasing of the question. The example does suggest that it may be worse to get answers to sexist questions than to have no answers at all, since we obtain a distorted picture when employing sexist methods. If you had a situation in which something was experienced as beneficial to one sex and as detrimental to the other, whose definition of the situation should prevail? The fact that in the example used above both female and male respondents were asked to respond to the statements does not alter the fact that they were both asked to respond in terms of an effect on the husband only.

I cannot possibly point out here all the various ways in which sexism can enter into the very methods we use to study a question, and the examples given are just that: suggestive examples. They should, however, suffice to demonstrate that our methods are by no means free from sexism, and where this is the case, we cannot possibly end up with an unbiased account of whatever it was we were studying. Our answers will never be better than our questions.

There is yet another way in which sexism can come into the research process even if all the methods employed are non-sexist and the language employed is non-sexist: through a sexist interpretation of results.

Sexist Interpretation of Results

Once data have been collected, they need to be interpreted. If they have been collected with sexist methods, the results will be sexist as well, no matter how the findings are interpreted. However, even if they have been collected in a non-sexist manner, they may nevertheless be interpreted in a sexist manner. Let us look at just one example from the area of primatology.

Perhaps the most telling example of bias concerns the famous juvenile female, Imo, a Japanese macaque living with her troop at Koshima Islet. Scientists provisioned the troop there with sweet potatoes. Imo discovered that washing sweet potatoes got the sand off. Her discovery quickly spread among the other juniors in the troop, who then taught their mothers, who in turn, taught their infants. Adult males never learned it. Next, scientists flung grains of wheat in the sand to see what the troop would do. Rather than laboriously picking the wheat out of the sand grain by grain, Imo discovered how to separate the wheat from the sand in one operation. Again this spread from Imo's peers to mothers and infants, and, again, adult males never learned it. The fact that these Japanese macaques had a rudimentary culture has been widely heralded. But what are we to make of the *way* culture spread in this troop?

If Imo had been male, we would never have heard the end of the "inventive" capacities of primate males, and since generalization spreads like prairie fire when the right sex is involved, no doubt their role in the evolution of tool use and — why not? — language as well. But the urge to grand theory withers when females are the primary actors, and when the task relates to food — at least food without killing. Imo has been described as "precocious" and left at that. (Precocious, indeed! How would you get the sand out of wheat?)*

*Imo took the wheat to the water where the wheat floated and the sand sank (Weisstein, 1982:46).

Conclusion

Altogether, then, we have looked at five ways in which sexism may enter into the research process: through the use of sexist language and sexist concepts, through the use of an androcentric perspective, through a sexist methodology, and, lastly, through a sexist interpretation of results. Often, all five types of sexism go together, but occasionally they do not. Research becomes sexist if any *one* of these types of sexism appears. We therefore need to work towards the elimination of all five types of sexism.

This means a re-orientation of research which would equal the re-orientation that had to take place when scholars realized that the sun does not revolve around the earth but the earth around the sun. I think that this is rather an apt parallel because, until now, we have really structured our social knowledge around men. In metaphorical terms, we have envisioned our social universe as if men were in the centre and everything and everybody — women, other men, children, social institutions, etc. — revolved around men. When feminist research is introduced, we sometimes get models that replace men with women. (This approach does not, of course, exhaust all forms of feminist research; it is merely one manifestation if it.)

When we introduce the concept of non-sexist research, we are suggesting that the social universe revolves around men *and* women, and this takes us completely out of the metaphor of a circle. Instead, we are dealing with an ellipse, meaning that all our previous assumptions, generalizations, and deductions no longer apply. They need to be re-considered and re-created to fit the model of an ellipse rather than that of a circle.

It is, therefore, a rather awe-inspiring task to rid science of sexism, since we are truly talking about a shift in paradigms. It is understandable if people wish to avoid such a major re-orientation. The alternative, however, is to fiddle around with existing models by trying to fit women into them without fundamentally changing them. The end result of such efforts are such convoluted systems of explanation that they become effectively unmanageable. This is precisely the type of process which Kuhn (1970) describes in his book about the structure of scientific revolutions. Over the long haul, therefore, it would be more complicated to try to adapt models which were created for a different purpose — in this case, for a social universe that was seen as revolving around men only — than to face the fact that we have to start out anew with respect to many issues. In any case, and at the risk of sounding "corny", the vast energy which is expended in such labour intensive tasks as research is only warranted if those who engage in it are convinced that they are, in some fashion or other, pursuing the truth. Once we have recognized the simple fact that there are two sexes in this world and that they are of equal importance, it becomes necessary to rid research of sexism.

Quite simply put, sexist research is bad research, since it distorts what it claims to observe and explain. To the degree that the public supports research through tax monies I think that we have the right to expect that the best efforts are made to do research in the best possible manner — and I therefore believe that we should stop using public monies to support sexist research. To achieve this, I would propose that a standard item in all grant application assessment forms should be a question which screens out sexist elements in proposals, and that monies should only be given if the research design and presentation have been cleared as non-sexist. Of course, other criteria would also have to be considered, as is the case now. Being non-sexist is a necessary, but not, by itself, a sufficient, aspect of any good research project.

Looking beyond the concern to obtain good research, which should be an aim in itself, we must also consider the fact that sexist research serves to maintain sexist social structures. There is an intimate relationship between power and knowledge. Those in power control knowledge, but, on the other hand, by obtaining knowledge, one may be able to alter the power structure.

Let us consider an example of how sexist knowledge has been utilized in order to exclude women from certain types of positions. The fact of menstruation has long been used as an excuse for not admitting women to some high prestige, high stress, high reward occupations. At the same time, the hormonal cycles of men were neither thoroughly studied nor considered relevant for those same jobs in which female hormonal cycles were considered debilitating factors. Now that male hormonal fluctuations have also been studied and men have also been found to have cyclical fluctuations in their hormonal balance, these arguments have withered away with regard to both sexes.

Let me give you an example of something we do *not* yet know. Current social welfare practise requires that a family on family benefits receive one cheque only. If there is an adult male "head of the household", that cheque will go in its entirety to him. To my knowledge, there has never been a study which looks at how this money is actually distributed *within* the family. The *assumption* which economists make is that it will be used for joint expenses and distributed equitably. However, there is some evidence from Australia which suggests that money which comes to one person does not necessarily benefit all family members equally (Edwards, 1981). If we had a Canadian study which examined how the monies that are given to one person on behalf of an entire family are actually used within different families, we might be able to argue convincingly that welfare cheques should be made out to the two adults (if such is the case) within a family.

Another example which has recently been much in the news concerns wife battering. Until just a few years ago the existence of wife battering was a well kept secret. It was assumed that, within a family, people — men and women, adults and children — found security, peace, love, support, etc. However, it now turns out that the family home may be the most insecure, physically dangerous, and psychically debilitating place in which to be for many women, and probably for many children as well — in fact, more dangerous than many a dark alley. People who have, in the past, argued that wives need protection (in the form of shelters, for instance) were in an extremely weak position because, when asked to produce evidence of the risk, they could not supply it. The evidence did not exist in a researched, accessible form. Even if we had had such studies we still might not have had shelters, but the position of those arguing for them would have been easier. Incidentally, we still do not have a single representative study of wife battering in Canada, although we now do have some appreciation of the scope of the phenomenon (cf. MacLeod, 1980). Incest, which is primarily a crime perpetrated by adult males on female children, has just barely started to penetrate the awareness of policy makers as a problem that needs attention. Again, we have never had a representative study of incest in Canada which would allow us to estimate what proportion of children is at risk.

Having good research on these topics does *not* imply that the policies will change or that these behaviours will stop, but at least it would be vastly easier to fight for the necessary changes. Non-sexist research, then, will not *necessarily* result in better policies, but sexist research is extremely likely to lead to or maintain existing sexist policies.

Freeing research from sexism, then, is an integral aspect of the fight for equality for women. It is, in my opinion, one of the great tasks of our times.

References

Adler, Hans J. and Oli Hawrylyshyn, "Estimates of the Value of Household Work Canada, 1961 and 1971", *The Review of Income and Wealth,* Series 24, No. 4, Dec. 1978, pp. 333-355.

Edwards, Meredith, *Financial Arrangements Within Families.* A Research Report of the National Women's Advisory Council. N.P.: 1981.

Eichler, Margrit, *Canadian Families Today. Recent Changes and Their Policy Consequences.* Toronto: Gage, 1983.

Eichler, Margrit and Carol Ann Nelson, "History and Historiography: The Treatment in American Histories of Significant Events Concerning the Status of Women", *The Historian,* Vol. 40, No. 1, 1977, pp. 1-15.

Gilligan, Carol, "Woman's Place in Men's Life Cycle", *Harvard Educational Review,* Vol. 49, No. 4, 1979, pp. 431-446.

Gilpatrick, Naomi, "The Secret Life of Beatrix Potter", *Natural History,* Vol. 81, No. 8, 1972, pp. 38-41 + 88, 90, 92-97.

Hanmer, Jalna and Diana Leonard, "Men and Culture: The Sociological Intelligentsia and the Maintenance of Male Domination: or Superman Meets the Invisible Woman", paper delivered at the British Sociological Association Conference, April 1980.

Jaffe, A.J., "Labour Force: Definitions and Measurement", *International Encyclopedia of the Social Sciences.* New York: Macmillan and Free Press, 1972, Vol. 8, pp. 469-474.

Kincaid, Pat, *The Omitted Reality: Husband-Wife Violence in Ontario and Policy Implications for Education.* Ed.D. thesis, University of Toronto, Toronto, 1981.

King, Karl, Thomas J. Abernathy, Jr., and Ann H. Chapman, "Do Adolescents Believe the Employment of Wives is a Threat to Marital Relationships?", *The Family Coordinator,* Vol. 27, No. 3, 1978, p. 231-235.

Kuhn, Thomas S., *The Structure of Scientific Revolutions.* Chicago: University of Chicago Press, 1970.

Lupri, Eugene and James Frideres, "The Quality of Marriage and the Passage of Time: Marital Satisfaction over the Family Life Cycle", *Canadian Journal of Sociology,* Vol. 6, No. 3, 1981, pp. 283-305.

McInnes-Hayman, Sasha, "Representation of Female and Male Artists in Canadian Art History Texts Used in the Visual Arts Department, University of Western Ontario, 1980-1981: A Report". Ottawa: Status of Women Canada, unpublished paper, 1981.

MacLeod, Linda, *Wife Battering in Canada: The Vicious Circle*. Ottawa: Canadian Advisory Council on the Status of Women, 1980.

Miller, Casey and Kate Swift, *The Handbook of Nonsexist Writing*. New York: Lippincott and Corwell, 1980.

Morgan, David, "Men, masculinity and the process of sociological enquiry", in Helen Roberts (ed.) *Doing Feminist Research*. London: Routledge and Kegan Paul, 1981, pp. 83-113.

Moulton, Janic, "The Myth of the Neutral 'Man' '', in Mary Vetterling-Braggin (ed.) *Sexist Language. A Modern Philosophical Analysis*. [Totowa, N.J.]: Littlefield, Adams and Co., 1981, pp. 100-115.

Schneider, Joseph W. and Sally L. Hacker, "Sex Role Imagery and Use of the Generic 'Man' in Introductory Texts: A Case in the Sociology of Sociology", *American Sociologist*, Vol. 8, No. 1, 1973, pp. 12-18.

Silveira, Jeanette, "Generic masculine words and thinking", *Women's Studies International Quarterly*, Vol. 3, No. 2/3, 1980, pp. 165-178.

Spender, Dale, *Man Made Language*. London: Routledge and Kegan Paul, 1980.

Spender, Dale, "The gatekeepers: a feminist critique of academic publishing", in Helen Roberts (ed.) *Doing Feminist Research*. London: Routledge and Kegan Paul, 1981, pp. 186-202.

Weisstein, Naomi, "Tired of Arguing About Biological Inferiority?", *Ms.*, Vol. 11, No. 5, Nov. 1982, pp. 41-42, 45-46 + 85.

Woodward, Diana and Lynne Chisholm, "The expert's view? The sociological analysis of graduates' occupational and domestic roles", in Helen Roberts (ed.) *Doing Feminist Research*. London: Routledge and Kegan Paul, 1981, pp. 159-185.

Yaguello, Marina, *Les mots et les femmes. Essai d'approche socio-linguistique de la condition féminine*. Paris: Payot, 1979.

Sexism in Language: Does it Matter?

Sexism in Naming The World: Consciousness in a Patriarchal Iceberg

ANGÉLINE MARTEL and LINDA PETERAT

Introduction

There is an odd paradox between the vision of women and language that are held by men and society on the one hand and women and feminists on the other. History and popular belief tell us that women are loquacious, talkative and verbose. To the constant flow of words is added the frivolous, unimportant nature of such speech. In the English language, we talk and we chat, we jabber and we chatter while men speak, proclaim and express concerns. In the French language, "elle parlote, babille, bavarde, jase, cause" while men "parlent, discourent, discutent".[1] Male writers have perpetuated this belief:

> Sir, a woman's preaching is like a dog's walking on his hinder legs. It is not done well; but you are surprised to find it done at all.
>
> Samuel Johnson (*Life of Johnson*,
> quoted in *Collins' Gem*, p. 250)

> De wimmin, dey does de talkin' en de flyin', en de mens, dey does de walkin' en de pryin' en betwixt en betweest em, dey ain't much dat don't come out.
>
> Joel Chandler Hassis (*Brother Rabbit and his Famous Foot*,
> quoted in *Collins' Gem*, p. 221)

43

Jamais vous ne la trouvez à court de réplique, à moins de la choisir sans langue.

(Shakespeare, quoted in Mariella
Righini, 1978, p. 166)

Etre une femme et se taire sont deux choses incompatibles.

(Tirso de Molina, quoted in
Mariella Righini, p. 166)

On the other hand, feminists, in their efforts to achieve consciousness, speak of language as a form, an expression of and a propagation medium inherent in patriarchy. We speak of language as foreign to us.

Mon langage ne m'appartient pas. Toute juste autorisée à jouer avec tes mots et tes idées, à penser et à parler au masculin.

(Mariella Righini, 1978, p. 141)

Others speak of forced bilingualism (Françoise Guénette, 1982, p. 60). We speak the language of patriarchy, we translate our experiences in a form foreign and deprecative to us.

Coincées entre le sens que nous donnons à la réalité, et le non-sens que constitue pour nous la réalité patriarcale, nous sommes le plus souvent forcées d'adapter nos vies à la traduction simultanée que nous faisons de la langue étrangère.

(Nicole Brossard, quoted in
Françoise Guénette, p. 49)

And we all speak with an accent.

The issue of language is an intensely discomforting one for feminists. The questions are numerous, profound and reach to the root of our being. However, the paradox between men's attitude and women's perception points to more than a superficial disagreement in perspectives. It tells a tale of insecurity and of uncomfortable dwelling in a language-abode where quantity seeks to compensate for the fundamental inability to express feminine experience through foreign words.

Our task in the present paper is threefold. Firstly, we wish to review language in its French and English expressions and recapitulate the well-known thesis of sexism in language. Secondly, in an effort to achieve consciousness, we wish to question language as a form of expression and uproot its characteristics. This leads us to the construction of an inventory of the modalities of foreign-ness and to the presentation of an alternative, counter form of expression. Thirdly, in an effort to be valuative and ontological, we wish to inventorize (be inventive and take stock of) our assets.

Sexism in Language

This section, without belabouring the generally accepted position on sexism in language, attempts to bring into focus examples drawn from our lives in both French and English.

Lexicon, as word choice, evidences two dimensions of sexism. The term "sexism" itself indicates the exclusion of one sex. This exclusion is seen in terms of possession or devaluation. Firstly, sexism is evident in the usage of words. It is in the context of language usage that masculine possession is shown, indicating feminine non-possession. Expressions such as "man and wife" and "Mrs." easily flow in our conversation, and men, more comfortably than women, claim possession of children (my son, my daughter), of co-workers (my staff, my secretary) and of objects (my house, my fence, la ferme de Monsieur Untel, la maison de mon voisin).

Further to possession, language usage chooses words that have different connotative values for men and women.

A business man is aggressive;
A business woman is pushy.

He is a man of the world;
She's been around.

He's close-mouthed;
She's secretive.

(Paula Caplan, 1981, p. 147)

"Aggressive" and "pushy" are used to present a similar context, with gender as the determining factor for word choice. Using language is like playing cards. You know that, when you draw a Queen, the King will always be bigger and better and the card value is always in relation to the might of patriarchy. Word choice reflects this constant underlying relationship.

Secondly, lexicon itself exhibits sexism, that is, it already places, by its very substance, women in a dispossessed and devalued position. In French, for example, the terms "muse" and "égérie" are feminine only, thereby presenting the view that women are, at most, relegated to the role of inspirers of speech, poetry, and action, all of which are performed by men in the roles of "écrivain, auteur, homme de lettres, littérateur, reporter, conteur," for which there are no feminine counterparts, except for the perjorative "conteuse" as a "tattle-tale" or liar.

In English we have attempted to alter words such as chairman, conductor, and manager, to open them to the inclusion of women as well as men. However, this inclusion is always a reformulation of feminine in terms of the masculine: for example, "manageress" is derived from manager, and a woman becomes a *lady*-doctor. Furthermore, by implication and by lack of male counterparts in expression, our language abounds with words deprecative of women: chick, fluff, sugar, witch, bitch, etc. and terms through which women are degraded through references to men: bastard, son-of-a-bitch.

Morphology, which in French is a more important part of the language than in English, further reveals sexism as inherent. The feminine is again derived from the masculine, and even efforts at non-sexist language do not reach the root of the problem. "Auteur" and "écrivain" can be created into new words as "auteure" and "écrivaine", but the basic structure remains. The feminine is always an addendum to masculine, as "woman" is an addendum to "man" in English. Note the following grammar lesson:

— Teacher: In French, how is the feminine formed?
— Student: From the masculine, just like Eve was created from one

of Adam's ribs. "Destructeur" becomes "destructrice" and "poète" becomes "poétesse".

— Teacher: And what is the agreement of the adjective?
— Student: The adjective agrees in gender and number with the noun.
— Teacher: And if it agrees with a feminine and a masculine noun?
— Student: Masculine plus feminine equals masculine.
— Teacher: And if you have 300,000 women and a man?
— Student: The adjective will be masculine plural. The masculine is always stronger.
— Teacher: Very good. You know your language lesson well.

Despite our efforts at non-sexist language, we forget that it is grounded so deeply in patriarchy that it can hardly be dislodged. Our consciousness, although growing, is still unable to cope with patriarchy. As an example, the following was heard:

> Nous aimerions remercier tous les collaborateurs et collaboratrices de cette émission.

(Radio-Canada, September 15, 1982)

The basic morphological problem still remains for women. The determiner "tous" is still in the masculine only, and the feminine form of "collaborateurs" has been placed, as if naturally, in second position.

Syntax itself is also integral to a patriarchal mode of thought. The basic sentence pattern (subject + verb + object) exhibits a linearity which forces us to think primarily in terms of a person acting upon the world. It prohibits a view of collaboration and dialogue. It fosters a behavioristic rather than holistic view of the world. It is not incidental that one of the main topics of philosophical discourse in the occidental world is the sempiternal dichotomy subject-object. As women and as researchers, we wrestle with the ideal of restoring a holistic perspective, not realizing that our language, whether French or English, spells out our concerns in two poles joined only by action (the verb) or by possession (the verb "avoir" or "to have").

The poles of action and passivity, of doer and receiver, are structured in our language and in our consciousness. We need to look beyond our own language to examples of the Chinese and native North American cultures, which can express holistic ideas with greater ease. In her book *The Aquarian Conspiracy*, Marilyn Ferguson points out that the Hopi person would not say, for example, "the light flashed", but would say "Reh-pi", "flash". The light and flash are one, subject and object are one.

Language, more particularly the French and English languages, is the tip and base of a patriarchal iceberg. As the tip, it is an evidence of the workings of patriarchy. As the base, it is a medium for propagating a system which, so rigidly frozen in words, morphology and syntax, shapes our consciousness into its mould. Language rejoins, supports and indoctrinates into patriarchy. It is the tip and the base of an ideology.

Language is ideology. The term "ideology", in its historical unfolding, speaks of the feminine saga. Shortly after its creation, the term was used pejoratively to condemn any thinker who might be a threat to the established system (Olivier Reboul, 1981, pp. 16-21). Similarly, language deprecates women and insures their subservience. For example, the moment of conception is labelled "reproduction", as if there were not alternatives to the established system. Under such labelling, we, in what can be seen as an act of creation, merely produce again what already exists: we re-produce. In childbirth we are taken from the "case room" into a room where the doctor "delivers" our children, as if they needed to be taken away from us. "Deliver us from evil", they say in prayer. And our children are "delivered" from us. To minimize the importance of our life-giving act, we are indoctrinated to live it as the patriarchy wants us to live it. We have taken pre-natal classes and have been taught to keep "under control": a willed dominance. Pain killers are administered, for pain is bad. It is a punishment for the "original sin" because, again, we sinned: we were the first guilty of disobedience to the status quo and must now and forever give birth in pain, so we are told.

So intricately are language and ideology (as a menace to the status quo) linked that the fibre of mythologies and thought is soaked (imbibé) with deprecative and pejorative terms and contexts for women. Giving birth is one among many examples. Mariella Righini cries out in despair: "Tout mon vécu est imprégné de tes clichés." She discloses the marxian meaning later given to ideology. From an abuse (une injure) thrown at dissenters, the term came to mean its opposite: the complex system of beliefs and opinions legitimating the established social order. In this sense, language is again ideology. Language subtly legitimates patriarchy through sexism. It weaves sexism into a complex web of myths, religions, practices and beliefs which exclude women or prejoratively label them. Furthermore, these labels are part of a language we learn and use; they mould our vision of ourselves and of the world. Just like the slave who confesses to being "no good" because she or he has learned to gauge personal worth according to the master's (seldom mistress') definition of a "good slave", we use a language which constantly judges our second rate worth — or worthlessness.

To recapitulate the thesis that French and English are sexist languages and to uncover examples from lexicon, morphology and syntax rooted in ideology, is to beg, with despondency, the question: What do we do about the power which language commands of our lives?

We wish to propose a twofold itinerary: first, a stock taking of impediments to a feminine language, and secondly, an inventory of the hope-full steps already taken.

The Impediments

Language as ideology speaks of two dimensions belittling women: the possessive and the pejorative. Thus language is not only an expression, but also a *form* of expression; one which rejoins the original meaning of ideology, that is, a menace to the status quo, a menace which must become subservient. Destutt de Tracy in 1796 created the word "ideology" simply to mean the faculty of thinking. Again, language is ideology, for it is a form of expression of a masculine mode of thought: rational, inauthentic and power-laden. Perhaps, by identifying the mesh formed around us, we can pose counter-alternatives closer to our experience.

Language is an embodiment of rationalism on two levels: the code and the lived experience. Let "rational" stand for the precedence given to the cognitive, abstract dimension of the mind. Without denying the significance of this dimension, we must, however, point to the over-emphasis and overimportance given to it by patriarchy.

As a code, language fosters rationalism by its very structure. Consider the following words: "rational, reason, classification, analytic and synthetic thought, sensible, raisonnable, réfléchi, logique, prédictible, prévisible". All of these connote detached and absolute wisdom, intelligence and discernment. To these expressions are contrasted the following, which are often associated with feminine modes of thought: "irraisonnable, irréfléchi, imprévisible, illogique, irrational, unpredictable, unreasonable, non-sensical, inconsistent". The feminine is, again, like the feminine nouns, derived from the masculine form. The feminine attribute is the absence of the male quality. Furthermore, the non-rational connotations are tied to "foolishness, feeble-mindedness, erratic, puerile, incompetent, idiotic, stupid". Again, we are defined according to patriarchal forms of thought.

The lived experience of language also reinforces the patriarchal mesh. Increasing pressures in academic and personal life are mounting. The aim is to implement, to dissect, to create a one-to-one correspondence between phenomenon and expression. Edmund Husserl's (1931) ideal of a totally conscious and manipulated language is becoming a strong drive in symbolic logic, science and research (natural and human) through operationalization. Our language has developed an overabundance of stark and empty expressions, sloganizing our lives with "bottom lines" and "zero-bases". Function, instrumental action, exchange theories and competencies direct our consciousness, moulding our valuative frame. The decreased popularity of poetic expression is a further witness to the rationalizing of language. Abstract, rational and complex thought lead to the proliferation of econo-politico-juridico-scientifico systems. As each system demands further specialization, segmentation and separation in order to pursue mastery, it, in fact, like syntax, further isolates the subject from the object.

The rational paradigm solicits impersonalness. From the removal of personal experience as valued knowledge and as valid grounds for knowledge, emanates the objectifying, rational stance. The ideal of impersonal-ness facilitates an inauthentic mode of life, separating our thinking from our feeling, our acting from our living, and each of us from each other. Separation from our own selves and divisiveness among ourselves further enhances and assures the growth of the political, administrative structures. The resulting distrust and ever-expanding need for control ensures a suffocating structure. Bureaucracy and its language of systems management are witness to this. The more abstract and removed from ourselves we are, the less authentic is our life and the more powerful is the influence of the outer world. Dorothy Smith (1979) spoke of "exorcising the cold angels". She was, in effect, saying that the language of rationalism and abstractions must be placed in its lived context, evaluated and rethought according to our own way of seeing and living the world. Joining knowledge with our internal sources ensures the exorcising of separation and divisiveness.

In our lives, with increasing frequency, language is experienced as a manipulative power in itself. To speak is to manoeuvre, manipulate and direct the world; in the command of advertising, the logic of discourse, the argumentation of persuasion, the rhetoric of politics, the action of policies. Bureaucratic and professional languages formulate a jargon behind which we, as act-ers, hide, separating our actions from ourselves. We set policies and develop programmes like combatants in an arena, sacrificing to efficiency, task achievement and report filing. And we let our stories be told to us through advertising, debate and mass policy decisions. Language packages and delivers our feelings, thoughts, visions and ambitions and we need only act out the scripts, frozen in our dominated consciousness and in our dominating language.

How do we, women, relate in this language embodying a rational and deprecative form of thought? Dorothy Smith and

Mariella Righini have pointed to the coldness and foreigness of our language-abode:

> Je suis trop ancrée au concret de l'existence pour accepter de la sacrifier à tes constructions les plus abstraites ou à tes abstractions les plus construites.

(Mariella Righini, 1978, p. 155)

In the logical paradigm of patriarchy in which we have and will have increasingly a diminished thinking horizon despite our equality gains, we wish to propose a delectation, not in an illogical, unreasonable paradigm, but in an analogical way. To seek analogy, rather than difference, is perhaps a more authentic mode of thought for us. Our task is to transform the rationalizing prose into poetic manifestations. We must enfresh language with openness, suggestiveness, authenticity of experience and life. We can seek and revive the legitimacy of openness through analogy. We must contrast it to the narrowing grip of logical reasoning.

The Appraisal of Assets

> Je ne peux te dire aujourd'hui à quoi pourrait ressembler, une fois désserré l'étau viril, une culture authentiquement féminine.

> On ne peut définer que ce qui est fini. . . . Mais déjà, je puis observer, ici et là des tentatives féminines de repenser, un par un, tous les gestes de notre quotidien. Des ébauches de nouveaux langages qui collent davantage à nos corps. Des réévaluations, timides encore, de valeurs sous-estimées et qui nous sont vitales.

(Mariella Righini, 1978, p. 145)

Many signs are waving in the wind. The air continuously brings odours of freshness (des bouffées de fraîcheur). Language can change and is constantly being changed. It contains within itself the warmth of potential through which we may create, shape, and command our lives.

Our increasing criticalness of language and the sensitivity towards our own word usage are warming the frozen forms which have dominated us. More and more we question, together and in solitude, the hypotheses underlying the words we utter.

We critically question language in the light of our own experience and recognize the limitations it contains. We see ourselves as muzzled victims, raging with the unspoken, pre-formulated in expression. In our questioning and reaching out to each other, the private and public spheres are united. The rage of women has often formed a language of resistance. We speak of "sexism" and "chauvinism" and in doing so name the experience which was previously taken-for-granted, hidden. We speak out against the contexts which place women in economic difficulties, which mould them as battered wives. We dare rise against pornography, patriarchal religions, the myths of love and culture, the male ownership of our bodies. As rebels or as victims we speak an unconforming language, and that is a major asset and opening, a shifting in our consciousness of the limitations and potentials which language contains. The resistance, the rage and silence contain the valuative and ideological elements of emerging language forms.

We require a language in tune with our own creative experiences, a language in tune with our minds that can envision freedom, flowing relationships and change; a language in tune with our wombs, creative and life-giving. When we can once again command our own creativity we will no longer be spectators of our own lives.

We firstly must attend and listen to our primordial silence:

Le matin des magiciennes ne s'est pas encore levé. Le jour où notre savoir-faire spécifique pourra sortir de l'ombre et notre savoir-être propre émerger du *non-dit* et du sous-entendu, on commencera peut-être à parler de culture féminine. Pas avant.

(Mariella Righini, 1978, p. 146)

If language, as has been abundantly shown, is sexist — that is, it excludes our gender from its code and its ideology — then we must re-source ourselves in a pre-language world: in silence. It is customary to speak of "le mystère féminin". We suggest that we are still a mystery because we have been listening to the words of patriarchy. Yet, all the while, our experience, our lives have remained in silence. We must bring to manifestation the primordial silence of women.

Susan Griffin speaks of the silence which freezes and locks both mothers and daughters in a helpless position.

> The child's attempt at speech had touched an old buried place in her, and so she lingers, half turned to her daughter, half turned away, knowing she will never grasp that feeling and thus already having given up, yet not able to turn from it.
>
> (Susan Griffin, 1978, p. 112)

And so it is within the silence, within the recapturing of the feeling, that we may form our language anew.

Secondly, we must listen to the silence expressing itself in our daughters, who are often leading the way in a naively brilliant "prise de conscience". They refuse to see themselves as "docteur". They create new words: "docteuse", "constructeuse". They will tell you with admirable self-assurance: "I can do it if I wish" and they will add "*because* I am a girl" instead of the traditional "*even though* I am a girl". They will initiate the questioning of details that places aside our taken-for-grantedness. Why doesn't Jacques Cousteau have women on his boat? Who decided that kitchen counters should be like this? Why is the first sentence we learn to write at school: Luc va à l'école avec son chien Fido? Hurray for our daughters. Let us listen to them. We have much to learn yet.

Finally, we must view language as a net which clings to our consciousness. "Naming the world" is a di-stanciating view of language, a view which fosters the language as tool orientation, holding and freezing our thoughts and lives in patterns of resistance and turning them into condescension and appropriation. Taking stock of our richness, we have an incessant warmth, melting the frozen mass. Action is needed but consciousness must enter in dialogue, a more and more limpid, crystalline consciousness rejoining our language with our being. Deep in our bones, we feel disquietude but we have hope. We have hope, for our praxis is increasingly ours. We are commanding a creative consciousness which is individually and socially transformative.

Footnotes

1. To wit, the following nursery rhyme:

> La bavarde
> Ell' gigote
> Ell' zozote
> Babille babillant
> Elle a trois ans
>
> Ell' papote
> Ell' parlote
> Jacase jacacassant
> Elle a treize ans
>
> Ell' jabote
> Ell' marmotte
> Bavarde bavardant
> Elle a trente ans
>
> Ell' radote
> Ell' tricote
> Bredouille bredouillant
> Elle a cent ans

> Anne Froissart,
> *60 poésies, 60 comptines,*
> 1975 (no page)

Bibliography

Caplan, Paula, (1981). *Between Women, Lowering the Barriers,* Toronto: Personal Library.

Collins' Gem Dictionary of Quotations, (1971). London: Collins.

Ferguson, Marilyn, (1980). *The Aquarian Conspiracy,* Boston: Houghton-Mifflin.

Foissart, Anne, (1975). *60 Poésies, 60 comptines,* Paris: Pomme d'Api.

Griffin, Susan, (1978). *Women and Nature, the Roaring Inside Her,* New York: Harper and Row.

Guénette, Françoise, (1982). "Les faux plis de la culture," *La Vie en rose,* juin-juillet 1982, pp. 58-63.

Husserl, Edmund, (1931). *Ideas,* London: George Allen and Unwin Ltd.

Reboul, Olivier, (1980). *Langage et idéologie,* Paris: Presses Universitaires de France.

Righini, Mariella, (1978). *Ecoute ma différence,* Paris: Grosset.

Smith, Dorothy, (1979). "In Search of the Feminist Perspective: the Changing Pattern of Women," Proceedings of the Spring Conference of CRAIW, OISE.

Sexism in Language in The Curriculum of Ontario Schools: The Case of "Man in Society"

DONALD POWER, MARLENE STEWART and VIOLA NIKKILA

The purpose of this paper is to examine attitudes towards the meanings associated with a high school course guideline authorized by the Ontario Ministry of Education. The course guideline in question is the one entitled ''Man in Society''. Since 1965, courses of study based on this guideline have been taught at the grades eleven and twelve levels in Ontario schools; and, in 1980, over 40,000 students were enrolled in ''Man in Society'' (Minutes of the History Heads' Meeting, Scarborough Board of Education, Tuesday, November 10, 1981, Appendix B). When the Ontario Ministry of Education approved of ''Man in Society'' as a title for the guideline in 1965, there was little public awareness of the possibility of sexist bias in ordinary language, but, since then, many people have become more sensitive to the need for eliminating, or finding alternatives to sexist terms (Miller and Swift, 1976). During the winter and autumn of 1982, the authors decided to investigate the question, ''Do people consider the title of the Ministry guideline 'Man in Society' to be sexist?'' In this paper, the results of survey responses to this question will be presented and considered.

During the winter of 1981-1982, a group of twelve student teachers taking a Faculty of Education course on how to teach ''Man in Society'', were given an assignment in which they were to examine the degree to which people perceived the title of the guideline to have sexist connotations. Sexism was defined as words or actions that arbitrarily assign roles or characteristics to people on the basis of sex (Nilsen, 1977). In carrying out this assignment, the students garnered opinions from professors, educational officials, college instructors, teachers, other students and members of the general public. By means of letters, interviews, telephone conversations, and survey forms, the students elicited two hundred and sixty-eight responses to the question, "Should the title of the Ministry guideline "Man in Society" be changed because it has sexist connotations?" In reply, one hundred and seventy-eight respondents said that the title is sexist and should be changed; fifty-one said that the title is nonsexist and need not be changed; and thirty-nine had no opinion. Among those respondents who did say that the title should be changed, some recommended that the new title might be "Human Society", "People in Society", or "Sociology", with the most recommended title being "Human Society".

There were many reasons for the opinions given by those respondents who recommended a change in the title of the course guideline. One community college instructor said that "sexist language is language that excludes women or gives unequal treatment to women and men." She said that she believed that the title "Man in Society" is sexist and that it is time to be inclusive. The argument for inclusive language was raised during the annual convention of the National Council of Teachers of English in the United States, in 1974. At the convention, the Council passed a resolution to adopt a new set of guidelines for nonsexist language. In these new guidelines, it was reasoned that while "man" in its original sense carried the dual meaning of "adult human" and "adult male", its meaning has come to be so closely identified with "adult male" that the generic use of "man" and other words with masculine markers should be avoided whenever possible (Nilsen, 1977).

In response to the question of whether or not the title of the course guidelines is sexist, one mother said that she perceived it to be sexist. She said, "I am not concerned with how I interpret the word 'man', but with how others interpret it. I believe that the term 'man' is narrowly understood. I have two school-age daughters. I do not want them to be viewed as second-rate citizens." In support of this woman's view, research studies have shown that the word "man" is often interpreted to mean men only. In 1973, Aileen Pace Nilsen, of the University of Iowa, tested children in their perceptions of the word "man". Using a picture-selection technique with one hundred children ranging in grade level from nursery school through the seventh grade, the research showed that the word "man", when used in the sentences "Man must work in order to eat", and "Around the world man is happy", was interpreted to mean male people and not to mean female people. Two other researchers, Sally Hacker and Joseph Schneider, conducted a similar study with college students at Drake University and found similar results, namely, that the respondents tended to omit references to girls and women when talking about the activities of "man" in the world (Miller and Swift, 1976).

It was the expressed opinion of an Ontario Human Rights officer that "the definition of 'man' is supposedly 'humankind', but in actual fact the use of 'man' only reinforces the invisibility of women in matters of importance." She said that "a very important part of discrimination is the labelling process." Since, as part of her responsibilities, this officer works with women who have been victimized in the work place, she is conscious of the cause and effect relationships that exist among bias, prejudice and discrimination. Bias, as the inclination not to show concern for the members of a group, often leads to prejudicial judgements about them, and then to discrimination against them. It is the chain reaction from feeling to thinking and then to acting to which the Human Rights officer is referring when she objects to the title "Man in Society" by saying that a very important part of discrimination is the labelling process.

One sociologist was in favour of changing the title of the course guideline, but not because he perceived sexist bias in it. He said, "If the course were titled 'Women in Society' we would expect that it looked at women's issues alone. The title should reflect a general category. For example, 'Geography' is not called 'Geography of man'." By taking an analytical approach to the question, the sociologist used logic and reference to analogous thinking in saying that the title of the Ministry guideline is inappropriate.

A director of an Ontario Women's Centre stated that "man" is a sexist term perpetuating sexual inequality and sex-role stereotyping in our society. She said that the use of the word in the guideline "further exemplifies the dominance of the male species in our culture and society." Since strong impetus was given to the women's movement by the publication of the *Report of the Royal Commission on The Status of Women in Canada* (1970), the Ontario government has supported a policy of furthering women's rights in education and employment. As one who is committed to this cause, the director believed that the elimination of the guideline title "Man in Society" would be a step in the direction of greater equality.

Although one hundred and seventy-eight respondents said that the title of the Ministry guideline is sexist and should be changed, there were fifty-one respondents who saw no sexist bias in the title and recommended that it continue to be used. Many interesting reasons were given by those who supported the latter option. For example, a housewife said, "Man does not necessarily mean male," and she based her opinion on the authority of the dictionary. Thus, in *The Concise Oxford Dictionary* (1964), "man" is defined as (1) Human being (a man and a brother, fellowman); (indefinite or general application) person, as any, no man, some, few, men; (all) to a man, all without exception. (2) The human race (man is born into trouble; man is a political animal). In contrast to this opinion, it has been argued that dictionaries have often been held in the same esteem as the Bible, and that they perpetuate cultural sexism (Gershuny as quoted in Nilsen *et al.*, 1977).

A legal stenographer reflected back upon her own high school experience and said, "I took 'Man in Society' — the title never really offended me. If anything, it would probably be better to be called 'Sociology'. But personally, it makes no difference (I'm not actually liberated!)" Sensing her own social oppression, she answered the question with some indifference and apathy. Yet it is possible, however, for men and women to become more liberated as they become freer to use language to take control over their lives. As Paulo Freire says:

> Human existence cannot be silent, nor can it be nourished with false words, but only by true words, with which to transform the world. Once named, the world in its turn reappears to the namers as a problem and requires of them a new *naming*. [We] are not built in silence, but in word, in work, in action-reflection. . . Dialogue cannot occur between those who want to name the world and those who do not wish this naming — between those who deny others the right to speak their word and whose right to speak has been denied them. Those who have been denied their primordial right to speak their word must first reclaim their right and prevent the continuation of dehumanizing agression.

An anthropologist had some acerbic comments on the question of changing the title of the Ministry guideline. He said:

> It is interesting to note that there are always those who would scour the world clean of sexism by changing a word here and there. As an active anthropologist, both researcher and lecturer/assistant professor for the past dozen years or so, I can tell you that this idea goes back at least a decade or more, what strikes me as something humorous, is that it keeps cropping up repeatedly as a ''new'' concept.

> The world is full of real horror stories with sexist overtones. To my mind, perhaps the most awful situation presently requiring attention, is the persistent sexual mutilation of the most brutal fashion perpetrated on young girls throughout the horn of Africa. It is my understanding that the World Health Organization has been struggling with this disgusting situation for some time. So far, they have had a singular lack of success. Those who are concerned about calling this particular course ''Human Society'', if successful, will in half a decade I imagine, want to change it to ''Huwoman in Society''. Perhaps their time and effort could be better expended working on more tangible problems. Changing words doesn't change ideas.

One comment on the viewpoint expressed by the anthropologist is that Canadians first need to solve Canadian problems of bias, prejudice and discrimination against women, just as Africans need to work on solutions to their own problems. The most tangible problems are those which are most immediate within our own society, and there is a real possibility that the symbolic significance of using alternative language forms will create more equity between men and women.

The results of the pilot study were such that the authors considered it worthwhile to do a more extensive study of the topic in the autumn of 1982. To elicit more opinions from those who are directly involved with the Ontario school system, a questionnaire was administered to one hundred and eighty-two high school students enrolled in "Man in Society" classes in a community in northwestern Ontario (Table 1). In this sample, there were one hundred and five female and seventy-seven male respondents. Out of the sample, fifty-two female students favoured a title change; forty-seven said that the title of the guideline need not be changed; and six had no opinion. From the group of seventy-seven males who replied to the questionnaire, thirty-four said that they thought that the title should be changed; forty said that it should remain the same; and three had no opinion. A similar questionnaire was also administered to one hundred and fifty-six student teachers in a Faculty of Education in northwestern Ontario (Table 2). Among this group there were ninety-six female and sixty male respondents. A title change was recommended by forty-six of the female student teachers; forty-two of them said that they saw no reason to change the title; and eight had no opinion. Among the male student teachers, twenty-one recommended a title change; thirty-five were not in favour of a change in title; and four had no opinion to offer. Most of the school and university students who preferred a change in title to the guideline recommended that "Human Society" would be a suitable substitution for the title "Man in Society", with its perceived sexist connotation.

The high school students gave a variety of reasons to support the idea of changing the title of the Ministry guideline. One student said that, in his opinion, "the course name should be changed mainly to appease those who find the name 'Man in Society' sexist." He said that "the name 'Man in Society' refers to humans in general, but to some it may seem that man = male in the course title." There were other high school students who also took the view that, if many people are upset about the title because it is perceived to be sexist, then it would be better to change it. One problem with this interpretation is that it can lead to the conclusion that bias exists only in the eye of the beholder. It implies that we do not have to change the real material conditions which lead to discrimination, and bias against women can be overcome by aiming to reach conceptual clarification about the meaning of words. However, while the quest to reach a common understanding of meaning is important, it is not sufficient to eliminate discrimination against women in society.

Another high school student said that she saw the title ''as not really sexist'' even though it sounds like it is directed to the male sex. She said that since ''the course itself deals with men and women, 'Human Society' is the best title. It deals with all people''. This student, like others in the survey, was reluctant to consider the question in terms of sexist bias. Part of the explanation for this reluctance is that, during the 1970s, references to sexism often produced confrontation and hostility between men and women. In pursuing the advancement of individual human rights, conflict and debate were accepted as part of human reality. However, in the eighties, there is now a growing awareness of the need for reducing levels of conflict between individuals and groups as they strive for a fuller understanding of the meaning of community living. Many young students now tend to avoid situations or interpretations which could cause conflict among them. Since many young people, at this time, think that the term ''sexist'' is a word which evokes images of confrontation and polarization, they do not see analyses of sexism as being potentially useful.

The high school students who were not in favour of changing the title of the guideline also gave some interesting justifications for their points of view. One student said that she is not ''into women's lib. The title never hurt anybody ten years ago, so why should it hurt now. Just because some women think it makes them feel stronger if they have everything with 'Man', they want to change the title to 'Human'. What do they want?'' As in the case of this student, there were several others who referred to ''women's lib'' in tones of disdain. The reasons for this attitude include the backlash against some of the overly aggressive statements expressed by zealous proponents of the feminist movement; the conservative swing in politics in the United States which led to the defeat of the Equal Rights Amendment; the association of "women's liberation" with the liberation movements of other countries, some of which oppose Canadian government foreign policy; a paternalistic attitude which often invokes sarcasm and ridicule "to keep women in their place"; and the influences of academic movements, such as sociobiology, which reinforce the idea that human behaviour is better explained by "natural" rather than "environmental" hypotheses.

Religious interpretation was in the mind of another high school student when he considered the idea of changing the guideline title. He said, "It really doesn't matter to me about the title, and also I can't change it even if I wanted to — and, besides, man was first on earth." This student alluded to Genesis 1:26-27, "So God created man in his own image, in the image of God created he him; male and female created he them." In addition to the allegorical problems connected with Biblical translations, there has been some concern recently about how the word "God" has been translated from Hebrew into English. As Gershuny (quoted in Nilsen *et al.*, 1977, p. 111) claims, there has been a distortion in translating the Hebrew word for God "Elohim" into the English that is used in the King James Version of the Bible (1611) and the New English Bible (1970). Through an error of translation, the word "God" has come to be understood in the masculine sense alone. In English translations of the Bible, the word "man" has been associated with Adam, the first man, who was made in the image of a masculine God. "The naming power goes from God to 'Adam'; Woman, not included in the English 'Adam' names nothing. . . Woman is neither given the dignity of a proper name in Genesis 2 nor the privilege of naming others" (Gershuny, *op. cit.*, p. 111). This linguistic problem has been considered by the United Church of Canada whose General Council Executive has recommended that inclusive language be used whenever possible when communicating the Gospel (The

General Council Executive of the United Church of Canada, November, 1981, *Guidelines for Inclusive Language,* p. 10).

Traditional male chauvinism appeared in the survey when one student saw the title of the guideline as a symbol of male dominance of females, and he aimed to justify it as such by saying that the title should not be changed "because men are stronger than women, and we are f------better workers." Today, many male students seem less sympathetic to the goals of the feminist movement than their counterparts were ten years ago. As the unemployment rates increase, many students of both sexes tend to be receptive to the idea that traditional occupation roles should be followed. As men become more critical of women who "take" jobs from them, many women shy away from being assertive in the search for jobs. Because of their own self interest, young men often revert back to the kind of sexist thinking which was common during the days of the Depression in the thirties. But with this suppression of feminist freedom in a time of economic crisis, there is the danger of a corresponding increase and support for neo-fascism.

There were interesting reasons given by the university students who supported changing the title of the course guideline. One student teacher recommended the title change, saying, "Women have been short-changed for too long. These simple changes may appear trivial, but the present title simply perpetuates the belief that education and other areas cater to men only. It may be a small change, but its a start on a long road to making society more equal *in all respects*!" Another student stated her opinion in this way:

> I think that the title "Man in Society" has sexist connotations. People are more aware of this sort of thing, e.g., the *role* of women in society and the whole issue of women's rights; and I believe we have to examine ourselves, our society and our vocabulary on this issue. The issue is not irrelevant, I don't think, because words have meanings for all of us. Whether we think of their meanings consciously or not, everyone is affected and influenced by the "word". Words that leave out women are cutting off at least fifty-one percent of the population and help keep "women" down.

As mentioned above, one out of every two university women was in favour of changing the title, whereas the approximate number of university men favouring the title change was one in three. One of the male students expressed the following traditional view on the subject: "The Bible states clearly (in fact I heard it this Sunday) that women came from the rib of man, etc., etc. Man has never meant anything other than the combination of both man and woman." A second male student stated: "Human society is referred to as mankind in books and other media. The term 'Man in Society' reflects such an outlook. If we start to change everything to incorporate the whims of the 'libers', where will we stop!"

Conclusion

Having considered a spread of opinion, and some of the reasons given in favour of changing and in favour of retaining the present title of the guideline, the question now to be considered is, "Is there a contradiction between the Ontario Ministry of Education policy on sex-role stereotyping, and the naming of the high school course guideline 'Man in Society'?" When "Man in Society" was authorized as a course guideline in 1965, the Ministry of Education had no well defined policy on sex-role stereotyping, but, since 1972, several Ministry documents have been issued in which it is affirmed that Ontario teachers have a duty and a responsibility to combat sex-role stereotyping in the schools, and to promote greater equality between the sexes through education. In the provincial curriculum policy statement for the primary and junior divisions (kindergarten to grade six), it is stated that "it is also the Policy of the Government of Ontario that education in the Primary and Junior Divisions be conducted so that each child may have the opportunity to develop abilities and aspirations without the limitations imposed by sex-role stereotypes" (*The Formative Years*, 1975). The expectations of the Ministry of Education with regard to programs developed at the local level, includes the prescription that "education must be conducted in such a way that each child may have the opportunity to develop abilities and aspirations without the limitations imposed by sex-role stereotypes or other forms of discrimination" (*Education in the Primary and Junior Divisions*, 1975). One year later, the Ministry authorized the publication of a resource list, sent to all schools in the province, to promote curriculum recognition of "the roles of girls and women in Canadian society and the world at large, and the contributions they have made to society in general" (*Girls and Women in Society*, 1976). This document is intended for use in the primary, junior and intermediate divisions (kindergarten to grade ten). In 1979, the Ministry issued a resource guide document for all divisions (kindergarten to grade thirteen), which illustrated how feminist studies could be integrated into eighteen areas of the curriculum (*Sex-Role Stereotyping and Women's Studies*, 1979). When the secondary school diploma requirements were issued under the authority of the Minister of Education, in 1979, there was the following reference to sex-role stereotyping included:

> The policy of the Government of Ontario is that there be equal educational opportunity in the province. Thus, it is inappropriate for any school to deny a student access to a course of study or program solely on the basis of the sex of the student. This does not make mixed classes of male and female student obligatory, but the policy underlines the fact that sex-role stereotyping of courses and programs is to be avoided. Similar courses may be given to mixed or unmixed classes so that students of either sex are free to participate in courses in all available subject areas. (*Circular H.S.1*, 1979-1981)

It is apparent, therefore, that the Ontario Ministry of Education has been making concerted efforts to use the school system to combat the effects of sexism in society.

After a period of time, the implementation of course guidelines which are authorized by the Minister of Education and utilized in the schools is open to provincial government review. In 1979-1980, the course guideline *Man in Society RP.48, 1965* and its implementation, were subject to provincial review conducted from the Ministry office in Sudbury. The purposes of the provincial review were to determine to what extent courses taught in the high schools were compatible with *Man in Society RP.48, 1965,* and what revisions of the guideline might be necessary to establish a suitable basis for "Man in Society" courses in the 1980s. The procedures used in the provincial review were as follows: Ministry personnel collected interview data from teachers of "Man in Society" and from a number of students; basic issues were investigated regarding the congruency of existing courses with the guideline and a needs assessment for the future; discussions revolving around content, teaching methods, skill development and student evaluation were held. Eighty-three secondary schools were used in the provincial sample.

One of the main conclusions that emanated from this review was that there is a need to bring "Man in Society" teachers together, perhaps more often than in the past, to have them discuss contents and methods of teaching which are congruent with the existing course guideline. It is interesting to note, however, that the question of the appropriateness, or lack of appropriateness, of the title of the guideline was not formally discussed during the review. It was taken for granted that "Man in Society" would remain the title during the eighties. Yet, as shown in this report, a substantial number of people now question the title of the guideline on the grounds of its perceived sexist bias.

In Ottawa in November 1982, at the Annual General Meeting and Conference of the Canadian Research Institute for the Advancement of Women, those attending the plenary session passed a resolution requesting the Ontario Ministry of Education to select a non-sexist title for the guideline "Man in Society", so as to be more consistent in the policy of using schools to combat sexism in society.

Table 1

The question was asked of high school students studying "Man in Society" in a community in northwestern Ontario, "Should the title of the course guideline 'Man in Society' be changed because it has sexist connotations?''

Responses	Female		Male	
	#	%	#	%
Yes	52	50	34	44
No	47	44	40	52
No Opinion	6	6	3	4
Totals	105	100	77	100

Table 2

The question was asked of university students in a Faculty of Education in northwestern Ontario, ''Should the title of the course guideline 'Man in Society' be changed because it has sexist connotations?''

Responses	Female		Male	
	#	%	#	%
Yes	46	48	21	35
No	42	44	35	58
No Opinion	8	8	4	7
Totals	96	100	60	100

Table 3

High school and university student responses to the question, ''Should the title of the course guideline 'Man in Society' be changed because it has sexist connotations?''

Responses	#	%
Yes	153	45
No	164	49
No Opinion	21	6
Totals	338	100

Table 4

Male and female student responses to the question, ''Should the title of the course guideline 'Man in Society' be changed because it has sexist connotations?''

Responses	Female		Male	
	#	%	#	%
Yes	98	49	55	40
No	89	44	75	55
No Opinion	14	7	7	5
Totals	201	100	137	100

Bibliography

Concise Oxford Dictionary (1964), Oxford University Press, London.

Freire, Paulo (1972), *Pedagogy of the Oppressed*, Herder and Herder, N.Y.

Interdivisional Task Force on the Changing Roles of Women and Men in Church and Society (1981), *Guidelines for Inclusive Language*, Toronto, United Church of Canada.

Miller, Casey and Swift, Kate (1976), *Words and Women*, Anchor Press, N.Y.

Nilsen, Aileen Pace; Bosmajian, Haig; Gershuny, H. Lee; Stanley, Julia P. (1977), *Sexism and Language*, National Council of Teachers of English, Urbana (Illinois).

Ontario Ministry of Education (1979-1981), *Circular H.S.1*, Toronto.

Ontario Ministry of Education (1975), *Education in the Primary and Junior Divisions*, Toronto.

Ontario Ministry of Education (1975), *The Formative Years*, Toronto.

Ontario Ministry of Education (1975), *Girls and Women in Society*, Toronto.

Ontario Ministry of Education (1975), *Sex-Role Stereotyping and Women's Studies*, Toronto.

Royal Commission on the Status of Women in Canada (1970), *Report of the Royal Commission on the Status of Women in Canada*, Information Canada, Ottawa.

What is Sexism in Research?

Females, Sport, and Biosocial Explanations

M. ANN HALL

For several years now much of my research and writing has been focussed on explaining why some females are attracted to sport and others are not. I am using the word "sport" here in what I consider to be its everyday sense: a spectrum of physical activities ranging from the more recreational, unorganized pursuits of relatively uncommitted individuals through to athletic competition at its highest levels, demanding not only arduous training but, often, unremitting and single-minded determination. For many women, sport is recreation, something done in one's free time. But for many others, sport is more than a leisure-time activity; it is a serioius commitment, sometimes a profession. Since by choice and training I am a "sport sociologist", my inclination has usually been to search for social rather than biological explanations of female athleticism.

However, a few years back, I read *Man & Woman Boy & Girl* by John Money and Anke Ehrhardt, and primarily through their work I became fascinated by the potential infleunce of prenatal hormonal factors on individual psychosocial development. One sentence in their book stood out above all the rest: ". . . one may sum up the current findings by saying that genetic females masculinized in utero and reared as girls have *a high chance of being tomboys in their behavior*" (p. 10, my emphasis). Money and Ehrhardt's definition of "tomboyism" included a preference for vigorous athletic activity, especially outdoor pursuits. Further to this was the "fact" that genetic females could be subject to prenatal androgen excess without any virilizing effect on the external genitalia, although the excess may be sufficient to influence the brain during critical periods of development. It was, of course, a quantum leap to suggest that women who enjoy sports or who are skilled athletes have been prenatally "programmed" by some quirk of nature or a misused drug. At one point I was discussing the evidence concerning the masculinizing effects of synthetic progestin with a class of athletically inclined females, who shortly thereafter contacted their mothers to ascertain if they had been treated with a synthetic steroid during pregnancy. I might add that none of them had been so treated, which made them immediately suspicious of my quantum leap; indeed, as it turns out, they should have been. I felt, nonetheless, that the whole matter had to be investigated further. For months I steeped myself in what was, to me, a very foreign literature. I wanted to know what sort of evidence existed for a hormonal basis to sexually dimorphic behaviour (i.e., having two forms, male and female), and particularly that behaviour characterized as "athletic" — outdoor, competitive, vigorous and involving high energy expenditure.

I shall come back to what I discovered presently, but first let me explain briefly what I intend to do in this paper. My overall objective is to examine the possibilities for a biosocial explanation of female athleticism because, in arguing for sex equality in sport, we simply cannot ignore biology. Firstly, I examine the evidence for a hormonal basis to sexually dimorphic behaviour arguing that this evidence is not nearly as unequivocal as it might initially appear to be, and that there are alternative explanations for some of the findings. I then go on to show that despite these problems, insightful research in behavioral endocrinology and neuroendocrinology cannot be dismissed in the same way that it is possible to discredit the biological determinism of sociology. Neither, however, should we posit some form of biological essentialism in our attempts to overcome cultural determinism. Nevertheless, biological processes influence and interact with our social situation, and to recognize this in no way concedes the case to biological determinism or to biological essentialism.[1] I conclude by examining the implications of biology for arguing sex equality in sport.

Sexually Dimorphic Behaviour

Based on my reading on sexually dimorphic behaviour, I came to the following conclusions.[2] Firstly, the evidence which points to a hormonal basis for sexually dimorphic behaviour differs substantially in both kind and quantity for animals and humans. Animal research is almost always experimental, whereas the evidence for humans comes primarily from clinical syndromes. The anomalous nature and relatively rare occurrence of these clinical syndromes presupposes that most of what we can surmise about prenatal hormonal effects in humans is predicated on experimental animal studies, the results of which, unfortunately, are far from consistent. For animals (primarily rats, mice, hamsters, guinea pigs, and rhesus monkeys), the evidence relating to the effect of androgen, a steroid produced by the early-differentiated testes, on *sexual or mating* behaviour is quite unequivocal. It has been amply demonstrated that the introduction of androgen during the critical period of development enhances male mating behaviour (e.g., mounting, intromission, ejaculation), whereas depriving the male of androgen augments the display of female sexual behaviour during adulthood (e.g., various soliciting behaviours and postures) with a concommitant reduction of male sexual behaviour (Reinisch, 1976). However, the evidence relating to the effect of androgen on *asexual* behaviours (such as play and threat, learning, aggression, avoidance acquisition, exploratory behaviour, and maternal behaviour) is not nearly so straightforward. There are many inconsistencies and contradictions in the animal data due to a multitude of reasons, perhaps the most important of which is the effect of learning and experience (see Reinisch, 1976). Therefore, to conclude *anything* about human behaviour from these animal studies is unwarranted.

Secondly, and as mentioned previously, the only evidence for humans comes through spontaneously occuring "experiments in nature". Clinical syndromes result either because of a genetically determined defect during the fetal stage (androgenital syndrome, Turner's syndrome, or androgen insensitivity) or because of the administration of synthetic progestins to the mother to prevent miscarriage.[3] When this practice began twenty to thirty years ago, it was not known that the progestin would have a virilizing effect on the female fetus. It is also this second group of clinical syndromes (progestin-induced hermaphroditism) which most closely approximates the induced prenatal androgenization in animal experiments.

Thirdly, although just about every psychology text and popular article I have ever read points out that there is a "masculiniza-tion" of behaviour in genetic females who have either the androgenital syndrome or progestin-induced syndrome, it is rarely mentioned that there is evidence to the contrary.[4] Moreover, where this "masculinization" of behaviour is observed, it is referred to as "tomboyism", meaning: a high level of physical energy-expenditure, especially in vigorous outdoor play, games and sports; a preference for male over female playmates; a preference for practical clothing and an indifference to personal adornments; a preference for toys traditionally reserved for boys; a lack of interest in dolls; little rehearsal of the traditional female role of wife and mother; a late interest in boyfriends and dating; and, eventually, the subordination of marriage to a career (Money and Ehrhardt, 1972). Tomboyism, so described, is a cultural phenomenon totally dependent on social and cultural attitudes. In fact, being a tomboy in our society today is universally acceptable since most girls (at least those from the middle and upper social classes) are involved in some form of organized sport, wear jeans everywhere, spurn frilly clothes, and, through the increasingly prominent example set by their mothers, see the possibility of combining marriage and a career. In sum, using tomboyism as an indication of sexually dimorphic behaviour is quite useless.

Fourthly, and finally, everyone who does research in this area talks about an "interactionist" approach to the nature-nurture controversy, according to which the development of each person depends on the specificities of the individual's environment interacting with the individual's genetic endowment. This is known as the "norm-of-reaction" concept (Lerner, 1976). Do boys and girls, for example, become differentially involved in sport because they are treated differently, or rather do boys and girls receive different encouragement to participate in sport because they demonstrate contrasting predispositions to become involved from the beginning? The answer is probably both. However, I eventually came to the conclusion that the puzzle is ultimately unsolvable, at least in any empirical sense. Although the norm-of-reaction concept is useful in conceptualizing the nature of heredity-environment interactions, we can only, at best, make statements about particular heredity-environment interactions *after* they have occurred (Lerner, 1976). Moreover, because every individual's genetic heritage is unique, all people will interact with their environments in unique, specific ways.[5]

Nonetheless, I had become convinced that there was at least some evidence for a hormonal basis to sexually dimorphic behaviour insofar as it related to participation in physical activities whose characteristics we normally describe as "athletic" — high energy expenditure, outdoor, competitive, and vigorous. I was also convinced that a biosocial explanation had certain inherent dangers. For instance, if the effect of the fetal gonadal hormones is to determine sexually-dimorphic behaviours in humans, and if we have already decided which behaviours are "masculine" (e.g., sports participation) and which are "feminine" (e.g., sedentary indoor activities), then how can we be certain that the behaviour is truly sexually dimorphic? The answer, of course, is that we cannot be certain. Linked to this problem was the concern that the evidence, conflicting and primitive as it was, could be used to argue that there really are stereotypical male and female attributes organized in the brain before birth, and that, therefore, imposing absolute equality between the sexes is useless.

At the same time that I was engaging in this research on sexual dimorphism and athleticism, sociobiology, in the form of Edward

Wilson's *Sociobiology: The New Synthesis* (1975) and his *On Human Nature* (1978), exploded on both the academic and popular scenes, and, in reaction to it, the marxist and feminist critiques also came to the fore. Coupled with this, was the publication in 1978 of Alice Rossi's "A Biosocial Perspective on Parenting", in which she argued that we have ignored the biological determinants to women's traditional role in childcare. This was a reversal from her previous position of arguing for absolute equality between the sexes. Her new argument is that equality is "quite compatible with the traditional (and, in fact, unequal) division of childcare between the sexes — a division which she now claims is ordained by biologically given differences in the responsiveness of men and women to children" (Sayers, 1982:148). Rossi's article was also accompanied by a loud feminist outcry. What has happened since, largely as a result of the critiques, is that all biological explanations of social behaviour are taken as problematic, at least by most feminists. More specifically, insightful research in behavioral endocrinology and neuroendocrinology is included in the same critique as sociobiology. I think this is wrong, and I intend now to argue why.

Biological Determinism

Janet Sayers, in her recent excellent book *Biological Politics*, suggests that we must distinguish between biological "determinist" and biological "essentialist" accounts of sexual inequality. In this section I shall deal with biological determinism. It has been around for a very long time, but the most recent revival stems from the social Darwinism of the nineteenth century, made popular in the twentieth century by proponents such as Ardrey, Lorenz, Morris, Tiger and Fox. Their thesis is that "human social organization represents natural human dispositions" (Sahlins, 1977:4). Although there are claims to more scientific rigour among the sociobiologists who follow, the thesis is still the same: there is a "one-to-one parallel between the character of human biological propensities and the properties of human social systems'' (Sahlins, 1977:5). In relation to women, the biological determinist argument runs as follows: ''because of biological factors, sexual equality can be achieved only at the cost of damage to women's reproductive functions'' (Sayers, 1982:7).

Much sexism and outright discrimination in sport, for example is based on the notion of inherent female inferiority, the belief in a ''weaker sex''. [6] In fact, in his book *On Human Nature,* Wilson uses the example of sport to buttress his argument that ''anatomy bears the imprint of the sexual division of labour'' (p. 126). He claims that:

> Pound for pound, they [men] are stronger and quicker in most categories of sport, their skeletal torsion, and the density of their muscles are particularly suited for running and throwing, the archaic specialities of the ancestral hunter-gatherer males. The world track records reflect the disparity. (p. 127)

He goes on to cite some statistics on male/female differentials in sport performance, no doubt correct when he was writing, but what of the most recent available evidence?

We all know that most women cannot run as fast, throw as far, or jump as high as most men. Even among the most superbly trained athletes, there are still some substantial performance differentials. For instance, men run the 100 metres eight per cent faster; they swim the same distance ten per cent faster; they can jump well over a foot higher, and so forth. However, it can be shown quite easily that over the past fifty years, and a much shorter period of time in some sports, the overall performance of female athletes has improved significantly relative to male performance. In other words, the gaps are closing fast, especially over the longer distances. There are even some predictions that performance *equality* between the sexes will be achieved in twenty or thirty years. For instance, Dyer (1982) shows that if the rate of decrease in performance differentials between the sexes seen throughout 1968-80 in track events were to be maintained, *it would disappear altogether by 1995.* [7]

Wilson and the sociobiologists are quite simply wrong. Women athletes are inferior, at present, not necessarily due to biological reasons, but because they have not benefited over the years from the same systematic and rigorous training as men. [8] Moreover, we know so little about the actual physical potential of girls and women that it is impossible to claim categorically that they are limited by their biology. As Janet Sayers puts it:

> Sociobiologists . . . often use the same social attitudes to corroborate aspects of their theory as they use to derive the theory in the first place. This is not to deny that writers like E.O. Wilson provide a wealth of detailed observations on animals in order to illustrate their claims about animal behaviour. They have, however, singularly failed to provide any systematic or comprehensive review of the ethnographic and historical data on human societies in order to make good their claim that certain features of these societies are also dictated for all time by biology (p. 58-9).

Biological Essentialism

Feminist theorists have sometimes been accused of neglecting and ignoring biology. If they posit some sort of cultural determinism, which some do, then this accusation would be correct. However, as Sayers (1982) points out, feminist theorists have, in fact, "suggested a number of ways of accommodating the facts of biology in their analysis of women's situation" (p. 107). One of these ways is through "biological essentialism":

> Women, they say, have become alienated from their essential nature as a result of living in a male-dominated society, and it is the task of feminism to enable women to get back in touch with their biologically given essence by, among other things, persuading society to construe and value femininity and female biology equally with masculinity and male biology (p. 147).

I mentioned earlier that, in 1978, the renowned American sociologist and feminist Alice Rossi published an article in which she argued for a biosocial perspective on parenting. What she meant was that the current sociological view of the family is distorted by its cultural determinism, and that, in order to rectify this bias, the traditional sociological approach to the family ought to be supplemented by bio-evolutionary theory as well as by recent findings from behavioral endocrinology. At the time, I was quite struck by what she wrote, because this was precisely the position I had put forward in my critique of our overt culturally deterministic explanations of female sport socialization (Hall, 1977). Here, I drew upon research in behavioral endocrinology and neuroendocrinology to show the potential for a biosocial explanation of female athleticism. However, as I have shown in the first section of this paper, the evidence of prenatal androgenization and the resultant "tomboyism" is quite equivocal, and we are on very dangerous ground when making causal assertions.

There is, however, another aspect to biological essentialism as it relates to female athleticism which is perhaps more dangerous, in that it does not serve women's interests. A theme which predominates the literature and research in this area is whether or not competitive sport "masculinizes" the female athlete psychologically and behaviorally. [9] In the early 1960s, Eleanor Metheny, an American physical educator, argued that the socially sanctioned image of what she called "feminine sports competition" was derived from several general principles (Metheny, 1965). The principles themselves were derived from "a conception of the female's role as a consequential force in the universe of space, time, mass and energy" (p. 52). For instance, she argued, it is not appropriate for women to engage in contests where there is an attempt to overcome an opponent by the direct application of bodily force. Metheny reasoned that since this prohibition "cuts across all cultural lines", then it must be traceable to some "biologically defined difference common to men and women of all social groups" (Metheny, 1965:52). The explanation, she reasoned, lay in the fact that within the act of procreation, the male may use his muscular powers to coerce the female and force her to submit to his will, whereas the passive, nurturing female cannot similarly coerce the male. By extension, she argued, it is *biologically appropriate* for the male to force another person to submit to his will by the direct application of muscular powers through bodily contact; conversely it is *biologically inappropriate* for the female to coerce or subdue another person by use of her muscular powers. Metheny willingly accepted the prohibition, as do many people today, as "a symbolic formulation of socially sanctioned female roles", roles for which women have some supposed biological predisposition. Therefore, Metheny wrongly evokes some sort of mythical feminine essence and uses it to justify blatant sex discrimination in sport. [10]

Biology and Sex Equality in Sport

In arguing for sex equality in sport, we cannot simply ignore biology. Women and men, less so female and male adolescents, are different in ways which often affect performance. Furthermore, females and males, on average, have distinctive athletic abilities. Females are smaller, more flexible, have a lower centre of gravity, and better insulation. Males have greater speed, size and strength. Most women would be at a physiological disadvantage if they participated with men in sports demanding these qualities, sports like football, basketball, baseball, and icehockey. Unfortunately, the "swifter, higher, stronger" ethos predominates the excessively professionalized and commercialized North American sport. On the other hand, the tremendous popular appeal of women's gymnastics and figure skating, and the inclusion of rhythmical gymnastics in the 1984 Olympics, are signs that our tastes in sport are broadening.

What we must not do, however, is to posit some sort of biological essentialism which "offers women the goal of achieving equality through pursuing an essentially different role from men" (Sayers, 1982: 153) in sport. In other words, everyone, male and female alike, has an equal right to what could be called the "basic benefits" of sport (e.g., health, fitness, fun, skill development). At the same time, male and female athletes must have equal access to the "scarce benefits" of sport, which include such tangible aspects as salary and prize money and the less tangible aspects of status and publicity. And yet, physical differences between the sexes alone prevent equal numbers of men and women from participating in all sports. Sex differences are frequently a justification for establishing separate competition groups. The rationale is usually that the interests of females can be served in no other way since they require protection due to their assumed physical inferiority. Where sex is not relevant to performance, the sport could be integrated; unfortunately, this is rarely the case. As we better understand whether existing sex differences in performance are due to physiological characteristics or to cultural and social inequalities, more and more sports will become integrated. More and more women and men, in future, will and should compete on an equal basis.

Footnotes

1. I am grateful to Sayers (1982) for helping me to recognize this point.
2. For more detail, see Hall (1977).
3. *Androgenital syndrome,* also known as congenital adrenal hyperplasia, is caused by malfunctioning adrenal glands which produce too much androgen. This results in the masculinization of the external genitalia if the fetus is female. *Turner's syndrome* is caused by a gonadal defect whereby no hormones are produced; thus the fetus develops as a female regardless of genetic sex. In *androgen insensitivity,* also called testicular feminization, the fetus is supplied with androgen but is unable to use it, thus resulting in a genetic male with feminized genitalia.
4. See Hall (1977) for the specific studies.
5. What is also interesting is that "interactionists", such as John Money, end up asserting some weird combination of both biological and environmental determinism. See Raymond (1977) for a discussion of this point.
6. See Hall and Richardson (1982), Chapter 5.
7. There is reason to be cautious about these sorts of predictions. Firstly, they apply to only a tiny proportion of the population. Secondly, the very fact that women athletes at least *appear* to be catching up to men may spur male athletes on to even greater heights. Thirdly, technology is playing an increasingly greater role in athletic performance and it may affect males and females differentially, to the advantage of the male athlete.
8. Wilson uses the example of East Germany, where, he claims, male and female athletes receive equal training, and yet the performance levels are still different. What he does not seem to know is that even East German women athletes vis-a-vis male athletes have only recently benefited from similar training and coaching, if indeed they are the same.
9. For my critique of this literature and research, see Hall (1981).

10. Nor was she cognizant of the political nature of her argument since the male's structural capacity to "coerce the female and force her to submit to his will" is not just an aspect of sexual intercourse, it is also fundamental to rape.

References

Dyer, K.F. (1982), *Challenging the Men: Women in Sport,* University of Queensland Press, St. Lucia.

Hall, M.A. (1977), Hormones, females and sport: The implication of prenatal androgenization for female sport socialization. Paper presented at the Canadian Association of Sport Sciences annual meeting, Winnipeg, 29 Sept.-1 Oct., 1977.

Hall, M.A. (1981), *Sport, Sex Roles and Sex Identity,* Canadian Research Institute for the Advancement of Women, Ottawa.

Hall, M.A., and Richardson, D.A. (1982), *Fair Ball: Towards Sex Equality in Canadian Sport,* Canadian Advisory Council on the Status of Women, Ottawa.

Lerner, R.M. (1976), *Concepts and Theories of Human Development,* Addison-Wesley, Reading, Mass.

Metheny, E. (1965), *Connotations of Movement in Sport and Dance,* Wm. C. Brown, Dubuque, Iowa.

Money, J., and Ehrhardt, A. (1972), *Man & Woman Boy & Girl,* The John Hopkins University Press, Baltimore.

Raymond, J. (1977), Transsexualism: The ultimate homage to sex-role power, *Chrysalis,* 3, 11-23.

Reinisch, J.M. (1976), Effects of prenatal hormone exposure on physical and psychological development in humans and animals: With a note on the state of the field. In *Hormones, Behaviour and Psychopathology* edited by E.J. Sachar, Raven Press, New York.

Reinisch, J.M., and Karow, W.G. (1977), Prenatal exposure to synthetic progestins and estrogens: Effects on human development, *Archives of Sexual Behaviour,* 6(4), 257-288.

Rossi, A. (1978), A biosocial perspective on parenting, *Daedalus,* 106(2), 1-31.

Sahlins, M. (1977), *The Use and Abuse of Biology,* Tavistock Publications, London.

Sayers, J. (1982), *Biological Politics,* Tavistock Publications, London.

Wilson, E.O. (1975), *Sociobiology: The New Synthesis,* Harvard University Press, Cambridge, Mass.

Wilson, E.O. (1978), *On Human Nature,* Harvard University Press, Cambridge, Mass.

Hegemony and Superstructure:
A Feminist Critique of Neo-Marxism

MARY O'BRIEN

It would be difficult to say which brand of neo-marxism best represents the mainstream of socialist thinking. Marxism spawns junior "isms" with a fertility which pays tribute to the vitality of the tradition and creates confusions for socialists. To women, Marxism speaks only in parenthetical whispers. Leninism, Stalinism, and Maoism are, for better or worse, represented in active political systems, none of which have taken the "women problem" very seriously. Trotskyism has taken up the role of conscience and fidelity to the truth of Marxism. Critical theory and Althusserian Structuralism remain at a level of abstraction which is essentially idealist. Hegemony theory is interesting in that it takes as its central problem the question of why the proletarian in bourgeois societies has failed to mount the longed-for revolution, and does so in terms of empirical investigation of the role of the State in ideological reproduction. The major interests of this group is in education, which is seen as the process of legitimation of knowledge and false consciousness, and the mobilization, active support of and consent to State power.

Hegemony theory, however, which developed in England, America and Canada as the New Sociology of Education, maintains that persistent disregard of women is a constant challenge to socialist feminists. [1] The analysis of the social processes of ideological reproduction and the centrality accorded to education in the reproduction of selected cultural traditions is appropriate enough when considering the "women problem".

Educational questions, Michael Apple argues, are always, in some quite specific sense, moral questions. [2] The process of reification embedded in commodity production obscures such issues: bureaucratic organization, to say nothing of bourgeois social science, loses sight of ethical issues in the fetishistic pursuit of "objectivity". Management models, of persons and of systems, project social relations in the symbolic languages of computer science, in which the fetishism of the representation of people as things advances to the representation of people as print-outs.

Hegemonists share with feminists the view that these issues have ethical dimensions, but ethics is, on the whole, a subject which makes Marxists nervous. Yet it can be demonstrated that, from its modern natality in the Puritan movement in the seventeenth century, feminism has asserted, with varying degrees of conviction, that women's morality is of a different and superior order to men's morality. The current name for such a conviction is "bourgeois deviation", at least among Marxists; the Right regards feminism very simply as sin. I do not want to argue this particular issue, but I do want to point out that hegemonic theory takes value systems to be something more complex than capitalist propaganda: it is concerned with uncovering and analyzing selective processes of the identification, formation and persistence of values, and the impact of class divisions on value issues and of value issues on class consciousness. This sort of analysis confirms that values are a strong factor in systems maintenance. However, it does not, as is the case with Parsonian structuralism, separate value systems from their economic roots or, like vulgar Marxism, bury them in the soil in which these roots germinate. Furthermore, there are clear indications that there are working class values created by working class practice, although these values do tend to be those of "the lads" and to be what bourgeois social scientists tend to think of as deviant.

Hegemonic analysis attempts to unpack such social processes without falling into the crevices of theology or economism. With such an approach, it is at least methodologically possible that hegemonic analysis might eventually cast some light on the conjoined questions of the social construction of gender identity and the differentiation of female and male value systems. Perhaps it will do so when it broadens its relational analysis to gender relations and to the impact of male supremacist ideology on both curriculum and the socio-sexual activities of working class men and women. It is important to do this for practical and political reasons. Feminists such as Jennifer Shaw, Jan Harding and Sheila Tobias have begun to question such sacred bulls as co-education and math/science astigmatisms. [3] Politically, the time has come to provide some scientific substance to the notion that the personal is political and to analyze the revolutionary potential of the private realm. Feminology must now lay the intellectual foundations of feminist education, feminist politics and feminist values. This cannot be done outside of intellectual history, for the strategies in question have as their objective historical change. I do not believe that cultural separatism can meet this objective, or address the social issues.

The question has always been: where do we start? The answer cannot be other than: where we are and with the conditions and problems which history presents to us. Thus neo-marxism, which marginalizes women but does not obliterate them, may hold heurestic and analytical possibilities which its current androcentrism conceals. For example, it may permit a deeper understanding of the relation of patriarchy and that complex abstraction which we call the State.

The attempt to rescue Marxist understanding of the state from the crude pincers of economism and reductionism has its own intellectual roots in the work of Antonio Gramsci. Gramsci aspired to produce a historical materialist analysis which would revitalize, elaborate and, above all, be tactically useful in the fight against Fascism; he also hoped to promote the understanding of the relation of theory to culture, ideology and to political practice. Like all competent dialectical logicians, he had to postulate his problematic in terms of a dialectic of universal and particular. Unlike Hegel, who opposes the universal spirit of Reason to particular historical understandings of rationality, or

Marx, who proceeds to the analysis of capitalism from the opposition of generalized commodity production and particular commodity, Gramsci proceeded from a different formulation, one which was historically developed by Marx himself but not adequately explicated.

Gramsci was concerned to analyze the relation of a historically generalized economic substructure and the complex particularity of superstructures. He argued that superstructures, in terms of culture and ideology, have their own dialectical dynamics, and that class antagonisms are mediated in cultural activities, both of social forms and class consciousness. This struggle takes place in a social arena which exists between the economic realm and the apparatus of ruling class coercion which is but one aspect of the State. Ideology is not a product of naked coercion but of social practice in the realm of everyday life and thought, where consciousness acts on the experiential social context in which the subject is immersed, and where men (sic) can only deal with the realities which history presents to them.

This complex theoretical project has two significant dimensions: for Gramsci, the rise of the "corporate" fascist State had thrown into stark relief the centrality of the State in superstructural and infrastructural formations; the State had developed historically into much more than the executive committee of the ruling class. On the other hand, Gramsci had studied Croce's polemic against materialism, and his positing of historicity as the essence of universal man was perceived by Gramsci to be the culmination of the defects of subjective idealism, an abstract individualism which lay like dead matter in the heart of the reality of community. He did not note that "universal man" was a male supremicist construct.

For Gramsci, what was important was the creation of a universal class, which meant the abolition of class as such. Gramsci understood class consciousness itself to be dialectically structured — the site of a struggle between "common sense", or acceptable knowledge, and "good sense", which has the potential to overthrow common sense and its ideological baggage in the revolutionary struggle to realize true consciousness.

Hegemony is the "motor" of common sense, defining reality and organizing consent to such ruling class definitions of truth, but in that very process it creates the possibility of counter-hegemony. [4] Hegemony relies on cultural relations. Education is especially vital to elaborate the axioms of practices of "common sense", yet in doing this it creates the critical "good sense" which challenges accepted definitions.

There is nothing at all abstract about Gramsci's epistemology. According to him, working class consciousness is based on economic reality, but this is not a reflexive nor a reductionist relation. It is a *mediated* relation, and the mediator is culture or, in Gramsci's terminology, civil society. The signficance of the hegemonic and mediative functions of the State becomes clear when the State takes a totalitarian form. Gramsci's understanding of the State is that of class rule working on two super-structural levels, [5] political society and civil society. These together constitute hegemony, the one protecting the hegemony of the ruling class "by the armour of coercion," [6] the other, civil society, representing the needs of individuals and standing between the political level of state and economic structures. For Gramsci, this is by no means a formal model, nor does he utilize it with particular consistency, but what he does understand clearly is that the relation between substructure and superstructure must be socially mediated in the living relations of proletarians and bourgeoisie.

The economic sub-structure not only produces goods, it "produces" social relations, [7] but the political drama and "organic unity" of these relations is played out in the realm of civil society where it creates autonomous cultural forms. The State attempts to control these cultural forms, and does so, when necessary, by summoning its coercive powers; but it cannot and does not need to produce detailed blue prints as long as it can prescribe acceptable outlines of common sense and elicit general consent to these. This has two implications for Gramsci. The first is that the working class must struggle to define and direct its own cultural formations. It can, in fact, initiate cultural changes *within civil society*, "pre-formations", in Gramsci's terminology, of the eventual destruction of the State and transformation of mode of production. Secondly, Gramsci insists the State *must* wither away if a universal classless society is to achieve its historic mission of the negation of class, for the State is no abstraction but the living totality of class division. Such a doctrine explains why Mussolini preferred to keep Gramsci locked up, but it hardly made him a hero in terms of Stalinism either.

This short summary lays no claim to be definitive: there is much debate about what Gramsci actually understood by "civil society", about his actual relation to Marx and Lenin's theoretical formulation, and whether he really believed that ideological/cultural relations were not only autonomous but were moments which took temporal precedence over the transformation of productive forces in changing a particular "historical bloc". [8] Such questions exercise Gramsci scholars as indeed they should: the question of whether a new form of State must *enforce* morality until such time as the masses stop resisting the displaced interpretation of morality is no small matter. It is, in part, an historical question in terms of whether all states have actually done this, but is also an ethical concern: is it necessary for new and *revolutionary* states to combine hegemony and force until they achieve classless consensus? Gramsci claims that, in practice, strong States rule more by hegemony — that is, consensual politics — than by tyranny.

Politics and education become inseparable in Gramsci's work: political action is education. In this broad sense, education is the key to the maintenance of hegemony, but it also leads to the breakdown of hegemony by challenging and, eventually, overthrowing consensus. Where, then, is this activity to be located? Both theoretically and in practice, it is found in that social space and in those social relations which Gramsci calls "civil society":

> What we can do for the moment, is to fix two major superstructural levels: the one that can be called "civil society" that is the ensemble of organisms commonly called private, and that of "political society" or "the State". These two levels correspond on the one hand to the function of "hegemony" which the dominant group exercises throughout society

and on the other hand to that of "direct domination" or command exercised through the State and juridical government. [9]

What is of great interest to feminists, I think, is Gramsci's notion that civil society not only can be but must be transformed in a concrete manner. [10] The concept of "civil society", so important to Enlightenment thought and to Hegel's notion of its transcendence by the university state, is not treated systematically by Gramsci. It is for him the realm of *needs* rather than the stern *necessity* for survival which governs economic activity. These needs are deeply felt, and their social expression is shaped by rather than emergent from the economic realm. It is needful but not necessary for the ruling class to perpetuate itself by controlling the state apparatus, just as it is needful but not necessary for the proletariat to prepare itself for the political struggles which will abolish particular man in the creation of universal man and abolish class antagonisms in the abolition of class itself. For such a project, proletarian man, in Gramsci's view, has a need for education: education is therefore a pre-condition of militant class consciousness and an active promise of the possibility of transforming false consciousness to true consciousness. The notion that patriarchy is or has been needful but not necessary is not part of Gramsci's analysis, but as "needs" is defined as historical, as opposed to "necessity" which is biological, the formulation raises some challenging theoretical and practical questions for feminists.

The opposition of particular man and universal man is the second axiom of Gramsci's dialectical logic, an opposition to be mediated only by the revolutionary class activity which will abolish the coercive State in favour of a universalized (that is, classless and stateless) Civil Society. Gramsci argues strenuously against all notions of "man-in-general": indeed he scorns all human nature theories. The quest to identify the "essence of man", so important in the history of political thought, is vehemently rejected: "man", for Gramsci, is not a concept, nor is he "natural". He is a social product, and his subjectivity is grounded in the "subjectivity of a social group."[11] However, Gramsci's perception of "man" at no time denies his masculinity *per se*; Gramsci no doubt thinks it is a non-generic form, but it is not, for Gramsci has no notion of patriarchal hegemony and the reality of gender conflict.

Non-antagonistic forms of social unity are to emerge from class struggle and the transformation of the production mode. The interesting point is that Gramsci argues that the political strategies which can bring this about involve a preliminary struggle to transform civil society. There is a clear relation between Gramsci's notion of civil and political society and feminist concern with private and public life, and his schema embodies at least some notion that the personal is political. Indeed, he has been criticized for a tendency to lapse into psychologism. However, apart from the obvious problem of the generic particularization of "universal man", Gramsci's notion of civil society is also circumscribed by his fixation on education and his neglect of family relations. He speaks of civil society as local culture centred on school and family but — at least in his translated works — has little to say about family.[12] He is more interested in the birth of organic intellectuals than in the birth of real live babies.

It is not at all clear whether Gramsci envisaged changes in the form and/or content of familial relations. It is one thing to claim that the nuclear form of family is the specific form developed in capitalist society: there is historical evidence for this theory. It is quite another thing to claim that the only content of family which is interesting for Marxists is the economic structure of households and the sexual division of labour, as Marxist feminists have been wont to affirm. This statement opens the possibility of reforming the economic life of women or even the level and strategy of political involvement for women, but still permits the dismissal of social relations of biological reproduction on the grounds that such an interest can serve only to steer enquiry into the muddy and unproductive waters of biological determinism.[13] The family is functional insofar as it reproduces labour power on an individual and species basis. It also reflects property relations, though less so in terms of corporate power and limited liability than in earlier historical forms of property relations. As understood by most Marxists, the relation of the family to mode of production is at best reflexive and at worst reductionist.[14] The family's role in ideological reproduction — in the socialization of young children, for example — is rarely examined, and its role in the reproduction of the social and ideological relations of male supremacy is thought to be exhausted in the concept of the sexual division of labour. There is thus a dogged evasion of the reality that women are oppressed by men.

The historical definition of "people" in general as "universal man" rests on the arbitrary conceptualization of certain *necessities* — such as the continuity of the species as a pre-condition of history — as mere *needs*. This sort of absurdity is the product of patriarchal hegemony, and it should be theorized as such. The determinant realm in the production of patriarchy is not the mode of production but the "ahuman" reality of biological reproduction. Patriarchy is a set of social relations, I would argue, grounded in the process of reproduction. All attempts to suggest that "universal" classless "man" will share *his* historic triumphs with women are as ideologically absurd as the canons of chivalry. They are absurd because women are not imperfect men with an inferior capacity for abstract thought and concrete action, nor is the oppression of women a sort of cultural by-product which illustrates the versatility of class hegemony. The concept of hegemony strongly points to the problem of ideology and popular consent in capitalist countries, then proceeds to define hegemony in the dialectically posed relations of economy, ideology and culture — the "mode of production" embracing relations of production, the reproduction of labour power and ideological reproduction. In collapsing the reproduction of labour power, that is, sustenance, into mode of production, the actual reproductive labour of women (what, indeed, women always understand in the first instance by the word "labour"), which ensures the birth of the individual and the continuity of the species, is negated.[15] In collapsing women's productive labour into labour in general, the actual exploitation of women workers by men workers is negated. In collapsing the particular ideology of male supremacy into the general category of ideological reproduction, the systematic denigration and, indeed, the physical violation of women in the name of that ideology, are negated. The results of this are twofold: in the first place, Marxism has nothing to say about the value of individuals; in the second place, it has nothing to say about gender struggle.

The question of the individual is one which produces a number of kneejerk responses from many Marxists: cries of bourgeois individualism, subjectivism and psychologism rend the air. To be sure, the polemic against liberal individualism, with its greedy sense of "I'm-all-right-Jack" and its inability to distinguish between free trade and free people, is one which has to be mounted. Marxist feminists have, on the whole, shared this polemic. We have not yet started to assert the need to pose our materialist problem specifically from our own experience, to ask the forbidden questions and to proclaim that, if the theory does not fit, then the theory is inadequate. For example, we do not ask what, if it is the case that all labour creates value, is the sort of value created by women's reproductive labour? Is it not, in some sense (a sense to be analysed), the value of the individual life poised in dialectical contradiction to the life of the species? Why are we nervous of claiming that feminine experience creates and, in the teeth of patriarchal hegemony, attempts to sustain certain moral values which may not sit comfortably with those whose political imagination chokes in the mouths of cannons? Why do we not give the lie to the claim that birth is merely a biological happening, when our sex has universally created a reproductive culture around this event, consisting of variable, identifiable and persistent sets of social relations among mothers, sisters, mid-wives, children and (usually rather transitorily) men? Why do we accept the absurd insistence that capitalism has abolished the distinction between private and public life when millions of women are suffering privatization and privation in households? Why should we accept the notion that ideological hegemony is sustained in schools and in political parties when we know quite well that the hand that rocks the cradle is making sure that the swaddling clothes are either pink or blue?

Marxist feminists have no difficulty at all in understanding that social change is a collective endeavour, but we must surely be a little more critical of a collectivity in which the individual members never get born. That women's labour is cheap labour is indisputable and must be changed. That life is cheap is not, I suggest, a careless indifference on the part of a ruling class, but a systematic indifference of a ruling sex to the value produced by women's reproductive labour. Only labour, Marx held, produced value, yet, by denying the capacity of women's reproductive labour power to produce value and failing to analyze and identify that value in social terms, we are left defenceless in the face of idealist claims that the value of a foetus is the same as the cultural value of a human being. There can be no human value without human labour, and no human value which is separate from the social relations which render it material.

All these issues are posed in a still preliminary way. Ironically, the understanding of how hegemony works might well be clarified in an ethnography of Marxist intellectuals. In Gramsci's terms, it may well be that Marxist intellectuals are now traditional because any claim they may have to be "organic" is destroyed in the vulgar teleology of the unicausality of productive modes on the one hand, and the refusal to come to terms with the social construction of the ideology of male supremacy on the other. This difficulty cannot be cured either by the extension of ethnographies to female sub-groups or by the limitation of Marxist-feminist enquiry to questions of women in the work force and to domestic labour. What is needed is an historical model which can give an account of male supremacy as an autonomous historical development. The crude superstructural model owes no debt to dialectical logic, and can get along quite well with positivist methodology. The dialectical relations, appearing by definition as class struggle, are found in both levels of structure, but the correction between the two levels is an unsolved problem. Hegemony theory goes some way towards resolution of this problem by Gramsci's positing of "civil society" as a mediating realm. What is being mediated, however, is a relation which is not dialectical, namely, the realm of economic necessity on the one hand and the need of a ruling class to control by means of violent coercion on the other. Quite apart from the obvious but unaddressed question of why hunger is epistemologically more important than sexuality, this relation is not even dichotomous, far less dialectical. Thus, the conception of civil society is partial, promising in form but very limited in content. The content of civil society cannot be circumscribed by the notions of political party experience as true education, or by faith in organic intellectuals bringing to the masses the knowledge which will make them withdraw consent to ruling class hegemony, the individual and the continuity of the race. Female reproductive consciousness is an integrative consciousness, linking the generations in a continuity over time and linking people as equal values. Its mediating force is physical labour as the ground of reproductive knowledge. Male reproductive consciousness, on the other hand, is an alienated consciousness. Paternity is essentially ideal: it is based on concept rather than experience, and dependent on a particular mode of reasoning, that of cause and effect. It is thus historical, for modes of reasoning are historical developments, and paternity must be understood as historical discovery. It is a problematic discovery: the discovery of integration in general species being is, at the same time, the discovery of material alienation from species being. Paternity is the discovery of uncertainty, materially grounded in alienation of the male seed. For men, physiology is fate, as I have remarked elsewhere. Paternal praxis arises in the context of efforts to mediate the alienation of the seed. These efforts generally take the forms of collusion with other men, the appropriation of children, and thus of women's reproductive labour, and the building of a hegemonic system to justify these procedures and to engineer consent to their interpretations of gender and knowledge. Historically, these efforts have been successful, and the condition of their success has lain in the involuntary component of women's reproductive labour. The fight for the control of reproductive power has been on the one hand a fight to resist the alienation of men from reproductive process, and on the other hand a struggle to maintain the involuntary nature of reproductive labour, to preserve men's reproductive freedom while cancelling their reproductive alienation. It is precisely because the involuntary component of reproductive labour is now challenged by technology (currently about as sophisticated as the water wheel) that the dialectics of reproduction emerge in a new social forms, which challenge patriarchal praxis as a denial of actual female reproductive experience and a wilful transformation of female reproductive consciousness. It is odd indeed that we have still to argue that reproduction is a form of knowledge with profound epistemological significance for women and men, and the fact that the argument must be made is itself a massive triumph for patriarchal hegemonic practice.

There can be no real analysis of hegemony unless it is recognized that cultural forms are subject to the articulation of consent of both a ruling class and a ruling sex. This recognition, in turn, cannot be accomplished on the grounds of economic determinism, however ameliorated or redivided. History has two infrastructures, one concerned with the daily reproduction of individuals (economic activity) and the other concerned with the reproduction of the species (the birth and sustenance of the new generation). Thus, if we are to be successful dialecticians and creative feminologists, we must develop a theoretical model which expresses these relations. Rather crudely, I would suggest that such a model would understand superstructures or, if one prefers, "civil society", as the level of mediation of the specific forms of contradiction emergent from three sources. The first of these is the economic substructure, in which contradiction emerges concretely as class struggle. The second is the reproductive substructure, in which contradiction emerges concretely as gender struggle. The third is the contradiction between these substructures, the contradiction between individual survival and genetic continuity, or the number of mouths to feed and the resources to feed them. Marxists, blinded by Malthusian antipathies, do not rate this latter question as "real", for they do not account demography a dialectical science. If they think at all about, for example, the fate of children in the Southern Sahara, the cliches of imperialist exploitation serve as adequate explanation. Meanwhile, the children die. The holistic character of dialectical materialism cannot cope, either, with analysis of the social relations of genital mutilation: this is a third world problem, we are told, and it would be impertinent to comment, far less interfere. Meanwhile, women suffer and die. The responsibility to conserve the natural environment is predicated on a concrete *genetic* relation to the future. Many men share in the social formation of an ethic of conservation, but, again, it is easier to lay the blame for destructiveness on capitalism rather than on men's alienated relation to the natural world.

The implications of a feminist model in terms of hegemony theory go far beyond the formulation of research questions or appropriate ethnographic samples. The question of consent is broadened from the public realm to the private realm: not only why and how a consensual working class consciousness develops, but why women consent to the ideology and practice of patriarchy. As the latter consensus shows more signs of erosion than the former, it appears to be a promising field for both research and political praxis. As far as education is concerned, the preoccupation with schooling must extend from public institutions to the locus of gender identification and reproductive knowledge in the family. Further, the question of violent coercion cannot be held in abeyance simply because the ruling classes do not find it necessary at a given moment to unsheathe their sabres publicly: violence in the private realm is an ongoing mode of social control which *may* be related to capitalism but *is*, overtly and unquestionably, related to male control of reproduction.

Questions of the social construction of reality must take into account, as Marx noted, such questions which history presents to us. What Marx did not note was that this is done selectively by men in general as well as by bourgeois men in particular. The ruling class and the ruling sex have, at this moment, a joint historical mission, but we cannot understand the current effort to get women back into conventional marriage and unpaid labour simply as emergent from the tribulations of capitalist crisis. We can understand far more clearly how this actually works if we examine, for example, the social production of popular culture.

One does not imagine that the State is sending out memos to songwriters to go back to sloppy lyrics about true romance, but they are being written. Why? The State is unlikely to encourage citizens to subvert the systems, yet this is certainly happening in America in terms of education in divine creation, abortion and homosexuality. In Britain, of course, class manipulation is generally much clearer, and the major effort at retraditionalizing women which was involved in the Royal Wedding is chiefly remarkable for its capacity to mask the crudity of the objective with the pomp of the execution. These are hegemonic activities which emerge from the reproductive substructure and must be understood as so doing. Only from the standpoint of feminist theory can we analyze how these activities work, and thus proceed to unify theory with knowledge in developing action for social change, a counter-hegemonic thrust which will challenge patriarchal power by translating the contention that "personal is political" from slogan to strategy, from private to public, from school to family and from theory to practice.

Footnotes

1. Angela McRobbie, "Settling Accounts with Subcultures", *Screen Education* 34, Spring 1980, p. 40. See also Madeleine Macdonald, *The Curriculum and Cultural Reproduction* (Milton Keynes, England, 1977).

2. Michael W. Apple, *Curriculum and Ideology* (London, Boston, Henley, 1979).

3. Jennifer Shaw, "Education and the Individual: School for Girls, or Mixed Schooling — A Mixed Blessing?" and Ian Harding, "Sex Differences in Performance in Science Examination", in *Schooling For Women's Work*, edited by Rosemary Deem (London, Boston, Henley, 1980); Sheila Tobias, *Overcoming Math Anxiety* (New York, 1978).

4. *Selections from the Prison Notebooks of Antonio Gramsci*, edited and translated by Quintin Hoare and Geoffrey Nowell Smith (London, 1971) (hereafter *P.N.*); Antonio Gramsci, *Letters from Prison*, selected, translated and introduced by Lynne Lawner (London, 1975); Antonio Gramsci, *The Modern Prince and Other Writings*, translated by Louis Marks (New York, 1975).

5. Hoare and Nowell Smith note (*P.N.*, p. 5, fn) that the Italian word "cet", which they translate at "Strata", does not mean quite that. Gramsci for

political reasons avoids the use of the word "class". "Levels" also suggest a hierarchical relation, where Gramsci clearly means to delineate a dialectical relation. Both political relations of the former to the ruling class is much more direct — although, of course, instrumentally individual proletarians do become soldiers and policemen/women.

6. *P.N.*, p. 263.

7. See, for example, Norberto Bobbio, "Gramsci and the Conception of Civil Society" and Jacques Texier, "Gramsci, Theoretician of the Superstructures", in *Gramsci and Marxist Theory* edited by Chantal Mouffe (London, Boston, Henley, 1979). For discussion of "historical bloc" and sex also see Waller L. Adamson, *Hegemony and Revolution* (Berkeley, Los Angeles, London, 1980), pp. 176-9.

8. See discussion by Leonard Paggi, "Gramsci's General Theory of Marxism" in Chantal Mouffe, *op. cit.*, pp. 122-3.

9. *P.N.*, p. 12.

10. In ". . . the enigmatic mosaic that Gramsci laboriously assembled in prison, the words 'State', 'Civil Society', 'Political Society', 'domination' or 'direction' all undergo a constant slippage." Perry Anderson, "The Antimonies of Antonio Gramsci", *New Left Review* 100, November 76-January 77.

11. Gramsci, *Il Materiali Storico e la filoso fia di Benedetto Croce*, p. 191. Quoted by Paggi, *op. cit.*, p. 123.

12. Gramsci's notion of schooling is traditional, centring on the primary need for literacy and a concern with discipline. Harold Enthwhistle appears to believe that Gramsci's quite conservative notions of curriculum undermine the radical integrity of the "new" sociology of education. See Harold Enthwhistle, *Antonio Gramsci: Conservative Schooling and Radical Politics* (London, Boston, Henley, 1979). It should be added that, in his personal life, Gramsci's concern for the welfare and education of his family is dignified and humane, as his moving *Letters from Prison* attest. He had two sons, no daughters.

13. Michele Barrett, *Women's Oppresion Today: Problems in Marxist Feminist Analysis* (London, 1980), pp. 12-3.

14. *Ibid.*, p. 12.

15. Mary O'Brien, *The Politics of Reproduction* (London, Boston, Henley, 1981), Chapter 1.

Sexism in Research: Anthropological Perspectives

ANNAMMA JOY

In a recent article on male bias in anthropological literature, the author, Milton (1979), wrote:

> Far from being a cultural universal, it is simply their [feminist anthropologists] own evaluation of the relation between the sexes. As such it is a product of their concern with their position in our own society and has little to contribute to the development of anthropology as a scientific discipline.

In this paper I will examine the concept of male bias, and explore the validity of a feminist critique utilizing it, in the study of culture and society. In order to do that I will summarize Milton's agrument and then follow it with a discussion of issues and problems raised in the literature on women.

Male Bias

In the initial stages of the feminist influence, general dissatisfaction with work done on and by women was expressed. The near invisibility of women in the ethnographic record was viewed with much concern and general recommendations to fill the lacunae were made. The few ethnographies that did exist, for instance, on Australian aborigines were viewed with great interest, as alternate models of society (Goodale 1971, Kaberry 1970).

Two basic sources of male bias in the literature have been identified by feminist anthropologists. The first exists in the theoretical frameworks that were formulated and used primarily

101

by men (and women) nurtured in a male dominated society. Secondly, it was argued, male bias exists in the cultures being studied. Together, then, these sources have worked to the detriment of knowledge about approximately one half the population of each society that is studied.

The next major theme that can be found in the feminist critique of anthropological literature is the concept that female subordination is more cultural than social. This viewpoint indicates that ideas of women (in a cultural sense) and men were thus more significant sources of data than what men and women did or how they acted. A corollary to this concept is the fact that in all societies women accepted the ideology of their own inferiority.

As Milton points out, there are several problems with the above arguments. First of all, merely studying women or employing women to study other women is not, methodologically, a solution. Indeed, it can be argued that a female bias merely replaces male bias. Secondly, the use of existing biased data as a case for demonstrating universal male dominance is itself problematic. Thirdly, if male bias is cultural rather than social, then evidence is mandatory for demonstrating the importance of one data base over the other in the interpretation. Fourthly, if, as some argue, male dominance is universal, then what is to be done with data that counters this proposition? For instance, Briggs (1974) and Reither (1975) argue that women do not always accept the ideology of male dominance: indeed, they go so far as to argue that women actively devalue their men. On a final note, if information is gathered from males who are indeed dominant in their culture, can the anthropologist be held responsible for presenting such data?

Another version of male bias in anthropological literature is presented by Ardener (1975). He makes the distinction between "dominant models" and "muted models" in a society. The implication is that the males who, through their mobility and experience, acquire power, thus create the dominant models of the society. In turn, women, who are less powerful, present the muted models of the society. Traditionally, as Ardener points out, anthropologists focussed on the former, and this created a sex bias in the literature. The solution, he argues, lies in studying women's models and focussing on women's spheres of activity, such as ritual and symbolic occupations.

Milton (1970) quite rightly challenges this description on the grounds that no clear criteria is used in identifying male and female models. What happens, for instance, when females use male models? The interpretation of the data thus becomes problematic. Ardener's solution is to claim that priority goes to those who formulated these models. In such an explanation, social reality is seen as fixed and individuals are seen as powerless in changing that reality. Needless to say, this raises other problems relating to social change as well.

In the light of such difficulties, it is not surprising that Milton deems as irrelevant and useless the concept of male bias in theory building. However, it is my purpose to demonstrate the validity of such a concept, in the light of new interpretations of the ethnographic record. It helps us to ask new questions, to challenge older assumptions and critique exiting theories.

In order to achieve my purpose, I will briefly refer to Eichler's (1980) definition of sexist science. According to Eichler (1980) sexist science is characterized by the following features:

1) Women are to a large degree ignored, yet conclusions and theories are phrased in such general terms that they purport to be applicable to all humanity.

2) If women are considered, they tend to be considered only in so far as they are important for and related to men, not by virtue of their own importance as human subjects.

3) Where both sexes are considered, the male is generally taken as the norm, and the female as the deviation from the norm.

4) Sexist content is mirrored in sexist language, as reflected, for instance, in the use of the generic "he" and the generic "man".

5) Sexist science is full of preconceived notions concerning a "masculine" and "feminine" nature. Consequently, identical behaviours or situations involving women and men are described and analyzed differently according to sex. In other words, we find a consistent double standard within sexist science.

6) By using sexist notions of human nature and employing a double standard in interpreting findings, sexist science itself becomes one

contributing factor in the maintenance of the sex structure from which it arose in the first place and in which it is grounded.

In the following sections I will discuss both the traditional theories of society and changes that have occurred in these theories as a result of a feminist perspective.

Biological and Evolutionary Theories

One of the major determinants, it has been argued, of universal male dominance is male physical strength and aggression. Goldberg (1973), in his book *The Inevitability of Patriarchy,* states that male dominance is physiologically based, i.e., it is associated with higher testosterone levels in the male, which gives the male an aggressive advantage. This in turn helps to institutionalize male authority and universally determines the higher status positions they hold. He even goes on to say that:

> it is the feminists' folly to believe that new knowledge will render the biological factor any less determinative.

Apart from being a grossly oversimplified single factor biological theory, Goldberg's assertion totally denies and ignores the historical and ethnographical record. For instance, women in matrilineal systems are seen as being under the control of some man, be it father, brother or spouse. Needless to add, in such a version of society, reality is fixed and change is impossible. While this represents one extreme end of the continuum, other evolutionary theories lay emphasis on aggression in the evolution of culture (Tiger 1969, 1971; Morris 1967).

Man The Hunter Hypothesis

The popular "Man the hunter" hypothesis clearly assigns centrality to hunting in the emergence of culture and the argument holds that cooperation between hunters fostered the development of male leadership and social organization (Tiger and Fox 1971). Women's work was generally considered boring, peripheral and not conducive to cooperation (Steward 1955).

The feminist perspective helped to expose the male bias in this kind of evolutionary theory (Slocum 1975). Isaac (1978) presents an alternate version of the theory of cooperation, using the link between the socio-biological concept of kin selection and sharing behaviour. In such an analysis food sharing does not even assume hunting. Zihlman (1981) and McGrew (1981) support the finding that the sharing of gathered food could have been established before extensive hunting began: indeed, it could have even facilitated the emergence of hunting. Contemporary evidence concerning hunters and gatherers such as the !Kung-San further reinforces the centrality of gathering in their diet.

As an extension of the above, it can be seen that food gathering and sharing must have also necessitated the use of utensils as food carriers. Oswalt (1976) argues that the perishable nature of such materials (i.e., bark and leaves) has prevented its survival. Kraybill (1977) likewise raises the problem of male archeologists who have not collected, described and categorized women's utensils and tools.

The concept of sharing was also extended to child care activities, which are incompatible with rigid dominance hierarchies or aggressive behaviour. Sharing also necessitated physical proximity, and the mother-child bond would have been the crucial social link within and among groups (see also Gough 1975). Isaac (1978) even includes communication as part of this sharing behaviour, i.e., between mother and child. This then calls into question the popular notion that the development of language was central to the need for planning and executing the hunt (see also Hockett and Ascher 1964 for a similar critique).

While most anthropologists agree that the sharing complex is related to the division of labour (Isaac 1978), there is no agreement on the "universal" image of Man the hunter. One interpretation of the image is that men do the arduous tasks such as hunting and warfare, and that these activities are incompatible with child bearing and rearing (Friedl 1975). Thus, men are thought to have evolved specialized adaptations to such activities. Leibowitz (1975), however, cautions against thinking of male strength and aggression as adaptive behaviour in the sphere of warfare and hunting. Using evidence from observation of non-human primates, she suggests that the smaller size and strength of the female may be an adaptation to child bearing — an efficient allocation of energy.

In any event, to think of hunting as a purely male activity ignores the ethonographic record (see, for instance, the cases of the Mbuti pygmies and the Agta). Also, the classification of hunting itself seems to be problematic. Lee (1968) categorizes shell fishing as gathering. Further, are trapping and fishing hunting? Thus theoretical and methodological problems exist in the interpretation of biological reasoning and evolutionary theories.

Furthermore, even if the image of ''Woman the gatherer'' helps to fill in gaps in our knowledge of hunting and gathering societies, it is still not sufficient to stop there. Rosaldo (1980), for instance, asks: why did hunting peoples never celebrate women's deeds, since they were crucial to human survival? Indeed, she goes on to say, that ''female sexuality'' in such contexts ''is seen more as a stimulant (demanding celebration) or an irritant (requiring control by rape) than as an active force in organizing social life.''

To carry the argument further, she points to a situation characterized by the emergence of a social hierarchy that ranks married men over unmarried men and encourages women to use their sexual appeal to undermine, support or stimulate initiatives by men. In such contexts, a sort of ''sexual politics'' appear to be central to women's lives. It is by posing such questions and making such arguments that the feminist perspective has contributed to the re-evaluation and re-interpretation of taken-for-granted explanations.

Theories of Universal Asymmetry

A well known theory of social organization states that the incest taboo and the exchange of women mark the beginnings of culture (Levi-strauss 1969, 1971). The assumption in this theory is that women are indeed subordinate; what is more, the necessity of establishing the assumption's validity does not even arise. Needless to say, in Levi-strauss' framework, forms such as matrilineal kinship are both unique and aberrant.

Using the premise of female subordination, Ortner (1974) expands on it and suggests that child bearing and child rearing activities link women with nature rather than culture. On a methodological note, she adds that the cultural realm precedes social actions and behaviours in theoretical and methodological importance. Thus, even when women use male models there is sufficient evidence to make the case for universal female inferiority (this is also implied by Ardener). Reiter's (1975) study questions this assumption. Also, as Quinn (1977) says, ignoring evidence of female insubordination is like choosing to examine only certain types of data. Sanday (1974), in a similar vein, argues that in the early stages of culture, "Female energy is concentrated in the reproduction and child rearing sphere whereas male energy is concentrated mainly in the subsistence sphere."

The low status of females in hunting and gathering societies is explained as a consequence of the assumption that women do not gain power unless they engage in productive activities (Sanday 1974: 194-195). Variations of this theme appear in the works of Friedl (1975) and Draper (1975). Whyte (1978), however, does not find any reason to assume that relative contribution to subsistence has any general status implication.

In a more recent article, Rosaldo (1980) cautions against uncritical use of the "universal" distinction between the domestic and public spheres of activity. She observes that the model as hitherto constructed (i.e., based on women's universal involvement in child bearing and rearing) is ahistorical and hides the diverse causes and contexts of gender roles. Gender relations in a culture reflect relations of power that remain unquestioned, if the separation of domestic and public is used uncritically and regarded as universal. For instance, the dichotomy does little to shed light on what women's lives were all about in hunting and gathering societies.

To speak of sexual asymmetry in hunting and gathering societies is not to make the claim that males are dominant.

> The pre-eminence enjoyed by men in groups like these appears to have as much to do with the significance of marriage for relationships among the men themselves — relationships that make wives something to achieve — as it does with sexual opposition or a more brute male dominance.

Thus women's status is itself not one thing but many things; as Quinn (1977) points out, it is a composite of measures that may not necessarily correlate with each other.

Theories of universal sexual asymmetry have brought to the fore key issues of feminism, such as the concept of sexuality and the creation of gender. In urging researchers to examine and study the political economy of sexual systems, Rubin (1975) recognizes its importance. The "exchange of women" is primarily a term used to express the social relations of a kinship system that specifies male rights over female kin, and in which women have no rights over themselves or over other male kin, she argues. Rubin's (1975) use of Levi-strauss's concepts as well as Freudian analysis helps to throw new light on the problem of sex inequality. It challenges the traditional Marxist explanation that reduces sex differences to differences merely in material conditions. The implication is that the elimination of sexual inequality no longer requires the elimination of men but rather the elimination of a social system that creates sexism and gender.

The Marxist Framework

Traditionally, Marxism has attempted to comprehend all social variance in class terms. Powerlessness is rooted in concrete and externally imposed structures which have to be removed in order to promote equality. To the extent that its method is dialectical materialism, Marxism gives secondary importance to "consciousness" or "thought processes". It also tends to equate reproduction of productive relations with biological reproduction, as if bodily differences account for women's subordination. The argument proposed is that the subordination of women results from the value placed on their reproductive capacity in societies where a greater productive potential makes an increase in population very desirable. Thus women as reproducers of producers become the object of competition among men.

From a Marxist perspective, the theories of universal asymmetry are questionable in their avoidance of the historical and ethnographic record. According to Leacock (1981), ignoring the changes that have taken place due to contact and colonization is highly problematic and a projection of our definition of power onto egalitarian tribes.

The basis for decision-making in band society is general consensus, and age and sex act as moderators in this process. Further, the band is the basic economic unit, and private property does not exist. If such is the character of band societies, then to project dyadic asymmetrical relations onto them is to view the world through our own lenses — a procedure which is both theoretically and methodologically unsound. It also implies a teleological and unilineal view of social evolution, in which our society is seen as the ultimate model.   Leacock (1981) proposes to rectify this biased viewpoint by examining societies organized in terms of relations of production, as well as in terms of relations set up among people. It is the latter (i.e., relations among people) as they engage in production, distribution and consumption, etc. that are crucial for understanding several inequalities. She therefore sets forth four broad types of production relations that have evolved over time. They are: 1) egalitarian; 2) ranking; 3) pre-industrial hierarchical societies; 4) industrial capitalist societies. In an egalitarian society, she maintains, reciprocity and complementarity between the sexes is central. It was only with colonization that this process was replaced by unequal relations. The development of ranking, she continues, was linked to the growth of trade, which became important enough to lead to specialization and reorganization of production relations, thus laying the basis for inequalities between men and women. In pre-industrial stratified societies, the existence of private property and the distinction between a class of producers and a class of consumers made women's work increasingly privatized. Finally, under capitalism and colonization, the subjugation of "people" generally implies the subjugation of women (Etienne and Leacock 1980).

By and large Leacock's work (1980, 1981) is thorough and critical. It cautions against the indiscriminate use of the concept of universal female subordination by feminist anthropologists (or others) and locates women's problems in surrounding material conditions. However, some issues are debatable, as Cohen (1981), in his reply to Leacock points out. According to him, it seems just as plausible, for instance, to argue that the fur trade enhanced, selected and emphasized qualities already present to a lesser degree, i.e., non-egalitarian characteristics. Also, to categorize all hunting and gathering societies as egalitarian is to ignore internal variations, which, ironically, also implies unilinear social evolution. Indeed, Begler (1978) demonstrates that egalitarian societies vary in terms of authority structures. For example, the !Kung-San and the Mbuti pygmies appear to be more egalitarian than the Inuit or the Australian aborigines. In her work Begler once again raises the issue of sexuality as power. According to her (1978: 587).

> the socially accepted legitimate use of power by the members of one sex to compel the behaviour of members of the opposite sex is evident in the frequent lack of support of male kin for a woman who is being overpowered by a male, the similar lack of support of female kin for a woman in a similar position and the occasional but analytically important, unprotested ganging up of men against a woman in certain culturally accepted situations.

While the Marxist perspective has brought to the fore the problems of ahistorical evaluation of female inferiority, it has yet to answer the challenge of incorporating the concept of sexuality as power into its own framework.

Conclusions

The ongoing debate over the cross-cultural roles and status of women is important in anthropological theory. While some writers alerted us to the invisibility of women in the earlier ethnographic records, others argued that it reflected a male bias.

The predominance of male anthropologists, and the use of male informants socialized in a sexually stratified milieu, have only exacerbated the situation.

This situation, in the opinion of some (Ardener for instance), could be rectified by focussing on women's models of society and women's spheres of activity (i.e., ritual and symbolic occupations). This is countered by the view that the separation and stratification of spheres of activity reflect state bias, as well as our own cultural values (Sacks 1979, Leacock 1981).

There has also been a tendency on the part of feminist anthropologists to describe women's status as universally inferior to that of men. Rosaldo and Lamphere (1974) emphasize the importance of child bearing and rearing, which creates the distinction between public/domestic spheres. Ortner (1974) also uses motherhood as a condition for making women analytically closer to nature than culture. Sanday (1974) likewise makes the case that child bearing and rearing are central factors in keeping women out of subsistence activities or the public sphere. In various ways these universal theories of women's subordination echo the views of Levi-strauss in his analysis of social organization.

Leacock's studies and those of a Marxist nature act as critiques of the above theories and emphasize the historical and ethnographic record. They invalidated the theory of universal asymmetry and called into focus the importance of not projecting our own models of power relations onto egalitarian societies. In the critical process the nature of the band, the public quality of band life and the complementary nature and autonomy of the sexes were highlighted. From Leacock's work, it can be seen that, while historical materialism was a useful and objective way of dealing with egalitarian societies as a category, it ignored the internal variations that were present.

In many of the societies lumped together as egalitarian, e.g., the Inuit, the !Kung-San, the Mbuti pygmies and the Australian aborigines, Begler (1978) makes a valid case that men as a group do indeed have authority over women, and emphasizes the centrality of sexuality and the creation of gender. However, the assumption that males have authority over females has been used uncritically as well. The Yanomamo, who are described as fierce, were not so a few hundred years ago. According to Leacock (1981), the Yanomamo probably first earned their reputation for fierceness in the 18th century when they fought off a Spanish expedition that was supposedly chasing fugitive sales. Furthermore, the assertion that higher amounts of testosterone contribute to aggression and the inevitability of patriarchy is particularly suspect as it is an ahistorical and single factor (i.e., biological) approach.

But there are sufficient reasons, such as those found in Begler's analysis, to see the treatment of sexuality as insignificant in the traditional Marxist framework. Sexuality is a form of power, manifested in the social construction of gender (McKinnon 1982). Sexuality, then, even in some egalitarian societies, can be seen as central to gender inequality.

The new wave of theorizing has suggested alternative explanations for evolutionary theory. "Sharing", as argued by Isaac (1978), does not assume hunting. All the corollaries to the "Man the hunter" hypothesis are therefore seen as being theoretically and methodologically problematic.

Feminist perspectives in anthropological literature have themselves undergone re-evaluation and have been central in the advancement of anthropology as both an objective and a humanistic discipline. The use of the concept of male bias (a feminist perspective) has brought to the fore the following issues:

a) research which ignores women, yet represents them in general conclusions;
b) research which does not treat them as important human subjects;
c) research which employs sexism in language and in theory building; and
d) research which uses preconceived notions of masculine and feminine nature.

As Quinn (1977) notes, what is clearest in the literature reviewed is the need for further investigation on the separate claims which have been made about women, their status and the conditions cited as evidence. What is most impressive about this literature is the overwhelming number of specific testable questions it has produced (Quinn 1977: 222).

Bibliography

Ardener, E. "The 'Problem' Revisited". *Perceiving Women*. (ed.) S. Ardener. London: Malaby Press, 1975.

Begler, E.B. "Sex, Status and Authority in Egalitarian Society." *American Anthropologist*. Vol. 80, 1978.

Briggs, J. "Eskimo Women: Makers of Men". *Many Sisters: Women in a Cross-Cultural Perspective*. (ed.) C.J. Mathiasson. New York: Free Press, 1974.

Brown, J.K. "A Note on the Division of Labour by Sex". *American Anthropologist*. Vol. 72, 1970.

Dahlberg, F. *Woman the Gatherer*. New Haven: Yale University Press, 1981.

Draper, P. "Kung Women: Contrasts in Sexual Egalitarianism and Sedentary Contexts". *Toward an Anthropology of Women*. (ed.) R. Reiter. New York: Monthly Review Press, 1975.

Eichler, M. *The Double Standard*. New York: St. Martins Press, 1980.

Etienne, M. and Leacock, E. (eds.) *Women and Colonization*. New York: Praeger Publications, 1980.

Faithorn, E. "The Concept of Pollution among the Kafe of the Papua New Guinea Highlands". *Toward an Anthropology of Women* (ed.) R. Reiter New York: Monthly Review Press, 1975.

Friedl, E. *Women and Men: An Anthropologist's View*. New York: Holt, Rhinehart and Winston, 1975.

Goldberg, S. *The Inevitability of Patriarchy*. New York: William Norrow, 1973.

Goodale, J. *Tiwi Wives*. Seattle: University of Washington Press, 1971.

Gough, K. "The Origin of the Family". *Toward an Anthropology of Women*. (ed.) R. Reiter. New York: Monthly Review Press, 1975.

Hockett, C.F. and Ascher, R. "The Human Revolution". *Current Anthropology*. Vol. 5, 1964.

Isaac, G.L. "Food sharing and human evolution: archaeological evidence from Paleo-pleistocene and East Africa". *Journal of Anthropological Research*. No. 34, 1978.

Kaberry, P. *Aboriginal Woman: Sacred and Profane*. 1939 report; London: Routledge and Kegan Paul, 1970.

Keller, E.F. "Feminism and Science". *Signs*. Vol. 7, No. 3, Spring 1982.

Kraybill, N. "Pre-agricultural tools for the preparation of foods in the old world". *Origins of Agriculture*. (ed.) C.A. Reed. Chicago: Aldine, 1977.

Leacock, E.B. *Myths of Male Dominance*. Collected Articles on Women, Cross-culturally. New York: Monthly Review Press, 1981.

Lee, R.B. "What Hunters do for a living or how to make out on scarce resources". *Man the Hunter*. (eds.) R.B. Lee and Irven De Vore. Chicago: Aldine, 1968.

Leibowitz, L. "Perspectives on the evolution of sex differences". *Toward an Anthropology of Women*. (ed.) R. Reiter. New York: Monthly Review Press, 1975.

Levi-strauss. *The Elementary Structures of Kinship*. Boston: Beacon Press, 1969.

Levi-strauss. "The Family". *Man, Culture and Society*. (ed.) H. Shapiro. London: Oxford University Press, 1971.

MacKinnon, C.H. "Feminism, Marxism, Method and the State: An Agenda for Theory". *Signs*. Vol. 7, No. 3, Spring 1982.

McGrew, W.C. "The female chimpanzee as a human evolutionary prototype". *Woman the Gatherer*. (ed.) F. Dahlberg. New Haven: Yale University Press, 1981.

Martin, M.K. & Voorhies, B. *Female of the Species*. New York: Columbia University Press, 1975.

Milton, K. "Male Bias in Anthropology". *Man*. New series, Vol. 14, No. 1, 1979.

Monis, D. (ed.) *Primate Ethnology*. London: Weidenfeld and Nicholson Press, 1967.

Ortner, S.B. "Is female to male as nature is to culture". *Women, Culture and Society*. (eds.) M.Z. Rosaldo and C. Lamphere. Stanford: Stanford University Press, 1974.

Oswalt, W.H. *An Anthropological Analysis of Food Getting Technology*. New York: Wiley, 1976.

Parker, S.E. & Parker, H. "The myth of male superiority: rise and demise". *American Anthropologist*. Vol. 81, 1979.

Quinn, N. "Anthropological studies on women's status". *Annual Review of Anthropology*. Palo Alto, California: Annual Reviews Inc., 1977.

Reiter, R. "Men and women in the south of France: Public and private domains". *Toward an Anthropology of Women*. (ed.) R. Reiter. New York: Monthly Review Press, 1975.

Reiter, R. (ed.) *Toward an Anthropology of Women*. New York: Monthly Review Press, 1975.

Rosaldo, M.Z. & Lamphere, L. (eds.) *Woman, Culture and Society*. Stanford: Stanford University Press, 1974.

Rosaldo, M.Z. "The use and abuse of Anthropology: Reflections on feminism and cross-cultural understanding". *Signs*. Vol. 5, No. 3, 1980.

Rubin, G. "The Traffic in Women". *Toward an Anthropology of Women*. (ed.) R. Reiter. New York: Monthly Review Press, 1975.

Sacks, K. *Sisters and Wives*. Westport, Connecticut: Greenwood Press, 1979.

Sacks, K. "Engels revisited: Women, the organization of production and private property". *Toward an Anthropology of Women*. (ed.) R. Reiter. New York: Monthly Review Press, 1975.

Sanday, P. "Toward a theory of the status of women". *American Anthropologist*. Vol. 75, 1973.

Sanday, P. "Female status in the public domain". *Woman, Culture and Society*. (eds.) M.Z. Rosaldo & L. Lamphere. Stanford: Stanford University Press, 1974.

Slocum, S. "Woman the gatherer: Male Bias in Anthropology". *Toward an Anthropology of Women*. (ed.) R. Reiter. New York: Monthly Review Press, 1975.

Steward, J. *Theory of Culture Change: The Methodology of Multi-Linear Evolution*. Urbana: University of Illinois Press, 1955.

Tiger, L. *Men in Groups*. New York: Random House, 1969.

Tiger, L. & Fox, R. *The Imperial Animal*. New York: Holt, Rinehart & Winston, 1971.

Whyte, M.K. *The Status of Women in Pre-industrial Societies*. New York: Princeton University Press, 1978.

Zihlman. A. "Women as shapers of the human adaptation". *Woman the Gatherer*. (ed.) F. Dahlberg. New Haven: Yale University Press, 1981.

Zihlman, A. and Tanner, N. "Gathering and hominid adaptation". *Female Hierarchies*. (ed.) L. Tiger & H. Fowler. Chicago: Beresford Book Service, 1978.

Sexism in Psychological Research

CHERYL MALMO

In psychology, as in other social sciences, a sexist perspective predominates. That an obvious bias toward males existed in psychology, was evidenced by Carlson and Carlson whose analysis of personality research in 1960 demonstrated:

1. an imbalance of sampling in research — "males are selected far more often than females as research subjects" (p. 482);
2. the paucity of tests for sex differences; and
3. the inadequacy of reporting the sex composition of research samples.

More than a decade later, in 1971 and 1972, Carlson demonstrated that personality research continued to focus on males and failed to test for sex differences. Another ten years have passed and we see a great increase in the number of psychological studies on women, carried out largely by feminists. However, while psychologists appear to have become more aware of the need to include females in their research samples, they do not necessarily understand either the importance or the limitations of sex differences. On the one hand we still see research which fails to report (let alone try to account for) sex differences. On the other hand we have a burgeoning new field of study on "sex differences", which continues to debate the relevance of miniscual differences in males and females, which often confuses sex and gender differences, which typically ignores the fact that average differences between males and females are less significant than variations found within each sex, and which consequently dismisses the vast number of similarities between the sexes — similarities which seem to reflect our

116

common humaness. Frieze *et al.* (1978) claim that the failure to report findings which show no sex differences has distorted psychological theory. There may exist a great body of research which demonstrates no difference between the sexes, but because these findings are "not significant", the results have not been published.

Sexism in psychological research has far more complex ramifications than this since data gathered on male subjects only have been the basis of many concepts and theories. Theorists have assumed that male behaviour is the norm — the model for what is human. Silveira (1973) maintains that when behaviour of female subjects does not fit the male norm, it is commonly written off as "error". When female subjects are excluded, or the "deviant" data from female subjects are ignored, the theory based on data gathered from male subjects may be biased and oversimplified. For example, when McClelland began his studies of achievement motivation he dispensed with female subjects because they did not fit his model. His theory was later demonstrated to be both biased and simplistic by Horner (1971, 1972). She introduced another motive that seemed to be present — the "fear of success" — after she explored how women respond to achievement motivation tasks. Horner's theory, although eventually criticized for perpetuating a trait theory of personality, remains significant as a starting point in the study of the psychology of women. From this beginning has developed a more comprehensive and complex understanding of women and motivation — theory which takes into account women's values and the social forces which affect them (Sherif, 1979b). As another example, the career development of women was, for a long time, ignored, because, not fitting the male model, women were seen to "complicate" the research. Males were the norm, and females were deviant, so they did not have to be accounted for. The theory of career development was not considered limited, however, until feminists demonstrated its inadequacy with regard to women's career development. Feminist research on dual career marriages continues to be sexist in that the definition of career is still based on the traditional male model.

The term "career", as it is currently used, does not account for the possibility that a woman may be nursing a baby, that either parent may be staying home with a sick child, or that either partner may value equally activities unrelated to her or his career.

The psychology of women has also been distorted by male bias when concepts based on data from research on males have been unsuccessfully applied to females. One example is Freud's application of the Oedipus complex (originating from his study of male development) to females. Though he encountered much difficulty in making the concept "fit" females, he nevertheless applied the male-based concept to females and then concluded that the female superego was less developed than the male superego (Klein, 1971). The criticism of Freudian theory as it applies to women has been vast and predates the latest wave of feminism. Karen Horney, Freud's contemporary, criticized his concept of penis envy as wrongly attributed to the biological difference of the sexes and as evident instead of women's dissatisfaction with the status quo. But not many psychologists took Horney seriously. Hannah Lerman (1980) has recently come up with a very interesting analysis of Freud's development of the Oedipal theory as applied to females. Examining the 24 volumes of the Standard Edition of Freud's works plus the volumes of his letters to various persons and the autobiographies of his disciples, she has ascertained that Freud originally theorized the female neurosis resulted from sexual seduction and trauma in childhood, fathers frequently being the perpetrators. However, Freud wrote to his intimate friend, Wilhelm Fliess, that he felt uncomfortable with this concept, troubled as he was with his own sister's neurosis and the probability of his father's involvement. Also, Freud was disturbed by a dream, he reported to Fliess, in which he himself experienced "overaffectionate" feelings toward one of his daughters. This he interpreted to mean that he was uncomfortable with the trauma concept of female neurosis. At this point he shifted to the Oedipal theory of neurosis (i.e., applying the theory of the origin of male neurosis to females), thus resolving his discomfort about his father and himself. Examining Freud's theories of neurosis in their final form,

Lerman observes that whereas the mother is seen to be the seducer of the son, it is the daughter who is the potential seducer of the father. Proceeding from this theory, Freud no longer believed his female patients when they complained of parental seduction. Thus, concludes Lerman, "The result was that psychoanalytic theory, which had started from an observational base, lost its connection to that base" (1980, p. 113). For females the basis became male experience. Psychiatrists today, who have not been taught to examine critically Freud's theories and practises, continue to disbelieve women. In my own practise, women who were incest victims have reported to me that male psychiatrists, after listening to them describe their sexual abuse as children, responded with remarks such as "You must have fantasized it", "You must have invited it", or "He must have been gentle with you so it couldn't have been that bad". In other words, the message to women has been: I can't deal with your experience so I'll negate it.

Another example of theory building based on a male model of humanity is Kohlberg's theory of moral development. Like McClelland, Kohlberg tested only male subjects but generalized his results to include females as well as males. Then, speculating on the moral development of the "average" North American, he placed females at a "less developed" level than males (Gilligan, 1977). Thus, he drew the same conclusions as did Freud. However, Freud admitted that he did not understand women and that he was dissatisfied with the conventional terms used to explain the nature of women. He states:

> That is all I have to say to you about femininity. It is certainly incomplete and fragmentary and does not always sound friendly. . . . If you want to know more about femininity, inquire from your own experiences in life, or turn to the poets, or wait until science can give you deeper and more coherent information. (Freud, cited by Mitchell, 1975, p. 119)

Kohlberg, on the other hand, gave no indication that he failed to research or understand women's moral development, despite the fact that his data were based exclusively on male behaviour. Carolyn Gilligan (1977) has recently researched the moral development of women, producing results which challenge both the sexist and class-biased basis of Kohlberg's theory. Her theory forces those who will listen to consider the limitations of Kohlberg's theory, not just for females, but also for males, i.e., for humans. Some listen only haphazardly, however, and then use Gilligan's findings on women to justify their belief that women are different from men because of their sex. The description of a difference is used as a rationalization for a belief in the sex stereotypes: women behave the way they do because they are women. Margrit Eichler, in her book *The Double Standard*, explains why this circular kind of argument is inadequate. She states: "To draw any inferences about biological differences — of whatever kind — to social differences without giving careful attention to the culture through which such biological differences are mediated is to commit a grave error" (1980, p. 12).

Another kind of sexism in psychological research results from theorists making interpretations about female and male behavior which simply reflect sex-role stereotypes. The Neo-Freudian, Erik Erikson, based his theory of child development on biological difference and assumed a male mode, as did Freud. Firstly, he differentiated female and male identity on the basis of their genital organs. From this basis he defined femininity as passive and masculinity as active, and theorized that:

1. women are passive and men are active.
2. women's identity is based primarily on their need to "fill their inner space" (have children), and
3. women are necessarily dependent on men because men achieve an identity based on what they do, whereas women achieve an identity based on their relationship to men.

Thus, Erikson assumed a male model of humanity and perceived women as an exception to the male norm. Further, like the traditional anthropologists, he assumed civilization to be a masculine derivative. That Erikson failed to explore beyond lay stereotypes of female and male behaviour; that his theory is based on individual interpretation which reflects cultural bias, more than on scientific investigation; and that his theory of female development is inadequate, is considered self-evident by many feminists (Douvan and Adelson, 1966; Gilligan, 1977; Millet, 1969; Spricer, 1979; Weisstein, 1971). In the words of Weisstein,

> These views from men who are assumed to be experts reflect, in a surprisingly transparent way, the cultural consensus. They not only asset that a woman is defined by her ability to attract men, they see no alternative definitions. They think that the definition of a woman in terms of a man is the way it should be. (p. 69)

According to Weisstein (1971), the failure of male psychologists to understand female dynamics is compounded by their insistence on looking for inner traits which agree with the stereotypes, and their failure to examine social context. Reviewing Erikson's theory, amongst others, she concludes,

> It is obvious that a study of human behaviour requires first and foremost, a study of the social contexts within which people move, the expectations as to how they will behave, and the authority which tells them who they are and what they are supposed to do. (p. 77)

In response to the obvious inadequacies of Erikson's theory and the limitations placed upon women by the feminine stereotype, Bem (1974) began an investigation of the traditional concepts of "femininity" and "masculinity" which resulted in the concept of androgeny. The creation of this concept was an important step in our understanding that neither females nor males need be limited in their behaviours by their physiological sex, as Erikson had proposed. It also taught us that behaviours need not be absolute and exclusive. However, the concept of androgeny is limited in so far as it does not question the original basis for the categorization of human identifies or behaviours on the basis of sex, nor does it contend with the fact that the so-called feminine characteristics are less valued. Further, it is a limited concept because it fails to account for the social norms and structural inequalities which define and limit males' and females' participation in society; instead, it attributes differences in behaviour simply to personality traits.

Psychological theories such as those of Freud, Kohlberg and Erikson that simply reflect cultural attitudes and values of the time are problematic in that they do not further our understanding of women's (or of human) experience. They are problematic, too, because they reinforce the stereotypes and support a status quo perception of women as subordinate and men as dominant. The description of the images and roles becomes a prescription for behaviour. That psychologists attribute different values to supposed masculine and feminine traits, in keeping with society's higher valuation of males, is also evidenced. In a study of male bias in psychotherapeutic practice, Broverman *et al.* (1970) demonstrated that clinicians have a double-standard of mental health for women and men. The clinicians (both female and male) not only described healthy women and men in different terms which parallel the sex stereotypes, but also described a healthy man as similar to a healthy adult and a healthy woman as different from a healthy adult. About these results, Silveira (1973) concludes, "Again, male is equated with human and healthy, female is not" (p. 102).

Traditional researchers have also contaminated psychological theory by using tests oriented to males, using tests which bias findings, or employing testing situations which are male-oriented. For example, McClelland, in his tests of achievement motivation, frequently used test questions related to military experiences. Because the military was (and, to a great extent, still is) a male domain, men, of course, were more likely to identify with these questions than were females. McClelland's conclusion, however, was that something was missing in women, not that something was wrong with his tests. Consequently, his first text, *The Achievement Motive* (1953) devoted only eight of its nearly 400 pages to studies of women (Alper, 1974). Vocational tests have also reflected sex stereotypes, as many of you probably know from experience. As a result of tests which were biased from the start, many women achieved results which portrayed their interests as fitting the stereotype — they could be nurses, elementary school teachers, secretaries, airline stewardesses or waitresses. If they showed some interest in math they could teach it to children, not become a mathematician or an engineer.

Test items have also been demonstrated to be biased in the

research on suggestibility, thus challenging the conclusion drawn in many social psychology texts, that women are more susceptible to persuasive influences or suggestions that are men. Examination of the test items revealed that the topics in the items were of interest to men but not to women. Further research demonstrated that women are easily influenced on topics not interesting to them or not involving their personal integrity. Similarly, men are easily influenced in areas not interesting or important to them. It was further discovered that the sex of the researcher affected how easily the subjects could be swayed. Men were more easily persuaded by female researchers on topics socially defined as interesting to females, while women were more easily influenced by male researchers on topics socially defined as interesting to males. In other words, the apparent credibility of the researcher on the topic was an important factor in whether or not women and men could be influenced (Sherif, 1979a). Recently the notion of innate male aggression has been challenged as a result of close examination of the testing situation in which male children were more aggressive when an adult was present, but when the adult left the room, female children were equally aggressive. The authors of the investigation conclude that, in the presence of an adult, conformity rather than aggression was actually being tested. Once again, Naomi Weisstein's (1971) belief that circumstantial factors are a much stronger factor than sex difference in determining behaviour, is supported.

Studies of sexism in language have made feminists aware of the difficulty of doing nonsexist research (Strainchamps, 1972). In psychology, the study of "mothering" is based on a number of sexist assumptions about women — about their *natural* ability to nurture and about their proper place in society. This research also supports the status quo in that it also assumes that men parent differently, that their role as parents is less important and that they properly belong in the world outside of the home.

Understanding the limitations and dangers of sexist language in psychology, the Canadian Psychological Association and the Psychological Association of Alberta have outlined for its members, rules for the use of nonsexist language. However, a male professor in my department jokes about these rulings and maintains to his students that it is his individual right to reject these rules and be himself, i.e., sexist. Clearly, there remains a lack of understanding of sexism and its ramifications.

Another bias in psychological research, which some feminists interpret as a masculine bias, is the logical empiricist approach to knowledge. This approach holds that knowledge is inherently neutral, and that the researcher and research method are impartial. Some feminists perceive a link between different ways of knowing (i.e., methods of gaining insight) and the male and female stereotypes and their differing valuations. Carlson (1972) associated the prestige associated with "hard data" to the prestige generally conferred upon men in society. Bernard (1973) attributes the focus on empirical research, with its inherent attention to mastery and control, separation, manipulation, and power relationships, to the masculine principle and a male preoccupation, calling it the "machismo element in research" (p. 23). Similarly, Millman and Kanter (1975) attribute the objective, controlled approach to establish "neutral facts", to a masculine ideal. They state, "the more conventional quantitative approaches, which deal with variables rather than persons . . . may be associated with an unpleasantly exaggerated masculine style of control and manipulation" (p. xvi). In other words, the empirical method, with its claim to objectivity, its focus on variables rather than persons, and its preference for quantitative information — "hard data" — parallels the masculine stereotype. It is rational, intellectual, unemotional, distant, powerful, etc. Further, the valuing of empirical methods and data as superior to the qualitative types, parallels society's valuing of masculine attributes.

The association of the dominant scientific method with the dominant male stereotype is not limited to feminists or to present day thinking. Before contemporary feminists equated a neutral objective science with masculine behaviour and values, Simmel (cited by Coser, 1977) associated the ideas of standard values, neutral knowledge, and objective science with the dominant male. He explains:

> We measure the achievements and commitments . . . of males and females in terms of specific norms and values; but these norms are not neutral, standing above the contrasts of the sexes; they have themselves a male character. . . . The standards of art and demands of patriotism, the general mores and the specific social ideas, the equity of practical judgments and the objectivity of theoretical knowledge, . . . — all these categories are formally generically human, but are in fact masculine in terms of their actual historical formation. If we call ideas that claim absolute validity objectively binding, then it is a fact that in the historical life of our species there operates the equation: objectivity = male. (p. 872)

Given the above, feminists' analyses and criticisms of the assumptions of science appear crucial. Vaughter (1976) insists that it is imperative that feminists analyze methodology as well as theoretical models of science, because the feminist perspective requires that the research enterprise itself be put into a social and political context. Limitations of the empirical method must be understood. In psychology it does not, for example, allow for the study of the meaning of behaviour to individuals, of the relevance of the wider social context of experience, or of life as an on-going process. The method itself limits the questions of investigation. Therefore, to understand human experience in its depth and complexity, other methods must be employed. When this happens we will find the boundaries of our separate academic disciplines merging. At the same time, development of the inter-disciplinary and cross-disciplinary approaches in feminist research may also engender recognition of the limited nature of the empirical approach for the proper study of women, and of humankind.

The empiricist notion that objective observers can remain detached from subject matter being researched is also being challenged by feminists. Lofland (1975) claims that observers not only selectively perceive, but also impose upon interpretations their own attitudes, beliefs and values. Consequently, she believes that male observers not only selectively perceive, but also impose upon interpretations, their attitudes, beliefs and values about women. Further, those male observers who are unable to empathize with the experience of their female subjects, are likely to interpret and judge women's behaviour from their own perspective. She concludes:

> To the degree that males and females . . . define each other as *other* and to the degree that the definition results in physical and psychological segregation, male researchers will be limited in their access to women's places and women's minds (and vice versa). (p. 159)

The danger to women of men misinterpreting and falsely judging their behaviour has been noted in relation to Freud's and other psychoanalysts' treatment of sexually abused women. As a therapist, I have been told numerous stories by female clients about how their former male therapists failed to understand their concerns and gave them advice which served to benefit males. For example, one client described how a male psychiatrist advised her to have surgery for breast enlargement because her husband complained that her breasts were too small. Leidig (1980) relates instances of males therapists getting erections as they listened to accounts of the experiences of retrospective incest victims. She concludes that, in cases of retrospective incest, males should not be permitted to counsel females.

That the sex of the researcher can affect the results of a study has already been mentioned in relation to the research on suggestibility. Placing the male researcher/female subject within the context of patriarchal society makes clear another aspect of the problem — the problem of female subjects withholding information from male researchers. Miller (1976) relates the failure of male researchers to elicit responses from female subjects to the power relationship which exists between the sexes. She maintains that women who are in a subordinate position to men are unlikely to reveal themselves to their so-called superiors. She states, "Put simply, subordinates won't tell" (p. 10). In my own research I have made attempts to determine whether or not my being female was an important factor to the women I interviewed and whether or not the content of the interview may have been altered by this factor. The topic of my research was

"What it Means to Women to be Women" and to this end I conducted in-depth interviews with thirteen Alberta women of varying ages, backgrounds, etc. After the interview proper was completed, I asked the women about the interview experience and the effect that my being female had. These are the results: Seven of the thirteen women interviewed stated that my being female was important to them, four stated that it made no difference and two qualified their answers. Regarding the seven who stated they preferred a female interviewer, the reasons given were as follows:

1. Four women would have felt uncomfortable speaking to a male interviewer about particular topics.

    Beret states:

    Yes, if you'd have been a man I don't think I would have felt as free to say maybe some of the things. Then I don't think I would have been as comfortable. I would have thought maybe twice about some things that we talked about — some things that I thought maybe they wouldn't be interested in because I don't think it would have meant anything much to them. And I would be really embarrassed about crying.

    Theresa states:

    The part of where we talked about my medical history, I guess I would have hesitated about being as open about it as I was with you, not because I would be afraid to say it to a man but I guess I wouldn't feel as comfortable. And if you don't feel comfortable there's some things you don't say.

    Marcela states:

    I wouldn't have talked about power as easily as I did. I wouldn't have talked about it. When the interview began, I was trying to let as many thoughts go through my mind as I could without restricting them, and I wouldn't have done that if you were a man. I would have felt obligated to be much more disciplined, rational.

    Sally states:

    Like I know I wouldn't feel too comfortable sitting and having an interview with a guy. I probably wouldn't say all the things I've said to you. No, I wouldn't.

2. Two women would have been afraid of being judged by a male interviewer, would be afraid a man could not understand them or would have questioned his motivations.

Sally states:

If you were a guy interviewing me, for sure I'd probably be nervous and wouldn't know what to say. Because of a man looking at me I'd be thinking that he'd be thinking, "Well, you're only a woman."

Joan states:

I couldn't tell a man. I don't know why. Maybe I would get the feeling that he was sort of putting me down or looking down on me. But I think, like with a woman I get the feeling that you may not have totally agreed with what I said, but you understand it, that you can understand how I might feel about it. Whereas a man, I don't think they'd understand at all. Because most women — at least I feel put down about certain things and I don't think a man would understand how I would feel put down about. Like they would not understand how I feel put down about my husband putting me down. Whereas I think you — you may not agree with me, but you can understand it. And I think women can understand that sort of thing. Whereas I don't think a man could. And besides, I'd wonder why the hell he was writing this book anyway.

3. Two women described how previous negative experiences with male psychiatrists would have made them reticent in talking to a male interviewer.

Mary states:

I just don't think I would let a man get that close to me. Not somebody that I didn't know. The one time I was talked to by a male psychiatrist was at University, and he utterly devastated me. He was a hideous person; he was really hideous and maybe that's why I have this reticence. My one contact with a male in this kind of context was really bad! I just don't think I would have been as relaxed.

Elizabeth states:

Hmmm. For sure! I would immediately feel like I was being exploited. For sure! Immediately! And a lot of that I think goes back to my psychiatric involvement, mostly with male psychiatrists. Because I recognize now the degree of exploitation that I suffered from male psychiatrists. I feel like I would be setting myself up to be distorted into his little, whatever he needed to prove about me, kind of thing. I just won't put up with it. And I think too that there are exceptions — men that don't need to make a case about women. I'm not sure that I could relate to any of them, because I wouldn't give them the benefit of the doubt. The probability is that any male interviewing me would be exploiting me, from my experience, and I know that. So I wouldn't trust a male interviewer. No. Because I would expect that they would probably exploit me.

It is important to understand, too, why the four women who stated that being interviewed by a male would not have made any difference to them, felt the way they did. Heidi made it clear, prior to the interview, that she had just finished telling her life story to a judge in front of a courtroom full of people. Alice and Christine would have felt relaxed talking to a male interviewer whom they assumed would also be a psychologist and who would therefore understand them. Madelaine explained that she likes to think of men as friends and finds that she can sometimes talk more easily to men than she can to women. Regarding the two women who qualified their answers, Denise stated that she would not change the content of her interview if the interview were male "whether it had been a bishop or whoever" because she is confident in herself. She did explain, however, that she may have been "a little more forceful towards standing up for women" and "a little more on my guard" with a male interviewer. Jean stated, "It would depend on the man", explaining that the personality and skills of the interviewer were more important to her than gender. The personality and behaviour of the interviewer were, in fact, judged by five women to have affected how openly they spoke about themselves.

There is just one more issue I wish to speak to in relation to sexist bias in psychological research, and that is the power relationship between the researcher and the subject, which parallels the power relationship between males and females, administrators and worker, the rich and the poor, etc. We are already aware that it is the people with power who benefit from the status quo. And we know, too, that knowledge is power. If researchers have knowledge about the subjects of their research and this knowledge is either purposely or inadvertently withheld, then the subjects are being exploited and the status quo is maintained. The empirical method in psychology supports the power relationship between researcher and subject in so far as knowledge is assumed to be neutral. That researchers selectively choose their topics, subjectively define variables and interpret results, and therefore grasp only certain aspects of reality, is hidden by this assumption. Meanwhile, behavioral psychologists, who are the most prestigious and powerful psychologists in North America (Sherif, 1979a), deliberately aim to manipulate, control, change, and predict the behaviour of others, typically without investigating the meaning of the behaviour to those individuals. It is not only feminists who are concerned with the dangers of such assumptions. Schroyer (1970) is concerned that contemporary science and technology have become dangerous in that they represent a new form of legitimating power and privilege. Therefore, feminists, who have a special interest in changing the structures of power and privilege which exclude women, must challenge not just the language, definitions, concepts, theories and interpretations of scientific research. We must also challenge the method of scientific investigation, and its claims of objectivity and neutrality, and thus expose the power relationship between researcher and subject. Further, we must find ways to bridge the gap between researchers and the people being researched, so that the power of our knowledge can be shared by all.

Bibliography

Alper, T.G. "Achievement Motivation in College Women." *American Psychologist,* March, 1974, pp. 194-203.

Bem, S. "The Measurement of Psychological Androgyny." *Journal of Consulting and Clinical Psychology,* 1974, *42*, pp. 165-172.

Bernard J. "My Four Revolutions: An Autobiographical History of the A.S.A." *American Journal of Sociology,* 1973, *78*(4), pp. 11-29.

Broverman, L.K., Broverman, D.M., Clarkson, F., Rosenkrantz, P. and Vogel, S. "Sex-role Stereotypes and Clinical Judgments of Mental Health." *Journal of Consulting and Clinical Psychology,* 1970, *34*, pp. 1-7.

Carlson, E.R. and Carlson, R. "Male and Female Subjects in Personality

Research." *Journal of Abnormal and Social Psychology*, 1960, *61*, pp. 482-483.

Carlson, R. "Understanding Women: Implications for Personality Research and Change." *The Journal of Social Issues*, 1972, *28*(2), pp. 17-32.

Carlson, R. "Where is the Person in Personality Research?" *Psychological Bulletin*, 1971, *75*, pp. 203-219.

Coser, L.A. "George Simmel's Neglected Contribution to the Sociology of Women." *Signs*, 1977, *2*(4), pp. 869-876.

Douvan, E.A. and Adelson, J. *The Adolescent Experience*. New York: John Wiley and Sons, 1966.

Eichler, M. *The Double Standard*. London: Croom Helm, 1980.

Erikson, E. "Inner and Outer Space: Reflections on Womanhood." *Daedalus*, 1964, *93*, 582-606.

Frieze, L.H., Parsons, J.E., Johnson, P.B., Ruble, D.N. and Zellman, G.L. *Women and Sex Roles*. New York: W.W. Norton and Co., 1978.

Gilligan, C. "In a Different Voice: Women's Conception of Self and Morality." *Harvard Educational Review*, 1977, *47*(4), pp. 481-517.

Horner, M.S. "Femininity and Successful Achievement A Basic Inconsistency," in M.H. Garskoff (ed.), *Roles Women Play: Readings Toward Women's Liberation*. Belmont, California Brooks/Cole, 1971.

Horner, M.S. "Toward an Understanding of Achievement-Related Conflicts in Women." *Journal of Social Issues* 1972 *28*(2), pp. 156-157.

Horney, K. *Feminine Psychology*. New York: W.W. Norton and Co. Inc., 1967.

Horney, K. *New Ways in Psychoanalysis*. New York: W.W. Norton and Co. Inc., 1939.

Klein, V. *The Feminine Character*. Urbana: University of Illinois Press, 1971.

Kohlberg, L. "Stage and Sequence: The Cognitive-Development Approach to Socialiation," in D.A. Goslin (ed.), *Handbook of Socialization Theory and Research*. Chicago: Rand McNally, 1969.

Leidig, M.W. *Retrospective Incest Therapy*. A paper presented at the Seventh Annual National Conference on Feminist Psychology, Association for Women in Psychology, Santa Monica, California, March 1980.

Lerman, H. *What Freud Couldn't Face: A Feminist Analysis of Freud and the Development of Psychoanalytic Theory*. A paper presented at the Seventh Annual National Conference on Feminist Psychology, Association for Women in Psychology, Association for Women in Psychology, Santa Monica, California, March, 1980.

Lofland, L.H. "The 'Thereness' of Women: A Selective Review of Urban Sociology," in M. Millman and R.M. Kanter (eds.), *Another Voice*. New York: Anchor Press/Doubleday, 1975.

McClelland, D.C., Atkinson, J.W., Clark, R.A. and Lowell, E.L. *The Achievement Motive*. New York: Appleton, 1953.

Miller, J.B. *Toward a New Psychology of Women*. Boston: Beacon Press, 1976.

Millet, K. *Sexual Politics*. New York: Equinox Books/Avon, 1969.

Millman, M. and Kanter, R.M. (Eds.), *Another Voice*. New York: Anchor Press/Doubleday, 1975.

Mitchell, J. *Psychoanalysis and Feminism*. New York: Vintage Books, 1975.

Schroyer, T. "Toward a Critical Theory for Advanced Industrial Society." *Recent Sociology No. 2*, 1970, pp. 210-234.

Schult, M.R. "The Semantic Derogation of Women," in B. Thorne & N. Henley (eds.), *Language and Sex*. Rowley, Massachusetts: Newbury House, 1975.

Sherif, C.W. "Bias in Psychology," in J.A. Sherman & E.T. Beck (eds.), *The Prism of Sex*. Madison, Wisconsin: The University of Wisconsin Press, 1979a, pp. 93-134.

Sherif, C.A. "What Every Intelligent Person Should Know About Psychology and Women," in E.C. Synder (ed.) *The Study of Women: Enlarging Perspectives of Social Reality*. New York: Harper & Row, 1979b, pp. 143-183.

Silveira, J. "Male Bias in Psychology," in J.R. Leppaluoto (ed.), *Women on the Move*. Pittsburgh: *KNOW* Inc., 1973.

Spricer, R. *Adulthood: The Developmental Tasks of Women*. Unpublished dissertation proposal. Department of Educational Psychology, University of Alberta, 1979.

Strainchamps. E. "Our sexist language," in V. Gornick & B. Moran (eds.), *Women in Sexist Society*. New York: New American Library (Signet), 1972.

Vaughter, R.M. "Review Essay: Psychology." *Signs*, 1976, *2*(1), pp. 120-146.

Weisstein, N. "Psychology Constructs the Female, or the Fantasy Life of the Male Psychologists," in M.H. Garskoff (ed.), *Roles Women Play: Readings Towards Women's Liberation*. Belmont, California: Brooks/Cole, 1971.

The Policy Consequences of Sexist Research

Labour Market Discrimination and Affirmative Action

BARBARA CAMERON

How one evaluates affirmative action programmes and other policies directed at eliminating sex discrimination in the labour market depends on one's analysis of the causes of that discrimination. There exists a variety of explanations of the causes and, therefore, also a range of opinions on the effectiveness of proposed policy approaches. The purpose of this paper is to outline the policy implications of some of the major theories of labour market discrimination and to propose criteria for evaluating policies drawn from several of the theories. For the purposes of our discussion, the theories of labour market discrimination can conveniently be divided into two categories: those that start from a model of a competitive capitalist economy, and those that begin with the premise of a monopoly dominated capitalist economy. This paper will first consider the competitive theories.

Many of the major arguments belonging to the competitive category appear in some form in a collection of essays recently published by the Vancouver-based Fraser Institute, entitled *Discrimination, Affirmative Action and Equal Opportunity* (Block and Walker, 1982). The influence of the competitive capitalist model on the editors and contributors to this volume is so strong that they completely ignore the considerable body of academic literature that focuses on the connection between segregation in labour markets and monopoly power. Instead, they base their analysis on work published in the 1950s, which opened up a debate among economists on labour market discrimination, and very carefully select from subsequent contributions to the debate only material by those authors who share their ideological assumptions.

Two chapters from an early work by Gary Becker, *The Economics of Discrimination* (Becker, 1957), are reprinted in the Fraser Institute volume. Becker's analysis is directed at showing the mistakes of those critics of capitalism who attribute labour market discrimination, particularly on grounds of race, to the desire of employers for profits. His theory centres around the concept of a "taste for discrimination", which exists when an individual "*acts as if* he were willing to pay something, either directly or in the form of reduced income, to be associated with some individuals instead of others" (Block and Walker, p. 130). Becker believes this formulation expresses the essence of discrimination in the market place. By using money as a measure of discrimination, he is able to determine the magnitude of either the taste for or the actual incidence of discrimination. He conducts this measurement by means of a "discrimination coefficient" (DC), which represents the costs to an employer, employee or consumer above those costs incurred or gained on the grounds of economic utility alone.

By defining discrimination in terms of a cost incurred in order to avoid contact with certain groups, Becker is easily able to show that capitalists cannot profit from discrimination. He illustrates this by hypothesizing two capitalist societies, one composed entirely of members of one, usually discriminated against group (N) and the other society composed of members of another, usually dominant group (W). He further hypothesizes that society (N) has a surplus of labour and society (W) has a surplus of capital, and argues that a refusal of (W) society to exchange capital for (N) labour can only result in economic loss for both (W) capitalists and (N) labour. The only individuals who stand to gain from this discrimination are the capitalists of (N) society and the workers of (W) society. Thus, he concludes, the charge that capitalists of a dominant group profit from discrimination and the workers of a dominant group lose is completely unfounded.

Becker's model contains the neo-classical economic assumption of the full utilization of both capital and labour under conditions of free competition. The belief is that, provided the unemployed are prepared to accept wages low enough to guarantee a profit, the supply of labour and the demand for it will be in equilibrium. The problem with Becker's analysis can be seen by changing his example to accord more closely with what happens on the real labour market. Suppose that (W) and (N) labour exist within one society and that there is a surplus of (N) labour. Suppose also that a capitalist, whether (W) or (N), who is motivated solely by profit, employs (N) labour, but at a lower wage than that received by (W) labour because of (N) labour's surplus situation. In this example, the capitalist benefits both from the lower wages paid to (N) and from the effect that (N) has on depressing the wages of (W) labour. Therefore, both (N) and (W) labour lose. According to Becker's definition, which limits discrimination to a refusal of contact with a disadvantaged group, the hiring of members of this group at lower wages would not be considered discrimination but good business. He thus precludes, by his definition, the exact situation to which women most strongly object: the hiring of women at lower wages to perform work of equal economic value to that of men.

The assumption of the equilibrium of supply and demand for labour in conditions of full competition is also fundamental to the arguments made by co-editors Walter Block and Michael Walker in their contributions to the Fraser Institute volume. Without this premise of supply/demand equilibrium, it is difficult to appreciate their enthusiastic description of the "willingness" of the disadvantaged to work for lower wages as "the traditional economic weapon of the downtrodden" (Block and Walker, p. 104). The premise also helps to explain, although it does not excuse, an illustration of the incompatibility of captialism and discrimination that many victims of inequality would find surprisingly naive. In their introduction, Block and Walker use redheads as the symbol for groups discriminated against on the basis of physical characteristics having no relation to economic productivity. They argue that the refusal of prejudiced employers to hire redheads would force these victims of discrimination to reduce their wage demands so that they were lower than those of blonde or brunette workers. Their lower wages would then make redheads particularly attractive to certain employers who, despite their prejudice, would be moved by their desire for profit to hire this source of cheap labour. In order to remain competitive, other employers would also be forced to hire redheads, and this would improve their bargaining position, finally resulting in the bidding up of their wage rates until they approximated those of other workers. The lesson Block and Walker draw from this example is that "The key to the redheads' escape from the full force of prejudice is their ability to offer other employers a profit possibly in the form of lower wages" (Block and Walker, p. 11).

The question that immediately occurs to any working woman is why the "willingness" of women to work for lower wages, demonstrated by the fact that they do so, has not resulted in an improvement in their position relative to men in the work force. To this, Block and Walker and the other contributors to this volume have a ready answer. The reason is that the conditions of full competition required by their model do not exist. If they did, then the conditions of the equilibrium of labour supply and demand would exist.

Returning once again to the real world of historical experience, the condition of full employment of adult workers rarely exists under capitalism. Indeed, if one considers the women who are outside the labour market because of home responsibilities, but whom can be drawn upon as a labour reserve in times of war and other conditions of great labour demand, full employment has never existed under capitalism. In the circumstances of a labour reserve, the effect of a completely competitive labour market is a decline in wages that is halted, not by an equilibrium being reached, but by the efforts of workers to control the labour supply. As Block and Walker contend, competition on the labour market is the great equalizer — but the equalization is downwards.

The analysis in other articles in *Discrimination, Affirmative Action and Equal Opportunity* is limited by the focus of neo-classical economists on the individual enterprise as the unit of analysis. As a result, some of the consequences of the private market as an economic *system* that contribute to inequality are omitted. One such consequence is the absence of quality, affordable day care, which would greatly improve women's competitive position on the labour market, but which cannot offer enough profit to attract capitalist investment. Because attention is focussed on the behaviour of the individual capitalist, the capitalist economic system as a whole is absolved of responsibility for the results of its operation. The discriminatory consequences are particularly evident in the anti-government interventionist form of capitalism advocated by the contributors to this volume.

This point can be illustrated by looking at two of the explanations for labour market discrimination advanced by these contributors. The first, the many inequalities attributed to discrimination are in fact the results of other causes. He uses as an example the differences in income and occupational distribution of men and women, and maintains that these should be seen as differences between married women and all others, including single women, rather than a result of sex discrimination. He states that "Obviously, a woman who re-enters the labour force after many years as a housewife is unlikely to earn as much as a man who has been working continuously" (Block and Walker, p. 51). From his perspective, the absence of women from the labour force is the result of personal, non-market choices, and he does not need to consider the discrimination implied in assigning to women the virtually exclusive responsibility for household labour. Nor does he need to consider whether or not the labour market under capitalism is structured so as to take advantage of the sexual division of labour that assigns women responsibility for child care. The same problems exist with the "investment in human capital" explanation outlined in the article by Walter Williams. He argues that women, "for reasons that need not concern us here", invest less in securing the training and skills necessary for the better jobs (Block and Walker, p. 75). The reasons that he considers inconsequential are directly related to an

unequal sexual division of labour, reinforced by the unwilling-
ness of capitalists to be taxed to cover the services and benefits
that would make such an investment a priority for young women.

These various theories of labour market discrimination are
presented to justify a specific political programme: opposition to
government or union-imposed restraints on the free operation of
the labour market. Minorities and women are encouraged to see
their interests as associated with the businessmen who are seeking
a return to a more competitive capitalist economy. Significantly,
the discussion of monopoly power in this volume focuses almost
entirely on union limitations on competition on the labour market
and government power. There are no proposals for breaking up
the power of monopoly corporations. Even if one accepted their
idealized view of the competitive capitalist system, one would
have to reject their programme as a prescription for disaster for
women since there is little likelihood that any other groups will
give up their control of labour and other markets. Now that others
have successfully used the state to better their position, women
and minorities are being advised to disarm themselves by
rejecting this avenue for improvement. An examination of the
experience of women workers in a period of laissez-faire
capitalism, however, quickly dispels any myths about the
neo-classical utopia. Unrestrained competition on the labour
market impoverished women as well as men workers, and only
benefitted those capitalists motivated by the desire for the
immediate maximization of profits.

The neo-classical economic explanations of labour market
discrimination discussed so far do not address seriously the
problem of the sex-typing of occupations, the female job ghettos.
Two women economists who work within the neo-classical
tradition and focus on the segregation of jobs along gender lines
as the central problem in sex discrimination are Barbara
Bergmann and Janice Madden. Despite their influence on much
of the debate about the economics of sex discrimination, there are
no references to the works of either in this volume. Bergmann
(1973) agrees with the neo-classical argument that, seen from the
perspective of economic utility, employers lose by sex discrimi-

nation. She maintains that the willingness of some employers to bear the costs is a result of the psychological rewards they receive by keeping women "in their place". These non-economic benefits have resulted in a marked dualism in labour markets that segregate women. It is the overcrowding of women into a small number of occupations that accounts for their low pay. Therefore, according to Bergmann, the best strategy for women is to press for access to traditionally male occupations rather than for equal pay for work of equal value legislation.

In contrast, Madden (1973) uses a monopsony model to argue that, under conditions of imperfect competition, labour market discrimination and profit-maximization are compatible. Madden's model applies to situations where an employer is able to exercise some degree of monopoly control over the labour market as a result either of concentration within an industry or the lack of mobility of labour power within a geographical area (Madden, pp. 73-76). For an employer who enjoys this monopoly power, two conditions are necessary for discrimination: (1) it must be possible to group the labour supply into separate labour pools; (2) these labour groups must have different elasticities of supply (Madden, p. 71). The opportunity to group men and women into separate labour pools arises for one or more of the following reasons: (1) men and woman have identifiably different biological characteristics; (2) they have gender-related lifetime working cycles; and (3) there are different socialization processes that result in different attitudes to work for men and women (Madden, pp. 77-79). Elasticity of labour supply refers to the capacity of a particular labour pool to respond to demand opportunities. Because of the requirements of women's non-market household responsibilities and the primacy of male labour market decisions for a family's welfare, women are seen by Madden to constitute a comparatively inelastic labour supply.

Madden's argument is that, in conditions of monopsony, employers can structure their demands for labour to take advantage of the special characteristics of the female pool of labour. The wage demands of this group are kept low because its members lack alternatives and because strong competition has resulted from crowding women into a restricted number of occupations. The elimination of the competition of female labour has the effect of increasing the wages of male workers. However, the total cost of labour to the employer is kept below what it would be in an unsegregated labour market.

Madden sees the monopoly power of employers in the labour market as a temporary and rare occurrence and one that can be undermined by the competitive tendencies inherent in capitalism. She suggests that, in situations where a number of employers share a labour market, segregation along sex lines is maintained by collusion among the employers. However, the temptation is strong for one employer to violate any agreement and attempt to maximize profit by attracting cheap labour to an unsegregated labour market. She therefore introduces other factors to explain why the discrimination motivation would outweigh the profit-maximization motivation. The factors promoting labour market segregation include government-enforced protective legislation, male dominated labour unions, a socialization process that selects men and women for gender specific jobs, and patterns of family decision-making that are biased against female labour force participation (Madden, p. 82). Her view of the normal, competitive situation, then, does not differ dramatically from that of the neo-classical economists.

The importance of the contributions of Bergmann and Madden is their identification of the segregation of labour markets as central to sex discrimination. In addition, Madden recognizes that certain characteristics of the female labour supply facilitate the creation of two labour markets. However, they are unable adequately to pursue these insights within the framework of neo-classical economics.

The alternate explanations of labour market discrimination — those that assume the existence and persistence of monopoly power — make the segregation of labour markets and the existence of distinct labour supplies the starting point of their analyses. We turn now to a brief consideration of some of these explanations.

Pat Connelly's exploration of labour market discrimination

against women (1978) directly addresses the issue of women as a source of cheap labour. Central to her analysis is the concept of the "reserve army of labour", which refers to a surplus population of workers that serves to regulate the law of supply and demand of labour under capitalism by providing a pool of cheap labour to be drawn on to depress the wages of employed workers or to fill new jobs in times of capitalist expansion. She maintains that the initial cause of the reserve army position of women is the split between the spheres of commodity production, located in the workplace, and of commodity consumption and the reproduction of labour power, centred in the home. On the basis of the division of labour between the sexes that prevailed at the time of industrialization, women were assigned responsibility for the non-market, household labour. Implicit in her analysis, although not clearly formulated, is the argument that the conflict between women's market and non-market labour activities placed them at a competitive disadvantage on the labour market. This resulted in women working for lower wages than men and being used by employers to lower wage rates. In order to defend their jobs and wages, male workers organized to control the labour supply by demanding the exclusion of women from certain occupations. The success of these efforts resulted in the creation of two separate labour markets, one male and one female, and the exclusion of married women from production as far as possible. These married women came to constitute an "institutionalized inactive reserve army" to be activated in times of capitalist expansion or unusual shortages of labour, which occur, for example, during wars. Due to the segregation of labour markets, married women have functioned as a reserve army for female jobs, only indirectly affecting male wage rates by being available to fill jobs in new sectors of the economy. Due to recent changes in the demand for female labour, associated with the expansion of the clerical and service sectors since the Second World War, and in the supply of female labour, caused by inflation, married women in the home are being transformed into an institutionalized active, rather than inactive, reserve of labour.

While Connelly distinguishes two sex-typed labour markets,

the dual labour market theorists analyze the position of women in terms of "primary" and "secondary" labour markets (or, sometimes, sub-markets described as "segments"). This framework has been outlined by Peter Doeringer and Michael Piore (1971, p. 165) as follows: "Jobs in the primary market possess several of the following characteristics: high wages, good working conditions, employment stability, chances of advancement, equity, and due process in the administration of work rules. Jobs in the secondary market, in contrast, tend to have low wages and fringe benefits, poor working conditions, high labour turnover, little chance of advancement, and often arbitrary and capricious supervision. There are distinctions between workers in the two sectors which parallel those between jobs: workers in the secondary sector, relative to those in the primary sector, exhibit greater turnover, higher rates of lateness and absenteeism, more insubordination, and engage more freely in petty theft and pilferage". Women are concentrated mainly, although not exclusively, in the secondary market, and share this location with young workers, minorities and immigrant workers. In their *Internal Labour Market and Manpower Policy* (1971), Doeringer and Piore associate the primary market with the existence of labour markets internal to companies. Access to these internal labour markets takes place through entry level positions at the bottom of a structured career ladder. Recruitment for higher level positions takes place from among those already employed in the primary jobs. In a refinement of the dual labour market theory, Piore distinguishes between an upper and lower tier of the primary market or segment, with professional and managerial positions belonging to the upper tier and industrial jobs to the lower tier (Edwards *et al.*, pp. 126-128).

Building on the dual labour market theory, Richard Edwards, Michael Reich and David Gordon (1975) provide a developmental interpretation of labour market segmentation. They situate the origins of this segmentation at the point of the emergence of monopoly capitalism out of competitive capitalism in the late nineteenth century. The persistence of a competitive capitalist sector within an economy dominated by monopoly corporations gave rise to two labour markets with different demands for labour and different rules of operation. The monopoly sector is characterized by a large investment in capital and the consequent need for a stable workforce to ensure the maximum utilization of this investment over the long term. The competitive capitalist sector is distinguished by a demand for labour on a cyclical, seasonal or otherwise less stable basis. The competitive capitalist sector continues to be motivated by the desire for immediate profit-maximization, while the monopoly sector is more concerned with the long term capture of product and labour markets.

The proponents of this model argue that the segmented labour market develops on the basis of already existing divisions within the workforce along gender, race or other lines. They maintain that employers consciously gear their labour demands to take advantage of these divisions and to create a labour market that responds to their particular needs. This practice, in turn, further institutionalizes and reinforces the divisions. Monopoly employers, for example, set entry level requirements that will attract a certain section of the work force, even if the qualifications demanded are not needed to carry out the work. Women and minority members who do find employment in the monopoly sector are concentrated into certain sex-typed or race-typed occupations having similar characteristics to secondary segment occupations. Workers excluded from employment in the monopoly sector must find work in the competitive sector.

The dual labour market theory in both variants discussed here has been used to explain labour market discrimination against minorities in the United States, and requires further elaboration to account fully for women's situation. A section of the female labour force is concentrated in the labour intensive competitive sector of the economy, both in manufacturing and service industries. But women are also found in the labour-intensive monopolized sectors, such as the electrical industry, and, more significantly, in the non-competitive financial and government sectors. As professional employees, especially teachers and nurses, women constitute an important part of the public sector.

In order to account for these circumstances, an adequate theory of labour market segmentation would emphasize the particular characteristics of the female labour supply. Unlike other types of cheap labour, women are divided along class lines and, despite unequal opportunity, tend to have as much and sometimes more education than men of their class. An important section of the female population, therefore, has been a source of labour that is not only cheap but also educated. As pointed out by the contributors to the volume *Women at Work, Ontario 1850-1930* (Canadian Women's Educational Press, 1974), single middle class women were the labour supply for the new professional positions in the expanding public sector at the inception of universal education and the welfare state in the late nineteenth and early twentieth centuries. Valerie Kincade Oppenheimer (1970) has stressed that the post-World War Two expansion of the government and financial sector created a demand for labour that was both educated *and* cheap. The customary sources of cheap labour for English Canada, non-English speaking immigrants, did not have the necessary literacy skills. The reserve of labour that was both educated and cheap was located among married women, who, until that point, were engaged as full-time wives and mothers in the home. Connelly's explanation of the structural reasons for the cheapness of female labour is therefore an important supplement to the dual market theories.

Building on Connelly's analysis and the developmental perspective of labour market segmentation, the analysis of affirmative action programmes in the final section of this paper will treat the unequal position of women in today's labour market as the historical product of the conflict between employers and workers over control of the labour market. Initially, the demand of industrial capitalism for labour was non-discriminatory, seeking only the cheapest supply of workers capable of doing a particular job. Due to the conflict between their labour market and non-market responsibilities, compounded by legal inequalities, women were in a weaker competitive position than men and, as a group, constituted an identifiable source of cheap labour. In response to employers' use of women to lower wages, male workers organized to exclude women from certain jobs and endorsed the principles of equal pay for equal work and the "living wage", a male wage high enough to support a wife and family. Their success in winning these restrictions came in those sectors of the economy where capitalists could make use of new technology to increase profits by using machines to improve productivity.

The exclusion of women from certain occupations resulted in the institutionalization of the unequal sexual division of labour that initially gave rise to the demands of workers and served to reinforce attitudes about the appropriate spheres of social activity for men and women. Today, labour markets are consciously structured by employers to take advantage of the labour supply characteristics of men and women related to their different roles in the family. Any analysis of the impact of policies on the inequality faced by women on the labour market must, therefore, account for the interaction of two sets of structural factors: (1) the position of married women as an institutionalized reserve army of labour; (2) the different labour demands of the various sectors of the economy.

In the evaluation that follows, the term "affirmative action" is used to cover both voluntary and compulsory programmes, including those that establish guidelines and goals to be met through active recruitment of qualified candidates and those that deliberately offer preferential treatment of candidates from disadvantaged groups, which might involve relaxing some of the established requirements. The impact of affirmative action programmes will be considered for the following sectors of the economy: (1) the monopoly sector; (2) the state sector; (3) the competitive sector. In the discussion below, the terms "primary" and "secondary" are employed to maintain continuity with the preceeding arguments. They are used here to refer to occupations with the characteristics outlined earlier in the article and not to refer to the behavioral characteristics of groups of workers.

The monopoly sector is "characterized by heavy capital investment per worker, by high productivity (the growth of which is responsible for most of the sector's growth), by growing control over a complex production and marketing process, sometimes from the raw material stage to the retail stage (called vertical integration), and by a restless takeover movement within single industries (horizontal integration) and across industries (conglomerates and holding companies)'' (Armstrong and Armstrong, 1981, p. 21). Within this sector women are concentrated in the financial institutions, where they made up 54% of the labour force in 1971 (Armstrong and Armstrong, p. 28). The labour market for the financial institutions is segmented along gender lines with women being confined to the clerical jobs. It should be noted that the labour-intensive character of clerical work is currently being transformed by microtechnology, which is being introduced rapidly in financial institutions. Clerical work within industrial establishments is also carried out by women. The majority of production workers in the monopoly sector are men.

Affirmative action programmes in hiring and promotion could be quite effective in the monopoly sector. As established earlier, the key problem here is access to entry level positions into the internal market that characterizes "primary" jobs.

In financial institutions recruitment for the primary jobs at the entry level has been from the external labour market with little or no possibility for women employed in the secondary segment jobs to transfer. Furthermore, primary jobs often require educational qualifications that the clerical workers may not possess. Affirmative action programmes in financial institutions would therefore need to be directed at seeking women in the external labour market for entry level primary jobs, as well as providing access to these jobs by clerical workers, which could involve relaxing unnecessary qualifications or making available re-training opportunities. The secondary segment jobs here are hurt by the availability of a female reserve army, which tends to depress wages. Unionization of these mainly unorganized workers would be necessary to counteract this pressure. Fear of just such action from workers in financial institutions is a factor in employers' interest in automation. The non-market labour responsibilities of women in the home will continue to have an effect on women's willingness to seek promotions, and so affirmative action policies will continue to be necessary even after women have gained access to primary entry positions.

Entry level jobs for many industrial jobs in the monopoly sector do not require any special education or training. Affirmative action programmes in hiring could have an effect on changing the gender balance in these branches of the economy. Promotion is usually regulated by collective agreements between management and labour, but active encouragement of women to pursue the available opportunities will probably be necessary. Arrangements would also be necessary to ensure that the office employees of these industries, who are often members of different unions, have access to the better-paid production jobs.

A major problem in this sector of the economy is that many of the manufacturing industries, such as the automotive industry, are in a state of crisis and will only survive by introducing new technology in order to become even more capital-intensive than they already are. As a result, rather than hiring, employers will be laying off workers in large numbers, and any women already employed will probably be among the permanently laid-off. Preferential lay-off provisions, similar to those negotiated by unions for elected union officials within plants, might have some impact, but the proportion of women already employed in these jobs is quite small. In all enterprises in the monopoly sector, including financial institutions, the trend will be a decline in employment due to automation. Of course, the industries that remain in the monopoly sector will have to replace members of their current workforce who leave through attrition, and affirmative action programmes for hiring should be in effect. But the already existing industries in the monopoly sector cannot be expected to provide alternative primary employment for the women concentrated today in sex-typed job ghettos.

The area that can be expected to provide new employment is the industries based on the new micro-technology. These are still in their infancy but can be expected to become the expanding area of the monopoly sector of the economy. As in the past, the female labour reserve will be drawn upon to fill some of the new positions that will be created. Unless some government or union-imposed restrictions are put up on the free operation of the labour market, however, there is every likelihood that the jobs in this industry will be as segregated along gender lines as those in the established industries. As the authors of *Microelectronics, Capitalist Technology and the Working Class* (CSE Microelectronics Group, 1981) have argued, this technology is just emerging from the skilled craft stage and undergoing the same fragmentation of the work process into specialized unskilled tasks that took place in previous industries. Historically, women have been recruited at this stage for the low-paid, least skilled industrial jobs. It is unlikely that affirmative action programmes will be needed to ensure women access to jobs in this sector. What will be required are measures to prevent the segmentation of jobs in this sector along gender lines, involving the exclusion of women from the best jobs. Unionization to counter the effects of the large female labour reserve is probably the single most important step women (and men) in these industries could take. Once unionized, employees in this sector could negotiate affirmative action programmes to ensure equal opportunity for women in hiring and promotion.

"Contract compliance" is a policy instrument for limiting the effects of the female labour reserve which enjoys some support. This approach requires that governments use their spending and taxation powers to force employers to implement affirmative action programmes. While such measures are desirable, the experience of women with equal pay and other legislation is that governments rarely appoint enough inspectors to make them effective. In the absence of governments with a strong commitment to ending labour market discrimination, it is likely that affirmative action programmes will be directed more at achieving the "rational utilization of human resources" than at full gender equality. Government legislation should be seen as a complement to, not a substitute for, the effective organization of women.

Like the financial institutions, the government bureaucracy expanded in the post-World War Two period on the basis of the reserve army of labour provided by the married woman in the home. The labour markets for government jobs is similarly segregated along gender lines, with the clerical positions being filled mainly by women and the technical, managerial and professional occupations mainly by men. The exception in the latter, primary, category is the large number of women employed in the sex-typed professions of teaching and nursing in government-funded institutions.

Many Canadian governments have implemented affirmative action programmes of various kinds. These include programmes to recruit women for the better paid positions, to encourage women to apply for promotions once employed, and to review the qualifications for jobs to ensure that the requirements are directly related to the work done. So far, the success of these programmes is limited by the commitment of some governments, for example the Ontario government, to them. However, the framework does exist for them to be strengthened through public pressure. Unlike the financial sector, government is highly unionized in Canada. This has had the effect of raising government wages for clerical workers above those offered in the private sector, which reacts to this competition for the female labour supply by launching regular attacks on ''overpaid'' government employees.

The third sector where women are employed is the competitive sector, which includes much of the service and trade industries and the labour-intensive manufacturing enterprises. Women comprise 57.6% of the labour force in community, business and personal services, with 44.4% of the total female labour force being employed here; women make up 36.7% of the trade division of the economy, with 17.6% of the total female labour force concentrated in these jobs, according to 1971 census figures. Women at that time accounted for 23.7% of people employed in manufacturing, which represented 15.3% of the female labour force (Armstrong and Armstrong, 1981, p. 25). With few exceptions, these women are employed in the labour-intensive manufacturing enterprises and many of them are new immigrants. Very often the industries in the competitive sector of the economy depend on the existence of a cheap pool of female labour for their survival. Even with the lower wages paid here, labour intensive industries in the clothing industry require government protection of the domestic market in order to withstand competition from cheaper labour in other countries.

Businesses in the services and trades division often employ women part-time, structuring their labour demands to take advantage of women's role in the family. The manufacturing industries in the competitive sector recruit their labour force on a cyclical or seasonal basis from among the labour reserve made up of women and/or immigrant workers. The most extreme exploitation of married women's position as a labour reserve occurs in this sector in the form of industrial "homework" for the garment industry (Johnson, 1982). Industrial home sewing in Canada is carried on with no effective protection from government. Most of the competitive sector either is non-unionized or has weak unions. Minimum working conditions are enforced in factories and stores through government regulation. As a result, this is the most competitive segment of the labour market. Efforts to control the effects of competition through unionization or legislation are hampered by the precarious situation of many of the industries in this sector. Affirmative action programmes could only help the women here by providing them with the means to escape into another sector of the economy, either through re-training courses or alternate job opportunities.

I have been arguing that affirmative action programmes in hiring and promotion can be useful in helping women gain access to traditionally "male" occupations under certain circumstances. The cases where they might be most effective are, first, in access to upper tier "primary" jobs (the technical, professional and managerial positions) by women who have the qualifications and have previously been excluded or who wish to transfer from "secondary" to "primary" segment positions; and, secondly, in access to entry level "primary" jobs in industry. To what extent, though, will this improved access solve the problem of the concentration of women in low paid, sex-typed job ghettos? For affirmative action to have an impact, women would have to be recruited in very large numbers to the jobs in the industries where most of the primary male workers are employed. But, as has been pointed out, the primary industrial jobs are in divisions of the economy that are increasingly capital intensive and unlikely to be providing many new jobs. The area of economic expansion in the monopoly sector in the future will be in the industries based on micro-technology. By the time mass industries develop in this division, most of the jobs will require a minimum of skill. Affirmative action programmes may not be necessary to encourage employers to recruit female workers. What will be required are effective measures, such as unionization, to control the effects of competition from the female labour reserve. Finally, affirmative action programmes for women will do little to eliminate the existing female job ghettos unless wages and working conditions are improved to attract male workers. The women who move from these ghettos into the primary sector jobs will very quickly be replaced by women from the labour reserve pool concentrated in the family.

So far I have considered women's reserve army of labour position only from the perspective of measures to control its negative effect on women's labour market position, such measures as unionization and government legislation. Another approach would be to attempt to eliminate the reserve army position altogether by abolishing the unequal sexual division of labour on which it is based. This would require a much more ambitious affirmative action programme, involving a system of universal child care and maternity benefits that do not penalize women in the labour force for their child bearing functions. These measures would diminish the pressure on women to go in and out of the labour market as dictated by family needs. A more equitable sharing of household labour between women and men would also be necessary to bring to a complete end women's disadvantage on the labour market. While governments cannot legislate this change, policies that eliminate sex-stereotyping in education and the media and, more significantly, that provide more leisure time to full-time workers, can facilitate it. An effective strategy to improve women's labour market position would involve measures both to minimize the effects of the reserve of cheap female labour and to eliminate this structural feature of women's relationship to the labour mearket.

The evaluation of policy options presented in this paper, therefore, differs sharply from those found in the Fraser Institute volume, *Discrimination, Affirmative Action, and Equal Opportunity*. The contributors to this collection ascribe the inequality of women on the labour market either to unprofitable ''tastes for discrimination'' or to government or union-imposed restrictions on a competitive labour market. They therefore argue that women's equality will come from dismantling legislative restrictions such as minimum wage laws and weakening union influence. According to the volume's contributors, the reforms advocated by women's organizations, such as equal pay for work of equal value legislation and affirmative action policies, will only compound a bad situation.

My argument is quite the opposite. I maintain that labour market equality, including the desegregation of occupations, requires that women take the same kind of steps to minimize the effects of competition from cheap female labour that men have taken. These include such measures as unionization and equal pay for work of equal value legislation. In addition, measures that are designed to eliminate the labour reserve position of married women are necessary. These will require greater state involvement in the provision of social services and in the enforcement of standards with respect to maternity leave. Affirmative action programmes in hiring and promotion are useful in promoting equality of opportunity for women but, unless they are very broadly conceived to include the measures proposed here, they will have little impact on the supply of cheap female labour. As argued in this paper, it is women's position as a reserve army of labour, and the structuring of labour markets to take advantage of it, rather than overcrowding, that are the causes of low wages. In the final analysis, public policies must therefore address not only the sex segregation in the labour market, but also the unequal division of labour in the family that is fundamental to it.

Bibliography

Armstrong, Pat and Armstrong, Hugh (1981), *The Double Ghetto: Canadian Women and Their Segregated Work*, McClelland and Stewart, Toronto.

Becker, Gary (1957), *The Economics of Discrimination*, University of Chicago Press, Chicago.

Bergmann, Barbara (1973), "The Economics of Women's Liberation", *Challenge*, May/June.

Block, W.E. and Walter, M.A., eds. (1982), *Discrimination, Affirmative Action and Equal Opportunity*, The Fraser Institute, Vancouver.

Canadian Women's Educational Press (1974), *Women at Work, Ontario 1850-1930*, Women's Press, Toronto.

Connelly, Patricia (1978), *Last Hired, First Fired. Women and the Canadian Work Force*, Women's Press, Toronto.

CSE Microelectronics Group (1981), *Microelectronics, Capitalist Technology and the Working Class*, London.

Doeringer, Peter and Piore, Michael (1971), *Internal Labour Markets and Manpower Analysis*, Lexington Books, Lexington, Mass.

Edwards, Richard C. and Reich, Michael and Gordon, David M. (1975), *Labor Market Segmentation*, Lexington Books, Lexington, Mass.

Johnson, Laura C. (1982), *The Seam Allowance: Industrial Home Sewing in Canada*, Women's Press, Toronto.

Madden, Janice F. (1973), *The Economics of Discrimination*, Lexington Books, Toronto.

Oppenheimer, Valerie Kincade (1970), *The Female Labour Force in the United States*, Institute of International Studies, Berkley, California.

Research on Child Abuse in Liberal Patriarchy

KATHLEEN A. LAHEY

Introduction

This paper brings together major themes developed in feminist theory and applies them to the phenomenon of child abuse. One theme is the rhetorical techniques that patriarchal culture has developed to disguise the messages of reality. Another theme is patriarchy's capacity to adopt and absorb changes in the social structure without losing its essential character: male prerogative. Child abuse has been chosen for the focus of this paper because its connection with patriarchal order is not as obvious as the connection between rape, for example, and patriarchy. In building up the interconnectedness of the definition and regulation of child abuse, the social role of mothers, and patriarchal studies of child abuse, we can delve deeper through the layers of deception that have become reality for children and women.

Radical Feminism as Critique

Traditional liberal critiques of child abuse tend toward description and categorization of the phenomenon, coupled with attempts to regulate overt abusive behaviour. Some of the critiques attempt to reach causal factors in a radical fashion, but are preoccupied with fixing up destructive effects of patriarchal order without disturbing that order itself. Radical feminism also tries to describe the phenomenon of child abuse and asks why it occurs. Unlike the liberal approach, it attempts however, to isolate underlying values that generate child abuse and considers alternative structures that would lead to results that are less destructive to human welfare. In this respect, radical feminism is similar to marxian critique of child abuse, which is also concerned with institutional factors.[1] Radical feminist critique takes on some features of marxian critique, but it is nonetheless more fluid, for it does not start out with an assumed ideal order of existence. Thus it is freer to consider alternatives and to search for optimal institutional arrangements.

Radical feminist critique differs from radical male critique — and from liberal feminism — in the order of values to which it gives priority in considering alternative institutional arrangements. Liberal feminism has become increasingly preoccupied with equalizing opportunities, wealth, power, etc. between women and men in the private and public spheres without necessarily affecting institutional arrangements as such.[2] Radical feminism[3] is concerned not only with issues of inequality, but also with the more generalized, more pervasive issues of values and influence in contemporary culture. Radical feminism seeks to deny not only male prerogative but also the values which male prerogative depends upon and implies. Patriarchal thinking — which focuses on concepts of hierarchy, right and wrong, restitution, rectification — is seen as depending on values such as autonomy, power, revenge, domination, compliance. In rejecting these values, radical feminism seeks to give expression to gynocentric values, which are not only antipatriarchal but which go further and affirm values that are traditionally associated with the special powers of women — values such as continuity, contextualized and relativistic decision processes, nurturance and social facilitation.[4] As Yolande Cohen has warned most eloquently, affirmation of these values is playing with fire, for historically they are the source of our special oppression. However, several Canadian feminists are now arguing that without this affirmation, we cannot have any meaningful impact on the institutions of patriarchy.[5] Although gynocentric values may well be associated with our historical oppression, the contradictions that their affirmation sets up can also be a source of political energy and the will to effect major cultural changes.

Patriarchy, Liberalism and Child Abuse

Many learned discussions of child abuse commence by noting that child abuse has always taken place, and indeed in more regretful or vicious forms than it does today, with perhaps the implication that more civilization is all that is needed in order to eliminate the problem entirely.[6] This view misses the point without necessarily being sexist — although it is not inconsistent with sexist research methodologies. The point is that written and documented history is largely the history of patriarchy. Relatively little information is available on child abuse in nonpatriarchal society, and that which is available is not referred to in the mainstream of literature on child abuse. Indeed, commentators can more easily resort to utopian feminist literature than to data on child abuse in nonpatriarchal social orders.[7]

What writers are really saying when they stress the constancy of child abuse is that child abuse is a feature of patriarchal order. These writers fail to make the obvious connection that child abuse has not been eliminated even in these enlightened times because the social order is still patriarchal and because child abuse still serves the patriarchal social order as well as ever. We may have moved from the era of feudal patriarchy to the era of capitalist, liberal or even antipatriarchal patriarchy, but the prevailing social order is nonetheless thoroughly patriarchal.[8]

The transition from feudal to liberal patriarchy has affected relationships between male people without significantly altering the content of their relationships with children or women. Two important contributors to the development of liberal ideology — Rousseau and Kant — explicitly integrated their concepts of democracy, freedom and human dignity into patriarchal thought. Rousseau, who is generally acknowledged as having a strong influence on the propagation of democracy, conceptualized the relationship between the state and the individual as analogous to the organization of the nuclear family. He used the notion of *parens patriae* to describe the power of the state with regard to individuals; *parens patriae* literally means "father of the country". Rousseau openly admits that the order of the state is patriarchal, and accords all power and freedoms to male members of the state.

Within the state composed of male members we find no independent women. They exist only to the extent that they belong to men. In Rousseau's ideal democratic patriarchy, the status of children is inferior even to that of women. They do not belong to male members of the state in the same sense that women belong; rather, they exist only as the object of the male-female relationship. While the function of women is to serve the physical and emotional needs of the male members of the state, children are accorded an even more dehumanized role. Children exist to form a vehicle by which male members of the state can transmit and control their property in the future. Women must be monogamously bound to individual men so that paternity can be determined factually or by legal presumption. Children to whom paternity attaches are then valued primarily as tools to carry male will into the future.[9]

Thus Rousseau articulates the concept of personal autonomy and freedom for men against the backdrop of the enslavement of women and children, who serve as the means by which male members of the state act out their autonomy and freedom. Early liberal writers did not seem to notice that this approach to equality was premised on institutionalized inequality. Instead, the contradiction that captured their imaginations was the conflict between the utter freedom that men sought for themselves and the constraints that government was seen to impose on the will of men. Given this formulation of the main issue of democracy, it is not entirely surprising that writers such as Kant could continue to vilify women as being mere spoiled children, not fit for participation in the world of affairs — the world of men — without noticing the astounding contradiction, the absolute nullification of said women and children.[10]

Early liberal patriarchal philosophers formulated their concepts of human rights and human dignity on the backs of children and women. Governmental interference was seen as a more serious derogation of human rights than was the subjugation of children and women. In this zero sum concept of dignity, children and women could only lose more or lose less dignity, but never gain dignity, for any gain in the dignity of children or women would equivalently derogate from the dignity of men.[11] By the time that liberal writers such as Mary Wollstonecraft, Harriet Taylor and others noticed the true contradiction of liberal patriarchy, the only way that they could express their outrage was in the imagery of liberal patriarchy. The equality they pursued was equality defined in liberal male terms; that is, equality in the public sphere. To achieve this equality, women have to become like men in reason, achievement and aspiration. Although Taylor and Wollstonecraft recognized the central fact of reproductive capacity and responsibility, their access to equality depended on becoming free from dependence on men and thereby achieving equal public status.

As a culture we have not yet moved beyond the aspirations of capitalist, liberal or socialist patriarchy. Feminist strategies are still preoccupied with obtaining equality for women in the public sphere and with eliciting help with housework and nurturance in the private sphere. Paradoxically, the steadily increasing number of single parent and same sex households still reproduce patriarchal social order. And patriarchal social order directly fosters child abuse — by treating children as pawns in the power structure, by the mystique of conforming children's behaviour to male defined norms, by treating children as an evil force that must be controlled. Although men may argue that women's involvement in child abuse proves that patriarchal social order has nothing to do with child abuse, a feminist analysis enables us to see through this particular deception.

A great deal of insight into the status of children in liberal patriarchy can be derived from reviewing legal attitudes toward child abuse. The traditional legal treatment of assault and battery of children reflects the belief that children are mere property and can be disciplined in any way necessary to conform their conduct to their parents' expectations or desires. Take, for example, the differing attitudes toward assault and battery of adult males and of children. Battery occurs whenever a person touches another without consent. Actual harm need not be proven; the only legally relevant fact is that there was no consent to the contact. Assault occurs when a person threatens to touch another person without consent. In order to succeed in an assault suit, the victim must be in apprehension of imminent harm. The relative size of the victim and assailant are relevant to determining that assault has occurred; actual contact need not be proven.

Numerous common law decisions make it quite clear that broad definitions of assault and battery are necessary in order to give human integrity the fullest possible protection, dignity and freedom. For example, a well known Texas case held that battery was committed when a restaurant manager snatched a plate out of an unwanted patron's hand. The patron was a black male.[12] Other batteries have been committed when one person has touched another person's car, chair or clothing — any object with which the victim is identified. However, if the victim of unconsenting or threatening contact is a child, patriarchy creates an exception to the law of assault and battery. Until family law reform came to Canada, the father was viewed as being the natural guardian of the child, excluding even the child's mother during the father's life. (How much legal reform has actually affected the balance of power within the family is open to question.)[13] One of the rights conferred by legal paternity is the right to determine the child's values, ethics, religion, education, deportment — almost every aspect of environment and behaviour. Another right conferred by legal paternity is the right to assault and batter the child to achieve the desired behaviour and attitudes. Children do not have the same rights to physical integrity and human dignity that most adult males and some adult females enjoy under liberal patriarchy. The legal mind approaches a case of intimidation or unconsenting contact not with a view to finding out if the child truly felt apprehension or withheld consent, but to determine whether the threat or contact was serious enough to justify "interference" by "paternalistic" government in the "rights" of the parents.

In order to ensure that softhearted judges do not sometimes forget that children have no right to physical integrity or human dignity, Canadian federal and provincial legislation creates exceptions to civil and criminal liability for assault and battery when a parent threatens or attacks a child. The federal criminal code expressly exonerates parents from criminal liability for child battery when the parent claims that the purpose of the battery is merely to discipline a child. This exception applies in favour of parents as well as anyone who has the care of a child, including siblings, other relatives, babysitters and teachers. Professor Backhouse has even found a 1792 Prince Edward Island statutory provision that exonerates a parent from a criminal charge of manslaughter if he happens to kill his child during chastisement.[14] Similarly, a child who seeks to bring a civil action against an assaulting or battering parent is precluded from doing so because of the doctrine of intrafamily tort immunity. In some Canadian jurisdictions, feminists have recently won partial abolition of that immunity for adult women like themselves, but no one has won such an exception for children. Only if extremely severe injuries result from so-called disciplinary battering can a child sue for damages, due to nonenforcement problems for mild injuries. Given the realities of how easily children are severely injured, such a child is likely to be permanently impaired or dead long before a suit could be filed.

Liberal patriarchy denies children legal safeguards for their integrity and dignity in other ways. The label of child abuse, which is applied when a parent or other caregiver inflicts clinically significant trauma, does not ordinarily connote other invasions which children suffer. Neglect, emotional deprivation, sexual interference and exploitation are not actionable except in very serious cases. Even when they are actionable, the child's integrity and dignity is certainly not treated as an absolute value. It is simply treated as a competing interest which must be weighed against other important social values — freedom of speech, for example, or the male prerogative to sexual gratification of any kind. Weak child protection laws translate into the right to neglect or deprive a child of almost every attribute of human existence except existence itself. Narrowly defined and arbitrarily prosecuted incest laws translate, in effect, into the right of a father to gratify himself with his child's body. Badly structured incest therapy programs translate into the mother's obligation to make her child's body available for sexual activity if hers is not. Political refusal to legislate against child pornography translates into the right of adult males to treat children as badly as they treat women in making works for commercial exploitation and in creating images for sexual gratification.[15]

Viewing the legal and cultural status of child abuse, the question is not what causes child abuse. Rather, we should be asking why some people do *not* abuse children, for abuse certainly appears to be the norm. Can we work more effectively toward eliminating child abuse if we can manage to engage in nonsexist rather than sexist research into child abuse? Or will nonsexist research that fails to question the essentially patriarchal structure of Canadian society be as misleading as research that has been done to date? The next part of this paper addresses this issue.

Research on Child Abuse

I have argued that contemporary legal responses to child abuse of whatever kind can be traced to the ideology of liberal patriarchy. Ideology is not the only source of law, however. An emerging source of law and of social policy that is implemented as law, is the research of social science investigators. Because the entire concept of law is itself an ideological tool, so-called reform laws that draw on social science documentation of the excesses of patriarchy can do no more than merely mediate the conflicts between patriarchy and its victims.[16] Thus it is not surprising that, after nearly two decades of research into the causes and treatment of child abuse, most research projects reflect the underlying premises of patriarchy, ask nonproductive questions and fail to give policymakers guidance which could lead to meaningful responses to child abuse. This results in research and laws that liberal feminists would call sexist; radical feminists would say that they simply serve the patriarchy by helping it to keep its worst abuses under control *without having to stop them*.

A brief review of mainstream research on the various types of abuse borne by children bears out this assertion. A peculiar thing about the literature is that, no matter who actually engages in child assault, battery, incest, neglect, etc., researchers manage to blame it on the child's mother. At least half of all battering parents are male, and not all battering is done by parents or even by family members. Yet mothers, who appear to account for less than 40% of all child battering, are blamed either directly or indirectly for the abusive behavior, for its continuation and for its ineradicability. The rest of this section documents this conclusion.

(1) *Research on Assault and Battery*

Take for example a recent study by Winifred Scott, a clinical psychologist who conducted an empirical study into the social history of mothers of battered children. She takes as her starting point the fact that most of the research on battery focuses on the interaction between mother and child. Ignoring other studies (which she mentions in passing) that have looked at parent-child interaction and not just mother-child interaction, she hypothesizes that child battery can be tied to attachment theory.[17] This narrow hypothesis is not in itself sexist, but her reason for focusing on attachment theory is:

> Mothers of abused children, rather than abusers, were selected for this study, since it is hypothesized that the mother plays a significant role in abuse, whether she injures or neglects the child herself or fails to protect him [sic] from another abuser.[18]

Dr. Scott goes on to argue that the antecedents for the battering or unprotective mother's behaviour can be traced to her own childhood, which shifts some of the blame from the battered child's mother to her mother's mother. The battered child's father (and grandfather) are completely invisible in this hypothesis; by inference they are blameless. Dr. Scott does not question this complete shifting of blame to mothers; apparently she accepts the male viewpoint that a mother who cannot protect her child from battering by a male (who is usually stronger than both the child and the mother) is more culpable than the male who is the actual abuser.

The Scott study is unique because it goes at least as far as male research in looking solely to the mother for family harmony, and warns once again of the dangers of cooptation in research, which is another aspect of sexism. The Scott study is also unique in that it sets up its elaborate hypothesis only to prove that almost any woman can become the parent of a child who will be battered. She found that mothers of battered children differed from those of nonbattered children in several significant social history indicators:

(1) separation from one or both parents in childhood
(2) abuse in childhood
(3) psychiatric problems
(4) drug or alcohol abuse
(5) police involvement
(6) illegitimate pregnancy
(7) assault by significant male in adulthood
(8) temporary separation from one or more children prior to the abuse incident[19]

Scott does not offer for comparison the proportion in the general population of women who have experienced one or more of the listed indicators. One can only suspect that it would be quite large, especially given factor (1) and escalating divorce rates.

Without actually saying so, Scott manages to suggest that mothers who had traumatic childhoods will reproduce that trama for their children, directly or indirectly. Ignoring the initiators of and contributors to that trauma, she is saying either that all trauma should be dealt with more effectively, or that mothers are largely to blame for child battering. I suspect that even if her point is that vast institutional changes have to be made if life is to be safe for women and thus for children, her study will simply be taken to say that some women are not fit to be mothers. And that is only a short step away from saying that male members of the state, who are the policymakers anyway, are better able to decide how children are to be raised and by whom. The whole concept of "fitness for motherhood" plays directly into the hands of judges and legislators, who would thus be able to resolve the patriarchal impulse toward control over women and reproduction.[20] Structuring feminist input into this aspect of the legal process is especially urgent, for until the entire concept of child abuse can be redefined, women are simply not free to decide how to nurture children without direct or indirect monitoring by men.

Scott is not alone in her preoccupation with the mother's direct or indirect responsibility for child abuse. Other researchers have looked for and found significant correlations between child battering by someone and that child's mother's immaturity, egocentricity, insensitivity, intrusiveness, coerciveness, inconsistency,[21] authoritarianism, rejection, interference and distancing.[22] The mother-character approach has been refined to the point where measurement of the mother's prenatal adaptive behaviour is used to predict which mothers will be maladaptive and in need of intervention or followup.[23] While it is certainly useful to understand how mothers influence the development of their children, the use of maternal attitude studies alone to predict maladjusted (abusive?) behaviour is somewhat suspect.

Even in general population studies, which avoid the small sample problem, fathers, other family members and nonfamily members are invisible. For example, a population survey of families with children between the ages of 1.5 and 4 years went out to mothers only. It concluded that child abuse was most clearly related to fatigue and premenstrual tension.[24] The methodology and conclusions of this particular study are interesting because, on the one hand, the authors surveyed only mothers, yet, on the other hand, they attributed the anger control techniques uncovered in the course of the study to all parents, which presumably includes men as well as women. The mothers who were surveyed made it quite clear that the factors that were associated with loss of control were strongly identified with the sex role of women: responsibility for training their children to eat, use the toilet and sleep on command; too much housework; marital disharmony; isolation in the house; financial worries. Nonetheless, the authors generalize their conclusions to fathers, and, perhaps more importantly, they ignore the relationship between sex role oppression and child abuse. This is symptomatic not only of sexism in research, but also of deep insensitivity to the horrors that patriarchal social organization holds for women and children.

Not all of the research on child abuse is premised on maternal inadequacy or culpability, or focusses exclusively on mother-child interaction. A general population survey by Murray Straus[25] manages to see beyond what battering mothers do to why they may do it, and in the process focusses on the sex role of the mother. He concludes that even though women are generally less violent than men, 17% of the women in the survey population batter children against 10% of the men. Instead of approaching these women as maladjusted and treating them as the guilty parties, the study sought out the reason for the percentage. He concluded that, due to sex roles, women have far more time at risk with children because of their primary responsibility as caregivers. In addition to more time at risk, Straus points to two other important factors. One is that increased time at risk is not often the result of free and voluntary choice on the mother's part; strong spousal and social expectations force mothers to assume overwhelming responsibility for children, which generates frustration. The other factor is that there are strong spousal and social expectations as to children's behaviour. If the child does not perform well enough, and no child (or mother) ever can perform perfectly, a high level of anxiety, frustration and guilt is inevitable.

Straus hypothesized that mothers who work outside the home would have a greater tendency toward child abuse because of the double role. However, women in the sample who worked outside the home were no more abusive than men. And these women were carrying the double burden of outside employment and continuing responsibility for the home. One is led to speculate that if women had only the single burden that men bear, they would be much less abusive than men under similar circumstances. This finding suggests that sexual division of labour is a very significant factor in child abuse, and that it would be more useful to study child battery from an institutional perspective than from the vantage point of the mother's adjustment.

Studies like these are valuable not only for their conclusions but also because they inevitably lead us to confront patriarchal assumptions that permeate institutional arrangements concerning child care. When researchers consistently observe that battered children are incredibly compliant and obedient, quiet, passive and unassertive, we are reminded of the attributes that men idealize in women.[26] It is research findings like this that stress — even when it is so obvious to feminists — that the function of violence in the family and in our culture at large is the containment and domination of "other". When that "other" is a child or a woman, violence erupts wherever our social structure brings the dominant group (frequently male persons) into contact with children or women. In the context of child abuse, the ultimate irony emerges when we see that even women — whose traditional role is as protector and nurturer of young people — can be forced to become transmitters of the domination-subjugation dichotomy that is so characteristic of North American gender-based social arrangements. The cowed and pliable battered child becomes the ultimate symbol of patriarchal patterns of domination.

(2) Research on Neglect

Mothers are not only held accountable for physical battering, but for physical and emotional neglect as well. An important development in the literature on child neglect is the use of the concept of "maternal deprivation" to refer to neglect. Again, this concept reflects the belief that it is mothers and mothers only who are responsible for nurturance of children. Therefore any failure of nurturance is the mother's fault. And if the depriving mother is not entirely responsible for inadequate nurture, then ultimate responsibility can be traced back to *her* mother.

Bias in studies of neglect is well disguised. Writers routinely stress that other factors play a role in neglect, naming the father, parental interaction, and social, economic and environmental factors in passing. But by focussing formal research on the so-called character disorders of mothers of neglected children, we are repeatedly assured that it is mother who is at fault.[27]

The findings of such research offer us a familiar image of mothers of neglected children. The mothers had disturbed childhoods, perform poorly as home centred workers, would like to be nurtured themselves, are severely isolated and markedly literal. They have problems in maintaining their self esteem and tend to be depressed, angry, helpless — even desperate.[28] Often the so-called character disorder is considered by male researchers to be so resistant to therapy that removal of the child is seen as the only useful treatment.

(3) *Research on Sexual Interference*

Sexual interference is a relatively new area of investigation. Denial operates strongly in relation to incest, and it has been reported that male medical practitioners routinely attribute reports of incest to overactive imaginations.[29] As with other forms of child abuse, sexual contact with children serves liberal patriarchy. In fact, the libertarian view of adult-child sexual activity is that there is nothing wrong with it, it is good for all parties and that legal regulation is highly inappropriate. Sexist attitudes pervade thinking about incest, and have also had profound influence on the legal response to incest.

Father-daughter sexual activity appears to be reported more frequently than other arrangements. Some writers estimate that brother-sister incest may be as much as five times as prevalent, but it is seldom reported and does not seem to evoke even the reaction that father-daughter contact does. Over 90% of the children involved in sexual activity with adults are female children; 97% of the abusers are male. Something like 75% of the abusers are known to the young woman (a statistic which is reminiscent of date rape data) and 27% live in the young woman's own home.[30]

Statistics alone suggest that sexual interference with children is simply one of the prerogatives of patriarchy despite recurring assertions that there is an incest taboo. Because the father or other male is directly engaged in the act in question, one would expect research to focus on what character defects distinguish the offending father from other more restrained males. That is not the case at all. Even when sexual activity takes place when the mother is miles from home, according to researchers, she somehow knows all about the activity; and knowing about it, she maliciously conspires and colludes in the incest in order to procure her daughter's cooperation. The mother is deemed to know everything that is going on and she is blamed for not using her supernatural powers to prevent or stop it.

The lengths to which researchers go in order to maintain this fiction are truly impressive. Kempe asserts that mothers either abet or arrange situations that are likely to make privacy between father and daughter easier to obtain, and that there simply is no such thing as an innocent mother in cases of longstanding incest.[31] He theorizes that the mother acts in this way in order to keep her husband happy, ensuring that he will not withdraw social and financial support. Apparently the mother's frigidity, promiscuity or sexual unattractiveness will drive her to this device. Other writers theorize that passive and ineffectual mothers collude in incestuous activity by pushing the daughter into becoming the central female figure in the household. Although the father is frequently described as domineering and patriarchal, the blame is shared by the colluding mother and the daughter, who is seen as actively encouraging the father to make sexual advances or at least as not resisting them.[32] Somewhat contradictorily, researchers also claim that maternal condonation takes the form of such a strong denial that the mother is unable to take any action to protect the daughter.

Lustig has discovered numerous explanations in the literature for father-daughter sexual activity, all of which implicate the mother.[33] It is a mechanism for the daughter's revenge against her nonnurturing mother, a role reversal between mother and daughter when the mother cannot fulfill her obligations, a device for reducing separation anxiety. If the father is latently homosexual, he can satisfy his female introjects through identification with his daughter. If the mother is latently homosexual, then she vicariously experiences lesbian incest through the father's action. On the other hand, the mother may identify with her daughter and thereby fulfill in fantasy her own childhood incestuous attachments. Finally, the mothers of the incestuous fathers may be at fault because they were overly seductive, which aroused the future fathers' incest anxieties. Rejecting all adult women in order to deal with this incest anxiety, the father turns to children, which somewhat paradoxically leads him to involvement with his own daughter.[34]

When mothers do report incestuous activity, male researchers charge that they do not do so because they object to the activity, but because they are angry for some other reason. Mothers, it is argued, collude too completely ever to object to incest, even when they actively take steps to stop it.[35]

Along with obscurity as to the causes of incest (since, according to men, it is not merely one of the less appealing features of the liberal patriarchal order) there is a certain ambiguity as to what constitutes incest. In Canada, the Criminal Code presently defines incest as sexual intercourse — penial penetration of the vagina — with a blood relative, including siblings, half siblings, parents and grandparents.[36] When there is a legal finding of incest, both parties regardless of age may be sentenced to up to fourteen years imprisonment. A child may avoid a prison sentence (but not conviction) once charges are laid only if the child can prove restraint, duress or fear of the person.[37]

This narrow legal concept is at variance with women's perceptions of incest. Nonpenial vaginal penetration, interlabial intercourse, nudity, lewd suggestions, fondling, kissing, unconcealed erection, penial play, oral contact have all led to reports of incest. These reports appear to have been disregarded as typical female paranoia or exaggeration. This difference in the legal and female perception of what constitutes incest has led one commentator to suggest that preoccupation with the vagina as the site of incest reflects the belief that, in terms of the politics of male ownership, it belongs to the future husband. Nothing else seems to matter.[38] Another commentator attributes the narrow definition of incest to the historical preoccupation with protection of the gene pool, not with the protection of children.[39]

Patriarchal attitudes carry over into the treatment of families in which incest occurs. The family therapy approach is premised upon establishing trust among family members, and requires each parent to acknowledge guilt and seek the daughter's forgiveness. Fathers appear to be less willing to make this confession than mothers, and frequently have to be threatened with legal prosecution to force them to it.[40] The Santa Clara County family therapy project boasts that it saves 90% of marriages, returns 95% of daughters to their homes and finds no recidivism in families that have at least ten hours of treatment,[41] despite the fact that reuniting the family is not widely perceived as the optimal resolution.

(4) *Research in Sexual Exploitation*

Sexual exploitation refers to commercial exploitation of children for the sexual gratification of adults. This problem has received much less attention than battery, neglect and incest. This is partly due to the covertness of much child pornography; it is also possible that it is attributable to the ghettoization of child prostitutes, which renders them invisible to the larger community.[42] Much of the recent public attention attracted by child pornography and sexual slavery has come from the legal sector. It is interesting to note that the legal articulation of the sexual exploitation issue has focused on the relationship between child pornography and the liberal doctrine of freedom of speech. Child sexual exploitation has not emerged in the legal literature as an aspect of child battery or incest, although, it is submitted, these are more appropriate viewpoints.

Feminists decry child pornography for the same reasons that they object to adult pornography. Yet attempts to regulate and restrict child pornography have raised objections from members of liberal patriarchy on the grounds that it violates the constitutional right to freedom of speech. Canada's federal parliament and several United States courts have declined the opportunity to outlaw trade in child pornography as a method of destroying its commercial value, all out of respect for freedom of speech and other constitutional doctrine.[43] This libertarian position may very well be strengthened in Canada with adoption of the charter.

Liberal patriarchy has an interesting fight on its hands with child sexual exploitation. To my knowledge no one — except provincial judges — has yet devised a theory that places responsibility for the practice of child pornography on mothers and mothering; perhaps it is just too preposterous to make such a charge.[44] Instead, pornographers are trying to use power and wealth, applied through the legislative and judicial systems, to protect their position. As long as the use of children as prostitutes or pornography participants does not violate the law, it is not a social problem with which social science and the law must deal. The proof that women and children are still the tools by which liberal patriarchy works out its social and economic objectives can be found in the fact that the abstract and exception-riddled doctrine of freedom of speech is accepted as a defense for criminal liability for such inhuman transactions as child pornography. Those of us who have taken seriously Rousseau and Kant's views on women and children are not surprised that child pornographers seek constitutional protection. To deny men their pleasure is to deny them both freedom and pleasure in that freedom, and men's freedoms are never to be constrained by an interfering state unless something else of crucial importance (to men) hangs in the balance.[45]

The existence of each type of child abuse can be traced back to the patriarchal organization of society. Assault and battery of children appears to serve the patriarchy as an outlet for the desire to dominate, to overpower and to put inferiors in their place,[46] as well as an outlet for frustration and aggression socially fostered by overwhelming expectations. Neglect may be attributable to such traumatization of traditional nurturers that they cannot fulfill the role assigned to them by sex. Incest is a microcosmic reenactment of the basic plot of patriarchy — the appropriation of women — with child pornography and prostitution bringing the essential dynamic of incest to those outside the home who can pay for it. As much blame as possible is placed on women, turning the helping agencies into abusers of women's consciences and self esteem and the legal system into a co-conspirator. The policy implications of child abuse in the patriarchy are simply that child abuse is here to stay as long as patriarchal order in any form persists.

As members of a patriarchally ordered social structure, it is difficult to imagine what the treatment of children would be like in a nonpatriarchal society. If a hypothetical nonpatriarchal society were structured around gynocentric values, however, we can at least sketch out some broad outlines within which we may want to speculate. Gynocentric values lay great emphasis on contextualized relativism in decision making instead of abstract rationality, continuity of relationships instead of autonomy, satisfaction of need rather than recognition of rights and promotion of harmony instead of acquisition of property. In a culture that has designed its institutions around these gynocentric principles, those people who have the power to create life would also have the power to protect it. The atomistic individualism that seems to be so central to the functioning of capitalist economies as well as to the liberal theory of the individual and the state would be seen as the destructive force that it is. An emerging respect for the needs of all people would replace the domination syndrome that men have refined over centuries of abuse. With the disappearance of domination — direct domination of women and indirect as well as direct domination of children — the treatment of children would have to move further to the side of nurturance and protection and away from the present model that focusses on out-and-out control. The last section of this paper struggles with the question of how to implement any gynocentric values in relation to the treatment of children in the absence of revolution (which does not yet appear to be imminent) and from within patriarchal social structures and institutions.

Policy Implications

It is apparent that sexism in studies of child abuse derives not so much from sexist hypotheses or data (although they are certainly present) but from the complexity of liberal patriarchy's ideological formations surrounding the role of children and women. These ideological formations are far more pervasive than terms such as "androcentricity" can ever suggest. Thus the policy implications of an analysis of child abuse in patriarchy are multifaceted and multilevel. We cannot point to specific sexist research projects and connect them directly with flawed but earnest social reform that has accidentally failed to end child abuse for all time. The problem is a much deeper one in the sense that the phenomenon of child abuse correlates with the powerlessness of women, the chattel status of children, the devaluation of nurturance. Patriarchal bias is reflected in the absence of meaningful institutional restraints on violence and authoritarianism; child abuse is fostered by the silence of the law, by the liberal theory of the state vs. individual will.

All these factors suggest that any program to eliminate child abuse must effect massive changes in institutional arrangements surrounding the care of children. This perception is reminiscent of the realization early in the women's movement that sexism was merely the symptom of fundamental patriarchal social organization. No one would argue that any one initiative — whether short-run or long-run — could satisfy all of the demands of feminism. Feminist analysis is instead engaged in a constant struggle to identify and influence the factors that support the sex role oppression of women.

So it is with child abuse as well. Short-run and long-run initiatives aimed at modifying institutional arrangements that contribute to abuse of children are needed. Every detail of those arrangements should be subjected to the same scrutiny that adult relations attract. Yet children are truly invisible from the day their birth is recorded by the birth attendant until the day that they come within the jurisdiction of educational enforcers. Invisibility must correlate strongly with abuse.

Policymakers should take several short-run steps immediately. All laws should be amended to give statutory expression to the duty of care owed to children. All physical or emotional abuse should be banned, and in enough detail to communicate rights and duties to children and their adult companions. Children should be entitled to sue for injury, give evidence, and remain entitled to support in another home, if they so wish. Children should have the same access to legal representation and partisan counselling that others enjoy. Abusers of all kinds should be treated to the full force of the law in order to impress upon everyone the seriousness of the dignity of children.[47] These are the minimum short-run changes that should be made.

Medium-run policy objectives should also be implemented. The invisibility of children should be brought to an end. Well-baby clinics can be established in every neighbourhood to facilitate compulsory examinations at regular intervals. Caregivers who have a positive legal duty to accompany their children for full scale examination every month or so in the first year and every four months until the age of six will doubtless take fewer liberties with their persons.[48] Child advocates whose sole professional function is to get to know preschool children and gauge their overall well being can be assigned to neighbourhoods, adding another safeguard against invisibility.[49] These minimal public health measures would not invade privacy or interfere with personal will any more than do restaurant health inspection or dogtag regulations, and are at least as much in the public interest. This analogy has been criticized because these kinds of measures are designed to protect people, not dogs. But to make this argument simply emphasizes that adults value themselves more than they value children.[50]

Abuse reporting laws and enforcement procedures can be improved, with the force of the law brought to bear on all who could have discovered or reported abuse. If medical practitioners, teachers, etc. can be made liable for failing to recognize abuse,[51] it is extremely likely that professional schools will add abuse detection instruction to their curricula.[52] Under present law, there is some obligation to report suspected child abuse, but the recent trend has been toward relaxation of this obligation.[53] Public awareness of the definition and consequences of abuse should be increased through ongoing media campaigns and educational initiatives. All caregivers should have relievers assigned to them so that they can count on "breathing space", even if only for a few hours a week.[54]

The short- and medium-run initiatives are relatively cheap, can be implemented easily and are consistent with widespread sensitivity to the well being of all members of a state. Their implementation should not arouse opposition because they would bring abuse under control without disturbing the other features of patriarchal order. They are consistent with the present approach to preventing child abuse and thus should be warmly received.[55]

Other medium-run initiatives should focus on long-run institutional changes, and may not be received so warmly. Educators and researchers should mount large scale projects to identify institutional arrangements that would altogether eliminate the possibility of child abuse of every type. Because we do not have easy access to social models in which there is no abuse, such research is likely to centre on two approaches: anthropological investigation and institutional experimentation. This avenue will be constrained by the realities of patriarchal order.[56]

These proposals are not, of course, without their difficulties. It is useful to consider briefly what those difficulties and objections will look like, for they help illuminate even further the relationship between patriarchal social order and the practice of child abuse.[57] One impediment to proposals such as these is that any legislation that involves compulsory examinations will run afoul of freedoms that are protected by liberal patriarchy. Unless power holders can be made to recognize the role that those freedoms play in the phenomenon of child abuse, this objection can well be a fatal one. Linked to this objection is the charge of fascism, which, it is argued, must arise whenever the freedoms of the individual are subjugated to the exercise of bureaucratic authority. This objection is similar to the complaints that women even now have about the exercise of arbitrary power by social workers, who can use their own discretion to remove children from any home that is not acceptably (and familiarly) middle class. Thus single mothers, student mothers, etc. — all those who are not well established in materially endowed homes — will be even more vulnerable to loss of their children if compulsory examination policies were implemented. Another impediment to these types of proposals is that there would be general resistance to a regular relief program for caregivers so long as liberal patriarchy does not recognize the value of work done in the home.

These objections are unified by a common theme — liberal patriarchy has strong arguments readily at hand against changing the institutional arrangements surrounding the care of its children. The very fact that these arguments spring so readily to mind should suggest that liberal patriarchy has a strong interest in maintaining the status quo, whether the proposal involves placing more value on the well being of children or on the labour involved in all phases of reproduction.

At the same time that these objections underline the importance of child abuse in the continuation of liberal patriarchy, however, they also emphasize that women and children in North America have a common interest in challenging patriarchal norms in all contexts. This does not mean that feminists should seek out political coalition with children; the powerless and devalued status of children makes the very suggestion ludicrous to those who are steeped in contemporary culture. What it means is that much of the task of accomplishing long-run changes that will eliminate child abuse will fall — as do many other tasks — on the shoulders of women. However, this is a matter of at least as much urgency to women as the goal of acquiring power and responsibility in the public sphere.[58] Unless we seek radical solutions to the plight of abused children at the same time as we are seeking more scope for ourselves, we will merely reproduce liberal patriarchy, not our visions. Eliminating conditions and attitudes that result in child abuse should be an important component of a feminist vision of compassion and joy in the fullest development of life.

Footnotes

I have received many helpful and challenging comments on this paper and earlier drafts from Sarah Salter, Diana Majury, Constance Backhouse, Rosalie Davies, Marion Perrin and Mickey.

1. See, for example, David Gil, "Confronting Societal Violence by Recreating Communal Institutions," (1979), 3 *Child Abuse and Neglect* 1-7.
2. For the clearest development of this theme, see generally Zillah Eisenstein, *The Radical Future of Liberal Feminism* (Longman, 1981).
3. Or what I choose to call radical feminism in this paper.
4. For the derivation of these values, see Carol Gilligan, *In a Different Voice* (Harvard University Press, 1981) and Nancy Chodorow, *The Reproduction of Mothering: Psychoanalysis and the Sociology of Gender* (University of California Press, 1978), discussed in Jeri Wine, "Gynocentric Values and Feminist Psychology," in A. Miles and G. Finn, eds., *Feminism in Canada* (Black Rose Press, 1983) at 67, 79-84.
5. Yolande Cohen, "Thoughts on Women and Power," in A. Miles and G. Finn, eds., *Feminism in Canada* (Black Rose Press, 1983).
6. See, for example, Samual Radhill, "Children in a World of Violence: A History of Child Abuse," in Henry Kempe and Ray Helfer, eds., *The Battered Child* (University of Chicago Press, 3d ed., 1980) at 1-20.
7. Charlotte Gilman, *Herland* (Pantheon Books, 1979; reprint) gives more insight into institutional structures that are incompatible with child abuse than traditional anthropological or crosscultural research such as that typified by Jill Korbin, "The Cross-Cultural Context of Child Abuse and Neglect," in Henry Kempe and Ray Helfer, eds., *The Battered Child* (University of Chicago Press, 3d ed., 1980) at 21-33. This obviously suggests that archeological, anthropological and sociological investigations into nonpatriarchal societies have been viewed by mainstream male powerholders as a rather anecdotal path of research rather than as a source of fundamental insight into social order.
8. See Zillah Eisenstein, *The Radical Future of Liberal Feminism* (Longman, 1981) at 33 *et seq.* for a description of these modes of patriarchy. Eisenstein actually uses the term "patriarchal antipatriarchalism" and develops it in relation to the emergence of liberal theory, but I prefer the more explicit formulation "antipatriarchal patriarchy," since we are talking about modes of patriarchy.

9. Jean-Jacques Rousseau, *The Social Contract and Discourses*, translated by G. Cole (Dent, 1973) at 117-118, 169-170; *Emile*, translated by B. Foxley (Dent, 1950) at 321-335; 347-352.

10. Immanual Kant, *Observations on the Feeling of the Beautiful and Sublime*, translated by J. Goldthwait (University of California Press, 1960); cf. *Fundamental Principles of the Metaphysic of Morals,* translated by T. Abbott (Liberal Arts Press, 1949) at 31, 45.

11. See Lester Thurow, *The Zero Sum Game* (Basic Books, 1979) for a discussion of the zero sum concept.

12. Fisher v. Carrousel Motor Hotel Inc., 424 SW 2d 627 (Tex 1967).

13. For example, despite the fact that Ontario family law has been amended recently, a child who is born of a married woman must bear the woman's spouse's last name (whether he is the genetic parent or not), whereas a child who is born of a single woman may bear the genetic male parent's last name only if he consents in writing.

14. "An Act relating to Treasons and Felonies," 33 Geo III (1792) chapter II section 4: "*Provided*, That this Act shall not extend to any Person who shall Kill any person in his own Defence, or by Misfortune, or in any other Manner than, as aforesaid, nor shall extend to any Person who in Keeping the Peace shall chance to commit Manslaughter, so as the said Manslaughter be not committed willingly and of Purpose, under Pretext and Colour of Keeping the Peace; nor shall extend to any person who in chastising or correcting his Child or Servant, shall besides his Purpose commit Manslaughter."

15. This paper does not try to convince feminists that child pornography is child abuse by setting out descriptions, data etc. It is sickening to write or read; check the male literature for that information. Nor does this section of the paper attempt to catalogue all of the relevant legal authorities; that aspect of this research project is still in progress.

16. Zillah Eisenstein, *The Radical Future of Liberal Feminism* (Longman, 1981) at 228-229.

17. Winifred Scott, "Attachment and Child Abuse: A Study of Social History Indicators among Mothers of Abused Children," in Gertrude Williams and John Money, eds., *Traumatic Abuse and Neglect of Children at Home* (Johns Hopkins Press, 1980) at 130.

18. *Id.* at 131.

19. *Id.* at 141.

20. See, for example, Donald Bross and Ann Meredyth, "Neglect of the Unborn: An Analysis Based on Law in the United States," in C. Kempe, A. Franklin, C. Cooper, eds., *The Abused Child in the Family and in the Community* (Pergamon Press, 1980) at 643, who argue varying degrees of legal intervention in pregnancy, including mandatory prenatal fetal monitoring, hospitalization for substance abusers and surgical delivery for herpes carriers.

21. See Clare Hyman, Robert Parr and Kevin Browne, "An Observational Study of Mother-Infant Interaction in Abusing Families," (1979) 3 *Child Abuse and Neglect* 241-246.

22. Esther Robinson and Frances Solomon, "Some Further Findings on the Treatment of the Mother-Child Dyad in Child Abuse," (1979) 3 *Child Abuse and Neglect* 247-251.

23. Jeanette Funke-Furber, "Predictive Study of Early Mother-Child Relationships," (1979) 3 *Child Abuse and Neglect* 259-267.

24. Neil Frude and Alison Goss, "Parental Anger: A General Population Survey," (1979) 3 *Child Abuse and Neglect* 331-333.

25. Murray Straus, "Family Patterns and Child Abuse in a Nationally Representative American Sample," (1979) 3 *Child Abuse and Neglect* 213-225.

26. Harold Martin and Patricia Beezeley, "Personality of Abused Children," in Harold Martin and Henry Kempe, eds., *The Abused Child* (Ballinger, 1976) at 105, 106, note that children who have been abused consistently exhibit the following traits: impaired capacity to enjoy life (66%), psychiatric symptoms (62%), low self-esteem (52%), school learning problems (38%), withdrawal (24%), opposition (24%), compulsivity (22%), hypervigilance (22%), pseudomature behavior (20%).

27. Mary Kerr, Jacqueline Boques, Douglas Kerr, "Psychosocial Functioning of Mothers of Malnourished Children," (1978) 62 *Pediatrics* 778-784; Joseph Fischhoff, Charles Whitten, Marion Pettit, "A Psychiatric Study of Mothers of Infants with Growth Failure Secondary to Maternal Deprivation," (1971) 79 *Journal of Pediatrics* 209-215.

28. Joseph Fischhoff, Charles Whitten, Marion Pettit, "A Psychiatric Study of Mothers of Infants with Growth Failure Secondary to Maternal Deprivation," (1971) 79 *Journal of Pediatrics* 209-215.

29. Henry Kempe, "Sexual Abuse, Another Hidden Pediatric Problem," (1978) 62 *Pediatrics* 382-389.

30. Joyce Askwith, "Sex in the Family," in Benjamin Schlesinger, ed., *Sexual Abuse of Children* (University of Toronto Press, 1981) at 11.

31. Henry Kempe, "Sexual Abuse, Another Hidden Pediatric Problem," (1978) 62 *Pediatrics* 382-389.

32. Ida Nakashima and Gloria Zakus, "Incest: Review and Clinical Experience," (1977) 60 *Pediatrics* 696-701. One might wonder how a passive and ineffectual mother could bring the other members of the family to comply with this particular design.

33. Noel Lustig, John Dresser, Seth Spellman, Thomas Murray, "Incest: A Family Group Survival Pattern," (1966) 14 *Arch Gen Psychiat* 31.

34. B. Glueck, "Psychodynamic Patterns in Sex Offenders," (1954) 28 *Psychiatric Quarterly* 1-21.

35. James Henderson, "Incest: A Synthesis of Data," (1972) 17 *Canadian Psychiatric Association Journal* 299-313.

36. This narrow definition may well be broadened in the near future.
37. Canadian Criminal Code section 150(3); this result would have been avoided if the proposed amendments that were discussed in the early 1980's had been enacted; however, the government decided not to follow through on this change.
38. Joyce Askwith, "Sex in the Family," in Benjamin Schlesinger, ed., *Sexual Abuse of Children* (University of Toronto Press, 1981) at 2. Women activists in both Canada and the United States have succeeded in persuading their federal governments to reconsider the type and scope of sexual offences that are actionable. See generally amendments to the Canadian Criminal Code and United States federal guidelines on sexual harrassment.
39. Diana Majury (private communication).
40. Judith Herman and Lisa Hirschman, "Father-Daughter Incest," in Leroy Schultz, ed., *The Sexual Victomology of Youth* (Charles Thomas, 1980) at 120.
41. Henry Kempe, "Sexual Abuse, Another Hidden Pediatric Problem," (1978) 62 *Pediatrics* 382-389.
42. Constance Backhouse has pointed out that child pornography and prostitution were also settled features of the social order in the nineteenth century; see generally Florence Rush, *The Best Kept Secret: Sexual Abuse of Children* (Prentice-Hall, 1980).
43. David Baker, "Preying on Playgrounds: The Sexploitation of Children in Pornography and Prostitution," in Leroy Schultz, ed., *The Sexual Victimology of Youth* (Charles Thomas, 1980) at 292, 309-323. Others have argued that censorship of pornography — including child pornography — merely increases its commercial value as it drives it underground. However, this reaction seems to point up the need for more complete regulation of that industry, and is not a persuasive argument for loose regulation or no regulation.
44. In one reported judicial decision, however, much of the blame appears to fall on the mother, who was also in the pictures, instead of on the male parent who took them. See Regina v. E and F, (1981) 61 CCC (2d) 278 (Ont. Co. Ct.) per McDermid Co. Ct. J.
45. Like defamation, hate literature, or the urge to cry fire in a crowded theater.
46. These words were suggested to me by Constance Backhouse (letter, November 12, 1982).
47. The legal definition of abuse will have to be drawn broadly as lawyers and doctors have a dramatic tendency to overlook or minimize abuse. See Jeanne Giovannoni and Rosina Becerra, *Defining Child Abuse* (Free Press, 1979) at 152.
48. This model was used successfully in China in eliminating the practice of footbinding, which has many parallels with forms of child abuse practiced in western cultures. Footbinding took place entirely in the private sphere; it was performed for the benefit of patriarchy; it was carried out by female

caregivers on female children in the service of patriarchy; it was brought to an end only when the state brought it out of the private sphere into the public sphere by compulsory examination. See Mary Daly, *Gyn/Ecology: The Metaethics of Radical Feminism* (Beacon Press, 1978) at 135-152, especially at 141-142 on how *not* to structure a program of compulsory examination.

49. Henry Kempe, "Approaches to Preventing Child Abuse: the Health Visitors Concept," in G. Williams and J. Money, eds., *Traumatic Abuse and Neglect of Children at Home* (Johns Hopkins Press, 1980) at 575, recommends post partum home visits; Ontario provides for such visits by public health workers in the first six weeks.

50. Liberal feminists who adopt the liberal patriarchal view that such measures would interfere with civil liberties are simply saying that healthy dogs are more important to adults than are healthy children. This position is reminiscent of the Mary Ellen case, in which the New York Society for the Prevention of Cruelty to Animals sought legal protection for the child Mary Ellen because child abuse had not yet been recognized as a public menace. Mary Van Stolk, *The Battered Child in Canada* (McClelland and Stewart, 1978) at 127, 177 note 26.

51. See Orville Endicott, "Civil Liability for Failure to Report Child Abuse," (1979) 3 *Child Abuse and Neglect* 633-641.

52. The defamation laws, etc., will also have to be reviewed to ensure that the risk of liability for reporting suspected abuse that has not actually occurred is no greater than the risk of liability for failure to report suspected abuse.

53. Recent amendments to the Ontario reporting laws increase the fines for nonreporting, but also reduce the class of people who are obliged to report; this was the recommendation of the judicial inquiry that followed the *Popen* case.

54. These two measures could be implemented without relying on legal measures to accomplish change.

55. Increased state involvement in the family will not pass uncontested. Women and minority group members have a legitimate concern that middle class bureaucrats will use their power to remove children to institutions that conform with their ideals. Children can be and are abused in foster homes and group homes. While these are legitimate concerns, they should not be used as a basis for retaining the status quo; rather, they indicate that child abuse must be defined more carefully than it is in contemporary legislative models, that social workers must be made conscious of their implicit middle class bias and that procedures for guarding against that bias must be developed. Neighbourhood centred services can go some distance in offsetting bureaucratization. Explicit protections for parents in oppressed groups can be built into laws if desired.

56. For example, Murray Straus, "Family Patterns and Child Abuse in a Nationally Representative American Sample," (1979) 3 *Child Abuse and*

Neglect at 213, has concluded that men who batter their spouses will be much more likely to batter their children than are other men. However, only a relatively few jurisdictions routinely remove such men from the home while requiring them to continue to support their families. At some point, the whole question of how to raise children will have to be reopened, including how to teach abusing women to nurture their children more effectively. Jill Korbin, "The Cross-Cultural Context of Child Abuse and Neglect," in Henry Kempe and Ray Helfer, eds., *The Battered Child* (University of Chicago Press, 3d ed., 1980) at 29-31, has concluded that western culture itself places children at risk with its limited indulgence of children, characterized by practices such as bottle feeding and early toilet training. Society at large will have to accept its responsibility to make childhood a more satisfying experience for all participants.

57. These difficulties have been identified by Marion Perrin, Rosalie Davies, Mickey and other readers.

58. We had better keep on discussing what that means as well, or we could fall into the abyss of total cooptation. See Jane Richards, *The Skeptical Feminist* (Penguin Books, 1982) at 299-302 for a preview of the abyss.

Sexism in Social Science Research on Aging

ELINOR J. BURWELL

In 1973, at a conference on older women, sociologist Pauline Bart recounted her experiences in 1967 when, as a new Ph.D., she was hunting for a job in academia (Bart, 1975a). "And of course no one, that is no one with the power to give me a job, was interested in the research I had done on middle-aged women" (p. 4). The study of older women was not of interest to male university professors, she claimed, because male scholars confused what they were personally interested in with what was important for the understanding of adult development and aging. Thus older women, having little power and status, and perceived as less than sexually attractive, were not considered worthy subjects of investigation by the academic establishment.

In 1975, Diane Beeson noted that social gerontology was beginning to pay attention to female subjects, but that because of certain methodological and theoretical assumptions, the process of aging for women was seen as less problematic and less traumatic than for men (Beeson, 1975).

In 1978, psychologists Rosalind Barnett and Grace Baruch drew our attention to the fact that both research and theory on women in the middle years of the human life cycle were replete with biases (Barnett and Baruch, 1978). They illustrated their argument that theories of adult development did not fit women's lives by referring to the stages of development proposed by Erik Erikson (1959) and by Daniel Levinson (1978). Both theories reflected male experience and both were inappropriate for understanding the sequence of events in women's lives. Barnett

185

and Baruch pointed out that because there was a tendency to see a woman's life only in terms of her reproductive role, empirical studies had focussed on the importance of menopause and the empty nest, and had neglected the variable of work (i.e. labour force participation) as relevant to women's well-being.

Finally, in a 1981 book on older women, Block, Davidson and Grambs claimed that women continued to be underrepresented as subjects of investigation in gerontological research (Block, Davidson, and Grambs, 1981). Like Bart fourteen years earlier, they attributed this situation, at least in part, to the tendency of male researchers to be more interested in the aging processes of males than of females.

In the fall of 1981, the publication *Hot Flash: A Newsletter for Mid-Life and Older Women* printed a small drawing of part of a blackberry bush, with the caption "Like blackberries, older women bear fruit in the fall, have thorns, and grow everywhere". We know from the demographic data on Canada's age structure and on the predicted age composition of our population in the early part of the next century, that older women do indeed "grow everywhere", and that in the future they will constitute an increasingly larger proportion of the population of older people. For example, according to one prediction, the proportion of people over 65 will have doubled by the year 2031 and the proportion of men to women over 65 will have changed from the current ratio of 100 men to 138 women, to an even more lopsided ratio of 100 men to 164 women (Denton and Spencer, 1980). We do "grow everywhere" but it appears that we are still almost invisible to those scientists who study aging.

My comments in this paper are directed at the work of social scientists who are involved in the study of the processes of aging and in the problems of older people. Nevertheless, it is worth noting that the accusation that older women have been neglected has been aimed not only at social scientists but at biological and medical scientists as well. For example, Robert Butler, former head of the U.S. National Institute on Aging, has called for the elimination of ageism and sexism both in the provision of medical services to the elderly and in the funding of research on those diseases and disabilities which have a high incidence in elderly women (e.g., osteoporosis, hypertension, stroke, diabetes, incontinence) (Butler, 1981). Similarly, Jane Porcino, speaking at the 1981 convention of the Gerontological Society of America, claimed that there has been a serious absence of research on the health problems unique to older women. One of the more startling statistics which Porcino offered to her audience was the American Cancer Society's estimate that one woman of every eleven will develop breast cancer at some time in her life — yet only 4.5 per cent of the funds spent on cancer research are allocated the breast cancer (Porcino, 1981).

One might hope that both scientists and journal editors would have responded, during the past decade, to the charges by feminist scholars that older women have been ignored and their life experiences misinterpreted. With this possibility in mind, I began my perusal of the gerontological literature by comparing the contents of the 1971 and 1981 issues of two widely read periodicals, *The International Journal of Aging and Human Development*, and the *Journal of Gerontology*. As an approximate index of the visibility of female subjects in gerontological research, I simply counted the number of studies in which the subjects were males only, females only, and both males and females. Only articles reporting empirical data were examined; in the case of the *Journal of Gerontology,* articles in the sections on Biological and Medical Sciences were omitted.

In the 1971 *Journal of Gerontology*, 36 per cent of the articles dealt with male subjects only, 7.5 per cent with females only, and 56.5 per cent with both males and females. By 1981, 78 per cent of the studies used both male and female subjects, and the remaining articles were neatly divided in an egalitarian manner: 11 per cent on males only, 11 per cent on females only.

The statistics for the *International Journal of Aging and Human Development* showed a somewhat different trend. In 1971 there were no studies which had used only female subjects, 20 per cent used males only, and 80 per cent used both males and females. By 1981, 8 per cent of the studies used only female subjects, 31 per cent used males only, and 61 per cent used both male and female subjects. To give a more accurate picture, it should be noted that the total number of articles reporting empirical data in 1981 was very small, 13 in all. Thus the figure of 8 per cent represents one article in which females only were subjects, compared with 4 in which males only were subjects.

Pooling the statistics from the two journals, one sees a modest decrease in research on males only (from 30 to 15 per cent) and modest increases in research on females only (from 4 to 10 per cent) and in studies using both male and female subjects (from 66 to 75 per cent).

The question that must be asked is whether this "number crunching" tells us anything at all about sexism in gerontological research. Does it really matter to us whether the psychologist studies paired-associates learning in males rather than in females? Probably not. What *is* of interest, however, is that, with one exception, all the studies using women subjects only were on topics in which gender is highly unlikely to be a variable of any significance, topics which would be unlikely to be of interest to any one but an academic psychologist interested in the finer points of the processes of perception and learning. Thus, studies with female subjects only dealt with age differences in verbal learning, paired-associate learning, odour identification, visual search, digit symbol substitution, mental rotation, and somatosensory evoked potentials. Studies with male subjects only were on similar topics, but in addition, males were subjects in studies of, for example, early retirement, the working retired, disengagement, personal adjustment to aging, age differences in the cancer patient's response to counselling, and self-concept. The studies which focussed on both men and women did, of course, include some which dealt with "human interest" topics, and they did yield some information about gender differences in aging. And in fairness one must acknowledge that by 1981, three-quarters of the studies were based on samples which included both men and women. But it is surely significant that of thirty-three studies which used a single sex design, eighteen of the thirty-three dealt with what I have referred to as human interest topics, and in seventeen of those eighteen the single sex was male!

So much for the quantitative data. The remainder of this paper will give examples of various forms of sexism in recent gerontological literature. No claim is made that my review has been systematic and comprehensive. It is admittedly impressionistic, and is based largely on books and journals which were readily available to me.

Sexism in language appears to be vanishing. Recent text books in adult development and aging no longer use the words "he", "him", "his", "himself" when the discussion is about an adult, sex unspecified. In the journals, workers are not automatically assumed to be males only, in contrast to a decade ago when, in one article, the older worker was routinely referred to as "he" (Stagner, 1971) and in another, the older driver was consistently referred to as "he" (Planek and Fowler, 1971). However, one still finds occasional slips in language usage in the periodicals. For example, a study of self-perception in elderly men and women found some interesting gender differences in old people's self-descriptions, yet the report contains sentences such as: "But there is also room to speculate whether an aged person participating in a psychological experiment actually sees himself in the way reported or only chooses to present himself in such a way" (Angleitner, 1977-78, p. 299). More surprising, perhaps, is a 1981 article which dealt with occupational stress in lawyers (Meltzer, 1981). Subjects were 130 lawyers in the age range 27 to 83. Despite the fact that women constituted 20 percent of the sample, the terms "he" and "his" were used throughout. Examples are: ". . . the lack of control which the practitioner has over his work schedule . . ." (p. 212); "he is entrusted with matters whose outcomes are highly important to clients" (p. 209); ". . . [clients] often feel no reluctance to call their lawyer many times during the day at his office, at his home, late at night and during weekends or holidays" (p. 215).

A few other examples could be given, but by and large the current gerontology journals merit a fairly high score on absence of sexist language.

A different picture emerges when one looks at the omission of women from studies of aging. Omission takes a number of forms. Usually, investigators acknowledge that their subject sample is not representative of the human race, and they restrict their generalizations to males only. In some cases, investigators seem to have forgotten that their samples did not include representatives of the opposite sex, and the findings are reported as though they could reasonably be applied to all adults. In still other cases, women are part of the subject pool, yet they seem to disappear when the data are analyzed and discussed. And of course there are topic areas in which women are seldom included.

An example of a study in which the findings were discussed as though they applied to both sexes, was an investigation of age differences in dreams. Based on an analysis of the dreams of males ranging in age from 27 to 64, the author concluded: "In any event, the decline in aggression and distortion means that as people age their dreams are somewhat less exciting"! (Zepelin, 1981, p. 40). There was no mention of the possibility that perhaps these findings would not hold true for women. Other gerontologists (e.g., Gutmann, 1977) have observed that women tend to become more assertive as they age. If that is true, one might speculate that as women grow older their dreams would become more exciting and aggressive . . . one would rather like to think so! But we will not know until the necessary studies are conducted.

In a similar vein is a report of age differences in personality structure (Costa and McCrae, 1977-78). Finding stability over time in the traits of anxiety and extraversion in males, the authors took that as evidence of the existence of an enduring and internally consistent self-image. In the discussion, there was no suggestion that a woman's self-image might be less stable over time. Given the evidence from many sources that women's lives involve more role change and discontinuities than do men's lives, a reasonable hypothesis might be that their self-image would be somewhat unstable. In any case, it would have been wise of the authors to have emphasized the restricted nature of their subject sample.

A third example is the report of an investigation of preretirement programs in which it was found that neither of two types of programs had any apparent impact on the retirement experience of male employees of a glass container manufacturing company (Glamser, 1981). The author referred to some limitations of the study, e.g., sample size, time and frequency of measurement, but failed to suggest that women workers might have responded differently to such programs. If one accepts the widely held belief that many women are unknowledgeable about financial matters, then one might reasonably hypothesize that preretirement programs, with their emphasis on investments and pension benefits, would have some influence on women's adjustment to retirement.

A similar criticism can be made of the discussion of the findings from a large scale study of the impact of retirement on age identity and well-being (Mutran and Reitzes, 1981). Subjects were males over 55 years of age. The major finding was that retirement was not directly associated with an older identity nor with psychological well-being. The authors do consistently refer to working men and retired men, but there is no suggestion of the possibility that the findings might have been different, had working women and retired women been studied as well. The omission is not trivial, since the research was interpreted in terms of its relevance to competing theories about the impact of retirement on people, gender unspecified.

The reasons for omitting women from studies are sometimes curious. For example, a 1971 study examined social and economic factors in reported chronic health problems (Osborn, 1971). The sample was drawn from a population of white, married couples, where the husband was in the 60 to 64 age range. Wives were excluded from the study because of ". . . the obvious influence of sex as a health variable and because of the variable nature of the female age structure of the study population" (p. 217). In other words, the study of women's health problems would have complicated the data analysis, presumably necessitating a separate analysis of factors in women's health status. This scarcely seems a sufficient reason for focussing on males only.

While the common pattern seems to be that investigators are aware that findings in single sex design studies may not be safely generalized to all adults, one notes that the titles of articles often lead one to believe that the contents will be relevant to both men and women. A case in point is a recent article entitled ''The etiology of alcoholism: A prospective viewpoint'' (Vaillant and Milofsky, 1982). The development of alcoholism in women has been largely ignored until relatively recently; thus a report with this title leads the reader to hope that the article may yield new insights into the predictors of this form of maladjustment in women and men. One quickly discovers that the study was based on a large sample of urban, poorly educated males, who had been studied from their teen years through to their late forties. The sampling bias is understandable, because the men had, in their adolescent years, been a non-delinquent control group for a study of juvenile delinquents. And in the 1940s and 1950s, juvenile delinquency was seen as being the province of males only. One of the predictors of alcoholism in the middle years turned out to be an ethnic factor, namely, coming from a culture which forbids drinking in children, but condones drunkenness in adults. Men of Irish extraction were much more likely to become alcoholics than were men from other ethnic backgrounds. One wonders if the findings would have been different had women been studied. My impression, from a very limited acquaintance with Irish culture, is that drunkenness in Irish men is tolerated or condoned while the same is not true for Irish women. (This comment is based on my observation, during a ten day visit to Ireland a few years ago, that many Irish pubs had no toilet facilities for women. *Moreover, some bartenders refused to serve me more than a half pint of Guinness*, while happily drawing a full pint for my male companion.) Humour aside, my point is that a life span perspective on the etiology of alcoholism is of considerable interest to the gerontologist. But is ethnicity a predisposing factor in the development of alcohol abuse in older women? Unfortunately, from the research that has been done to date, we do not have the answer to that question.

The disappearance of women during data analysis was illustrated in a paper in *The Psychology of Adult Development and Aging,* published in 1973 by the American Psychological Association. The article, by economist Burkhard Strümpel, dealt with the economic status of old people, and it concluded with a section on poverty among the aged. Strümpel presented a table of the correlates of poverty, based on data obtained in 1960 and 1968. His stated purpose was to ". . . single out the economic problem cases — the poorest among the aged — and try to locate as well as to describe them and to trace the basis of their unfavorable situation to causally related circumstances and characteristics" (p. 692). Earlier in the article, Strümpel had noted that the group of dependent aged consisted predominantly of single females, and he observed that "These data clearly identify the female aged, whether dependent or independent, as the primary soft spot within the aged population" (p. 682). ("Soft spot", in this context, presumably just means a very poor group.) Thus Strümpel was clearly aware of the financially disadvantaged status of elderly women. However, in his concluding section, where he identified the poorest of the elderly, sex as a variable was not included! In the table and discussion of the correlates of poverty, he examined disability, age (i.e., 65-74 vs. 75 and older), geographic region, type of community, race, and education, and he concluded that the two variables of overriding importance for the explanation of poverty were race and education. Somehow, old women just disappeared from his analysis of poverty. The unwary reader, or the reader whose consciousness has not been raised, finishes the article without receiving the clear message that the poorest of the poor are elderly women.

In a more recent review of the economic status of the elderly, economist Robert Clark made the point that the proportion of elderly persons in poverty in the United States dropped dramatically over the two decades prior to the late 1970s (Clark,

1981). While noting that the income of the elderly non-married is significantly lower than that of married couples, Clark made no reference to the fact that it is non-married women who are at the bottom of the financial heap. Indeed, the only reference to women in the entire article concerned the effect of a spouse's income on the retirement decision of a husband or wife. Once again, the financially disadvantaged status of elderly women is hidden from the reader's view. It may be harsh to suggest that this kind of omission is sexist, yet given the large number of elderly non-married women in the population, it is distressing that an article on the economic security of the elderly should fail to call attention to their unfortunate situation.

Of the many topic areas in gerontology where there has been little attention paid to women, I will comment only on three. In their review of the literature on stress, disease, aging and behaviour for the 1977 *Handbook of the Psychology of Aging,* Eisdorfer and Wilkie note that there have been relatively few studies which have looked at psychosocial factors related to diseases among women (Eisdorfer and Wilkie, 1977). Most of the research on psychosocial factors and cardiovascular disease, for example, has been on men under 65 years of age. The fact that more and more women are in competitive jobs in the labour force has led to the suggestion that in the future, occupational stress may increase the incidence of stress-related illnesses in women. It is thus most unfortunate that so few investigators have included female subjects in their studies.

One of the most glaring omissions in the gerontological literature has been the subject of women's adjustment to retirement. Although women have been a significant proportion of the labour force for many years, they were essentially absent from the literature. Work was not seen as being central to their lives. This point of view was made explicit in a chapter of the *Handbook of the Psychology of Aging.* The authors, citing only one reference, stated that "Women tend to hold lower work and achievement commitment than do men at all ages, and this is true for working women as well as for those not working" (Bengtson, Kasschau and Regan, 1977, p. 334). It follows that if the work role was regarded as being unimportant to women, retirement from it could scarcely be considered a source of stress. Thus women's retirement was not considered a subject worthy of investigation. The few studies which were done yielded conflicting findings (Atchley, 1976; Palmore, 1965). As recently as June of 1982, a large scale longitudinal study of changes in work expectations in later life omitted married women because "preliminary tests of the survey instrument revealed that the majority thought of retirement in terms of their husbands' stopping work" (Goudy, 1982, p. 143). This particular study looked at factors relating to whether workers, in the age range 60 to 64, changed their minds, over a four year period, about retiring or continuing to work. The omission of data on married women is unfortunate, since it would have been informative to discover whether married women workers changed their definitions of retirement as they themselves approached the age of retirement.

It must be noted that we are now beginning to see more studies of women and retirement. At the 1981 annual meeting of the Gerontological Society of America, at least two sessions were devoted to this topic. The reported findings came as no surprise. When groups of retired men and women were equated in terms of age, education, occupational status, work patterns before and after retirement, age at retirement, and reasons for retirement, it was found that there were no sex differences in adjustment to retirement (Schnore and Kirkland, 1981). In another study, two factors of great importance in women's retirement experience were those that are also of great importance to men, namely, health and income (Atchley, 1981). One's first reaction to these less than earth-shaking findings might well be astonishment that any one would bother to conduct research which would result in such obvious and predictable results. A moment's thought tempers this jaded reaction, however, when it is recalled that not so long ago retirement was considered to be a non-event for women. Instead of a picture of women happily returning to their rightful place, the domestic sphere, we now have it on authority that for women, as for men, life satisfaction in retirement is significantly influenced by income.

In 1977, Atchley and Corbett made the astute observation that because many women are late in starting careers (that is, giving full-time attention to careers only when their children had left home or, at least, were in school), their retirements were likely to occur before their career goals were achieved. This intriguing suggestion has not, to my knowledge, been followed up by research which would compare the life satisfaction, in retirement, of women who were committed to a career throughout their adult lives, and of women whose career commitment began relatively late in life.

A recent report of a study of gifted elderly women (Holahan, 1981) is, however, a beginning in the direction of understanding the implications, for life satisfaction, of varying career patterns throughout the adult life cycle. The subjects were 352 women (average age 66 years) who had been part of Lewis Terman's longitudinal study of gifted children. In their childhood, these women had been identified as unusually gifted intellectually. Some had been homemakers throughout their lives, some had been committed to careers, and others were job holders (that is, they had worked for needed income, but did not consider their work a career). The greatest discrepancy in life satisfaction both in earlier and later adult life was between job holders and career workers. The pursuit of a career, whether it was continuous or interrupted by childrearing, was related to greater satisfaction in aging than was simply working for needed income. Unfortunately, the data did not permit an analysis of early vs. late life career commitment. Moreover, as the author noted, the findings may not hold up when other samples of less gifted women are studied. Nevertheless, this study breaks new ground in its focus on the variations in the patterns of women's lives and their effects on levels of life satisfaction throughout the adult years.

Another under-researched topic, strangely enough, is menopause. Although middle-aged women have been described in terms of their reproductive roles (i.e., as premenopausal, menopausal, postmenopausal, or as suffering from the empty nest syndrome), the lack of research on menopause has been noted by a number of scholars (e.g., Laws and Schwartz, 1977; Posner,

1979; Sherman, 1971). Pauline Bart examined anthropological records of thirty societies to obtain data on women's menopause-associated problems. She found data on the menopause for only five of the societies. "Clearly, anthropologists are generally male and thus not interested in pursuing such information — or unble to, for when the anthropologists were female or when teams included females, information about menopause was reported" (Bart, 1975b, p. 157).

Judith Posner has observed that studies of menstruation are increasing in number, but that the study of menopause still seems to be avoided by social scientists and gerontologists, perhaps because the aging female has a low status in society. Interestingly, Posner indicted not only gerontologists and medical scientists, but also feminist scholars. The latter have not only paid minimal attention to older women but have also, like many medical practitioners, adopted a psychological model of menopause. Feminists have been eager to portray women as the victims of their gender role socialization rather than as being at the mercy of their hormonal systems. The dismissal of sex differences in physiological functioning as possible influences on gender differences in behaviour might itself be seen as a form of sexism. As Paula Weideger has said: "As long as women run away from the reality of the menstrual cycle, we are refusing to know ourselves and are accepting an external definition of ourselves" (Weideger 1977, p. 199). The same statement could be made about menopause. Well-designed research should enable us to understand the interactions between biological and psychological factors which are important at mid-life, and hopefully would enable us to reject two prevalent but contradictory views of the menopausal woman: either she is in the grip of a disease caused by estrogen deficiency, or suffering from symptoms which are all in the head.

Another form of sexism identified by feminist scholars concerns the masculine bias in choice of methods to be used in an investigation, as well as in the conceptualization of the issue to be investigated. In 1972, psychologist Rae Carlson argued persuasively that psychology should expand its methods of scientific inquiry to include not only the standard methodologies involving manipulating, controlling, ordering and quantifying, but also those methods of investigation which involve naturalistic observation, participant observation, and a sensitivity to the qualitative aspects of experience (Carlson, 1972). Using Bakan's terminology, she referred to the first approach as agentic, and the second, communal. The terms "agentic" and "communal" are similar to our stereotypes of "masculine" and "feminine". Carlson argued that without some combination of the agentic and communal approaches, psychology would fail in its attempts to understand the behaviour of women and men.

An example of reliance on agentic methodology is a recent study of the impact of widowhood on the social relations of older persons (Ferraro and Barresi, 1982). The focus was on only the *quantity* of interaction with family, friends and neighbours. The investigators recorded how often the widowed elderly got together with other people, but no attempt was made to assess the meaningfulness of these social interactions. One of the conclusions from this study was that widowers are not more socially isolated than widows. In fact, it was found that after the death of a spouse, males increased their interactions with friends and neighbours. If we are willing to define social isolation as meaning few social contacts, then we cannot quarrel with the manner in which the investigators have operationalized this concept. But what are we to understand about the impact of widowhood on women and men when the *qualitative* aspect of social interactions is completely ignored?

An earlier study (Powers and Bultena, 1976) which also looked at social interaction in the elderly, provides, in my view, a more comprehensive picture of the social networks of older men and women. Numbers of contacts with friends, relatives and neighbours were counted. But in addition the subjects were asked: "Is there any person you feel particularly close to? We are thinking of someone you feel you can really depend on; in other words, someone who is closer than 'just' a friend". The findings were similar to those of the study of widowhood, in that men had higher social interaction scores. However, men were less likely than women to have intimate friends, and they were less likely to make new friends. The authors' final statement is worth quoting: ''women have a diverse social world and many have intimate ties outside the immediate family. It is somewhat ironic that the last years of men's lives should be so precarious in a society that has been largely oriented toward the privileged position of men'' (Powers and Bultena, 1976, p. 746). The authors, in Carlson's words, have been sensitive to the qualitative aspects of experience. Exclusive reliance on the agentic or masculine approach, as in the widowhood study, surely tells us less than we would wish to know about the quality of life in late adulthood. One hesitates to term this approach sexist, yet it is difficult to avoid the speculation that a masculine bias has permitted the investigators to be comfortable with defining social isolation in terms of number of social contacts, and with ignoring the meaning of interpersonal relationships.

Another area of gerontology where this same form of sexism has reared its ugly head is in the study of families of later life. Sociologist Emily Nett has recently argued that the way in which the family is defined by social scientists is based on male models of family organization (Nett, 1982). For example, research on intergenerational relationships is largely restricted to studies of parents, children and grandchildren, based on a definition of family which would make sense to a male who sees family relationships in terms of his roles of provider and controller of family resources. In the male model, then, family relations take a lineal form. Women's definition of family, Nett stated, are rather different, in that they often include siblings, nieces and nephews, cousins, and other relatives. Women's kin networks may be very important to them, particularly in the years of late adulthood. Yet because studies of family relationships utilize questionnaires based on the male model of family, our literature has failed to give us an accurate picture of the lives of older women. Nett spelled out the possible policy implications of this distorted picture of older families, one of the implications being the placing of elderly women in situations of increased dependency.

Perhaps the most eloquent statement of psychology's failure to consider the female experience in theory and research on adult development has been made by Carol Gilligan. In a series of reports of her own research on the formation of moral values during the course of development from adolescence to adulthood, Gilligan has done a splendid critique of the concepts of maturity presented to us in the work of Lawrence Kohlberg, Daniel Levinson, and George Vaillant, among others (Gilligan, 1977; Gilligan, 1982a; Gilligan, 1982b; Gilligan, 1982c). Kohlberg's theory of the development of moral judgement envisages the individual progressing through a series of stages, with maturity of moral judgment being attained when moral dilemma situations are assessed in terms of universal principles of justice. In this ethic of human rights, Gilligan observed, there is a balancing of the claims of one's self against the claims of others; there is an element of separation from others. A morality which focusses on caring for and sensitivity to the needs of others is seen as belonging to a much lower stage of moral development, stage three of a possible six stages. "Stage 3 appears to be a stable adult stage for women" and is "a functional morality for housewives and mothers" (Kohlberg and Kramer, 1969, p. 108).

Kohlberg's theory was derived from research on men. Its emphasis on the separation of self from others as a criterion of maturity is similar, Gilligan noted, to the emphasis on automony and independence as the criteria of maturity in the research on adult males by Levinson (1978) and Vaillant (1977). In their studies, mature males were distant in their relationships with other people. The path to maturity involved achievement and, often, it involved separation from others. On the other hand, the studies which have been done on adult women (e.g., by Rubin, 1979, and by Hennig and Jardim, 1977) have found that women, even those in top managerial positions, are concerned about interpersonal relationships. As Gilligan said, women tend to define their identity through relationships of intimacy and caring. Theirs is an ethic of responsibility and care. Attachment, not separation, is primary.

Gilligan has also criticized the view, fostered by theorists such as Erik Erikson, that women arrive at midlife in a child-like state, dependent on others. Our theories of human development have taken shape as they have, believes Gilligan, because ". . . we have listened for centuries to the voices of men and the theories of development that their experience informs" (Gilligan, 1982b, p. 173).

From the foregoing, it follows that when women are assessed by scales which purport to measure maturity of moral judgement, or when their maturity is assessed in terms of a value system emphasizing autonomy and independence, they are seen as deficient, or, at best, as deviant. Gilligan believes that issues of responsibility and care must be built into our comprehension of what constitutes a mature adult. "Seen in a different light, the observation that women's embeddedness in lives of relationship, their orientation to independence, their subordination of achievement to care, and their conflicts over competitive success leave them personally at risk in midlife seems to be more a commentary on the society than a problem in women's development" (Gilligan, 1982a, p. 110).

Gilligan argues, of course, for theory and research in human development which would take account of the experiences and the perceptions of social reality of both men and women. We must begin to listen, she believes, to the voices of women. To date, most of the research on the development of morality and maturity through the years of adulthood has failed to do that — sexism on a rather large scale.

Another research area in which social scientists have sometimes neglected to listen to the voices of women is that of living environments for the elderly. In recent years, much has been written about the nature of residential facilities for older people. From survey research, we know a good deal about the kinds of neighbourhoods that older people wish to live in (Lawton, 1980; Regnier, 1975). We know something about the kinds of services that should be close to senior citizens' apartment buildings, or to "adults only" developments. Additionally, we know that most of the institutionalized elderly prefer living in a single room to sharing a room with others (Lawton and Bader, 1970). But, to the best of my knowledge, those doing research and planning on housing for the middle-aged and elderly have not conducted user surveys about optimal divisions of space in housing designed for "adults only". Senior citizens' apartments are designed for a married couple or a single individual. Dwellings for "adults only" have the usual larger master bedroom and one or two smaller bedrooms. These floor layouts are appropriate from the male's point of view. After all, in Canada 74 per cent of men over 65 are married, while only 39 per cent of elderly women are married. Furthermore, of all elderly persons living alone, 70 per cent are women (Statistics Canada, 1979). The possibility that two older women might wish to share accommodation seems not to have been considered. An appropriate housing design for some older women might well be one which featured two bedrooms of equal size, with, perhaps, a smaller third bedroom. In the years ahead, the number of non-married older women, relative to the numbers of non-married older men, will be steadily increasing. Housing shared by women would seem to address problems of loneliness and of financial difficulties. Surely the time has come when social scientists involved in research on housing for the elderly should investigate women's needs and wishes in this important area.

There is some evidence that gerontologists are beginning to realize that men and women may differ concerning the types of living environments which will enhance the quality of their lives in their senior years. Psychologist Rudolf Moos has been conducting research on the evaluation of sheltered care settings for older people (Moos, 1980). One set of factors involved in his proposed assessment model concerns the opportunities that institutional residents have for choice and control of activities. Women residents, he found, were more likely to live in settings which offered them opportunities to determine, to some extent, their own daily routines. "Surprisingly", said Moos, "the relative lack of such choices as to when to get up, go to bed, bathe and eat, and whether to do their own personal laundry, affected women more than men" (p. 90). Since most residential settings for the elderly offer very little in the way of choice and control, and since the population of such settings is overwhelmingly female, perhaps their finding will have some impact on the nature of future institutional programs and policies. The suggested interpretation which Moos offers for this sex difference seems commonsensical, namely, that most elderly women have spent their lives in their homes, rather than in the labour force, and have thus been accustomed to organizing their own daily routines. One cannot help feeling that this sex difference might have become apparent long ago if investigators had tried to see the world of the elderly through women's eyes as well as through men's eyes.

Apart from the neglect of specific topics of research on older women, it is the case that where longitudinal rather than cross-sectional designs were used, very few of the studies of age changes in physiological and psychological characteristics have included women in their samples. One large scale study on aging (the Baltimore longitudinal study) began in 1958, and added female subjects only a few years ago. In an attempt to compensate for the dearth of longitudinal studies of women's lives in 1982 an entire issue of the *Journal of Social Issues* was devoted to articles which provide techniques which will allow investigators to disentangle life-cycle-related personal changes from social changes, and to sort out historical, cohort, and developmental factors. There is a need for special techniques to study women's lives because women's lives typically show more role changes and more changes within roles than do men's lives (Stewart and Platt, 1982). This volume will undoubtedly prove to be a welcome addition to the methodological tool kit of the social scientist, and should spark some interest in the study of women and aging.

Another hopeful indicator that the neglect of women in studies of aging may be a disappearing phenomenon is the publication in 1982 of a volume, edited by Janet Giele, entitled *Women in the Middle Years: Current Knowledge and Directions for Research and Policy* (Giele, 1982). The book is the result of work done by a sub-group of a committee established by the U.S. Social Science Research Council to investigate work and personality in middle adulthood. Research is reported on a variety of physical, social and psychological factors influencing women's lives; new research strategies are recommended; and an appendix gives a valuable compendium of longitudinal and cross-sectional data sources on women in the middle years.

One last instance of sexism in the social science literature on aging must be mentioned. Although I have dealt with it elsewhere (Burwell, 1982), I cannot refrain from again drawing your attention to a recommendation made by gerontologists Edgar Borgatta and Martin Loeb, in a chapter of a recent book on aging and retirement (Borgatta and Loeb, 1981). Noting that the distribution of funds for research on and programs for the elderly must be guided by some kind of rational policy, Borgatta and Loeb came up with the amazing suggestion that priority should be given to the study of men's lives. Research on older women, they argued, would lead to services to improve the equality of life for older women. That, in turn, would increase women's life expectancy and thus lead to an even greater discrepancy in life expectancy for men and women. The fair thing, they suggested, would be to give priority to research which would yield knowledge on how to lengthen men's lives. This astonishing recommendation may have been a tongue-in-cheek attempt to try to provoke readers into thinking about the inequities involved in the distribution of scarce resources to various segments of the population. The failure to acknowledge the fact that research on older women has been minimal, the callous disregard of the present poor quality of life of many older women, and the ignoring of the implications of the suggested funding priorities for the lives of older women in the future, all add up to sexism. If the decision-makers in control of distributing research funds should happen to consider seriously the Borgatta and Loeb proposal (and this is at least a remote possibility, given the contra-feminist movements identified by Sharon Abu-Laban, 1981), then we might witness the disappearance of *all* research on women and aging, research of both the sexist and non-sexist varieties!

In summary: sexism in a variety of forms continues to be

present in the social science research on aging. Bias is present in subject selection, in methodology, in interpretation of findings, and in the nature of topics investigated, or omitted from investigation. Nevertheless, there does seem to be some reason for optimism. Sexism in language is disappearing. Older women are more likely to be the subject of research than they were ten years ago. A beginning is being made in the study of all facets of women's lives, including labour force participation and retirement. And techniques are being developed to facilitate the study of the complex pattern of roles and role changes which characterize the lives of most women. Masculine models of conceptualizing the human experience are being challenged by feminist scholars, with the promise that our knowledge of aging in both women and men will be enriched when we listen to the voices of women, as Carol Gilligan would say. This rosy view of the gerontological literature of the future could be shattered, of course, if, as Borgatta and Loeb has proposed, the funds for research on older women are shifted to studies of the factors which would increase the lengths of men's lives. But that is another story.

References

Abu-Laban, S.M. "Women and aging: A futurist perspective." *Psychology of Women Quarterly,* 1981, *6*, 85-98.

Angleitner, A. "Health, socioeconomic status and self-perception in the elderly: An application of the Interpersonal Checklist." *International Journal of Aging and Human Development,* 1977-78, *8*, 293-299.

Atchley, R.C. "Selected social and psychological differences between men and women in later life." *Journal of Gerontology,* 1976, *31*, 204-11.

Atchley, R.C. "Male-female differences in attitudes toward work and timing of retirement." Paper presented at 34th annual meeting of Gerontological Society of America, Toronto, Ontario, November 11, 1981.

Atchley, R.C. and Corbett, S.L. "Older women and jobs," in L.E. Troll,J. Israel and K. Israel (eds.) *Looking ahead: A woman's guide to the problems and joys of growing older.* Englewood Cliffs, N.J.: Prentice-Hall, 1977.

Barnett, R.C. and Baruch, G.K. "Women in the middle years: A critique of research and theory." *Psychology of Women Quarterly,* 1978, *3*, 187-197.

Bart, P.B. "Emotional and social status of the older woman," in *No longer young: The Older Woman in America*. Occasional Papers in Gerontology No. 11. Ann Arbor, Mich.: Institute of Gerontology, 1975(a).

Bart, P.B. "The loneliness of the long-distance mother," in J. Freeman (ed.) *Women: A feminist perspective*. Palo Alto, Calif.: Mayfield, 1975(b).

Beeson, D. "Women in studies of aging: A critique and suggestion." *Social Problems*, 1975, *23*, 52-59.

Bengtson, V.L., Kasschau, P.L. and Ragan, P.K. "The impact of social structure on aging individuals," in J.E. Birren and K.W. Schaie (eds.) *Handbook of the psychology of aging*. New York: Van Nostrand Reinhold, 1977.

Block, M.R., Davidson, J.L. and Grambs, J.D. *Women over forty: Visions and realities*. New York: Springer, 1981.

Borgatta, E.F. and Loeb, M.B. "Toward a policy for retired persons: Reflections on welfare and taxation," in N.G. McCluskey and E.F. Borgatta (eds.) *Aging and retirement: Prospects, planning and policy*. Beverly Hills, Calif.: Sage, 1981.

Burwell, E.J. "The handwriting on the wall: Older women in the future," *Resources for Feminist Research*, 1982, *11*, 208-209.

Butler, R.N. "Women, aging and health." General session address, 27th annual meeting of Western Gerontological Association, Seattle, Washington, April 13, 1981.

Carlson, R. "Understanding women: Implications for personality theory and research." *Journal of Social Issues*, 1972, *28*, 17-32.

Clark, R.L. "Aging, retirement, and the economic security of the elderly: An economic review," in C. Eisdorfer (ed.) *Annual Review of Gerontology and Geriatrics*, Vol. 2, New York: Springer, 1981.

Costa, P.I. and McRae, R.R. "Age differences in personality structure revisited: Studies in validity, reliability, and change." *International Journal of Aging and Human Development*, 1977-78, *8*, 261-275.

Denton, F.T. and Spencer, B.G. "Canada's population and labour force: Past, present and future," in V.W. Marshall (ed.) *Aging in Canada: Social perspectives*. Don Mills, Ont.: Fitzhenry and Whiteside, 1980.

Eisdorfer, C. and Wilkie, F. "Stress, disease, aging and behavior," in J.E. Birren and K.W. Schaie (eds.) *Handbook of the psychology of aging*. New York: Van Nostrand Reinhold, 1977.

Erikson, E. "Identity and the life cycle." *Psychological Issues*, 1959, *1*, 1-171.

Ferraro, K.F. and Barresi, C.M. "The impact of widowhood on the social relations of older persons." *Research on Aging*, 1982, *4*, 227-247.

Giele, J.Z. (ed.) *Women in the middle years: Current knowledge and directions for research and policy*. New York: Wiley, 1982.

Gilligan, C. "In a different voice: Women's conceptions of self and of morality." *Harvard Educational Review*, 1977, *47*, 481-517.

Gilligan, C. "Adult development and women's development: Arrangements for a marriage," in J.Z. Giele (ed.) *Women in the middle years: Current knowledge and directions for research and policy.* New York: Wiley, 1982(a).

Gilligan, C. *In a different voice: Psychological theory and women's development.* Cambridge, Mass.: Harvard University Press, 1982(b).

Gilligan, C. "Why should a woman be more like a man?" *Psychology Today,* 1982, *16,* 68-77. (c)

Glamser, F.D. "The impact of preretirement programs on the retirement experience." *Journal of Gerontology,* 1981, *36,* 244-250.

Goudy, W.J. "Antecedent factors related to changing work expectations: Evidence from the Retirement History Study." *Research on Aging,* 1982, *4,* 139-158.

Gutmann, D. "The cross-cultural perspective: Notes toward a comparative psychology of aging," in J.E. Birren and K.W. Schaie (eds.) *Handbook of the Psychology of Aging.* New York: Van Nostrand Reinhold, 1977.

Henning, M. and Jardim, A. *The managerial woman.* Garden City, N.Y.: Anchor, 1977.

Holahan, C.K. "Lifetime achievement patterns, retirement and life satisfaction of gifted aged women." *Journal of Gerontology,* 1981, *36,* 741-749.

Kohlberg, L. and Kramer, R. "Continuities and discontinuities in childhood and adult moral development." *Human Development,* 1969, *12,* 93-120.

Laws, J.L. and Schwartz, P. *Sexual scripts: The social construction of female sexuality.* Hinsdale, Ill.: Dryden, 1977.

Lawton, M.P. and Bader, J. "Wish for privacy by young and old." *Journal of Gerontology,* 1970, *25,* 48-54.

Lawton, M.P. *Environment and aging.* Monterey, Calif.: Brooks/Cole, 1980.

Levinson, D.J. *The seasons of a man's life.* New York: Ballatine, 1978.

Meltzer, M.W. "The reduction of occupational stress among elderly lawyers: The creation of a functional niche." *International Journal of Aging and Human Development,* 1981, *13,* 209-219.

Moos, R.H. "Specialized living environments for older people: A conceptual framework for evaluation." *Journal of Social Issues,* 1980, *36,* 2, 75-94.

Mutran, E. and Reitzes, D.C. "Retirement, identity and well-being: Realignment of role relationships." *Journal of Gerontology,* 1981, *36,* 733-740.

Nett, E.M. "Family studies of elders: Gerontological and feminist approaches." Paper presented at annual meeting of Canadian Sociology and Anthropology Association, Ottawa, Ontario, June 7, 1982.

Osborn, R.W. "Social and economic factors in reported chronic morbidity." *Journal of Gerontology,* 1971, 26, 217-223.

Palmore, E. "Differences in the retirement patterns of men and women." *The Gerontologist,* 1965, *1,* 4-8.

Planek, T.W. and Fowler, R.C. "Traffic accident problems and exposure characteristics of the aging driver." *Journal of Gerontology,* 1971, *26,* 224-230.

Porcino, J. "Health issues of older women." Paper presented at 34th annual meeting of Gerontological Society of America, Toronto, Ontario, November 9, 1981.

Posner, J. "It's all in your head: Feminist and medical models of menopause (strange bedfellows)." *Sex Roles,* 1979, *5,* 179-190.

Powers, E.A. and Bultena, G.L. "Sex differences in intimate friendships of old age." *Journal of Marriage and the Family,* 1976, *38,* 739-747.

Regnier, V. "Neighbourhood planning for the urban elderly," in D.S. Woodruff and J.E. Birren (eds.) *Aging: Scientific perspectives and social issues.* New York: Van Nostrand, 1975.

Rubin, L. *Women of a certain age: The Midlife search for self.* New York: Harper and Row, 1979.

Schnore, M.M. and Kirkland, J.B. "Sex differences in adjustment to retirement." Paper presented at 34th annual meeting of Gerontological Society of America, Toronto, Ontario, November 9, 1981.

Sherman, J.A. *On the psychology of women: A survey of empirical studies.* Springfield, Ill.: Charles C. Thomas, 1971.

Stagner, R. "An industrial psychologist looks at industrial gerontology." *Aging and Human Development,* 1971, *2,* 29-37.

Statistics Canada. *Canada's elderly.* Ottawa: Minister of Supply and Services Canada, 1979.

Stewart, A.J. and Platt, M.B. "Studying women in a changing world: An introduction." *Journal of Social Issues,* 1982, *38,* 1-16.

Strümpel, B. "The aged in an affluent economy," in C. Eisdorfer and M.P. Lawton (eds.) *The Psychology of Adult Development and Aging.* Washington, D.C.: American Psychological Association, 1973.

Vaillant, G.E. *Adaptation to life.* Boston: Little, Brown, 1977.

Vaillant, G.E. and Milofsky, E.S. "The etiology of alcoholism: A prospective viewpoint." *American Psychologist,* 1982, *37,* 494-503.

Weideger, P. *Menstruation and menopause: The physiology and psychology, the myth and the reality.* New York: Delta, 1977.

Zepelin, H. "Age differences in dreams. II. Distortion and other variables." *International Journal of Aging and Human Development,* 1981, *13,* 37-41.

Sexism in Policy Relating to Welfare Fraud

MARION PORTER and JOAN GULLEN

In recent years feminist historians have been critical of the mainstream historians of the family because of their sexist bias.[1] They assume that the nuclear family, with father as the head of the household, mother subordinate and dependent, and dependent children, is the natural, correct and inevitable state. This view is reflected in welfare law, whereby a woman who may have had financial responsibility for a long period of time both for her children and herself is presumed to become economically dependent as soon as she chooses to live with a man, regardless of the permanence of the relationship or of whether he is in fact contributing to her support. An example of this implicit sexist bias can be found in a serious history of the family published in 1975, where author Edward Shorter, as a synonym for the family, frequently refers to "Mom", "Dad" and "the kids".[2] Patriarchal attitudes die slowly and men are undoubtedly reluctant to admit that their superior position is being eroded. Still, it is surprising that a modern historian who is clearly aware of the sexual revolution which has taken place since the widespread availability of contraception, is not equally aware of the changing position of women.

The feminist historians claim that much family history is basically sexist because it borrows assumptions from sociological theory which is basically sexist. In particular, the structuralist functionalist theory, used by Talcott Parsons to describe the principal types of social structure, seems to imply that strains will develop in a society unless the roles that are appropriate for that type of society are followed. For example, in what Parsons calls the universalistic-achievement pattern, which, he says, is the type of structure central to industrial societies, the involvement of the conjugal family with the occupational system tends to be primarily focussed on the adult male. He admits that "the primary problems and strains centre on the role of the wife and mother." He suggests that "the 'easy' solution is for her to be completely excluded from the occupational system by confining herself to the role of housewife." However, he goes on, "In most industrialized societies there tends to be a good deal of adaptation and compromise relative to this solution."[3]

Parsons describes a stable society in a state of equilibrium where, though strains may exist, adaptations and compromises have been made. Christopher Lasch, however, in contemplating climbing divorce rates and intensifying generational conflict, poses the question of whether "these developments signify merely the 'strain' of the family's adaptation to changing social conditions" or whether "they portend a weakening of the social fabric, a drastic disorganization of all our social institutions."[4]

Whatever the interpretation, there can be little doubt that the family and the position of women in it is changing. Women's demand for equality, the need for a two pay cheque household in the present economy, the increase of marriage breakdown, and impermanent sexual relationships, mean that the traditional family with father as the breadwinner and mother as the housewife is less and less the norm. The reality today is that fewer and fewer families in fact consist of "Mom and Dad and the kids" living together in harmony.[5]

Whether related to marriage instability or not, the women's movement has been pressing for greater equality for women since the mid-sixties. Feminists believe that women's dependence has been a source of oppression.

What do these issues have to do with welfare fraud? As we mentioned earlier, welfare legislation assumes that, if a man and a woman are living together, then the man is head of the household and the woman and children are dependent on him. If a sole support mother is living with a man, she is ineligible for welfare in her own right, regardless of the man's capacity to contribute, or of his legal responsibility for the children. If she is receiving welfare and a man is found to be living regularly in the house, she can be charged with fraud under the criminal code. This is known as "the man in the house" rule.

In view of current sexual practices and changing attitudes towards the position of women this legislation is anachronistic. In addition, it is unjust because it can deprive a single mother of the opportunity to develop an emotional relationship with a man, and it imposes upon her a condition that the rest of society would not accept: an invasion of her privacy and a curtailment of her personal freedom. A man could well be frightened away from a woman if he knew that the consequence of a relationship with her would be that he would have to support her children. A woman must face the prospect of losing her benefits or risk going to jail.

A review of the situation in Ontario will illustrate the problems. Mothers' allowances have existed in Ontario since 1920, recognizing the need for long term income security (inadequate though it is) for women who have been deserted or widowed to allow them to raise their children. Unwed mothers were not eligible for mothers' allowances until 1955, a reflection, no doubt, of the fact that welfare was seen as a privilege and that only those who deserved it would get it. As we shall see, courts in Ontario have decided that economic/social factors, rather than moral grounds, should be the criteria used to determine whether a woman is eligible for benefits. However, the influence of sexual morality is still apparent in the decisions of the Social Assistance Review Board.

In 1966 the federal government introduced the Canada Assistance Plan to help the provinces provide assistance to people in need. In 1967 the Ontario government passed the Family Benefits Act to provide welfare to people who were un-employable as a result of having dependent children or being disabled. This lent support to the view that mothers should be given financial assistance to enable them to raise their children without having to enter the labour force.[6]

It is interesting to observe that Ontario is one of three provinces which retain two levels of welfare. Family Benefits are funded and administered by the province, while General Welfare Assistance is administered and partially funded by the municipalities for those considered to be in short term need. The level of assistance is considerably higher under the Family Benefits Act than under the General Welfare Assistance Act. The current Ministry has widened that discrepancy and, in so doing, has compounded the problem for women.

Family Benefits are crucial to many sole support mothers. After divorce or desertion it is usually the mother who keeps the children. In many cases, she gets little or no support from the father. If, as is true for a large number of divorced women, she has no skills, no work experience and little education, then she is obliged to go on welfare. Even if she is able to find a job in today's depressed economy, she is faced with the problem of what to do with her children in the absence of subsidized day care spaces. A pamphlet from the Family Benefits Work Group states that, in Ontario, there are 270,000 mothers in the work force with children under the age of five. There are about 120,000 mothers on family benefits. The total number of subsidized day care spaces is 17,000.[7]

How does the system work? The Family Benefits Act states that certain categories of female applicants/recipients are not eligible for an allowance if they "are not living as a single person". The Income Maintenance Branch of the Ontario Ministry of Community and Social Services has published some policy and procedural guidelines for its welfare officials.[8] According to these guidelines, "It is incumbent on the worker to report/and/or investigate any suspicions, allegations, written or oral complaints which imply that a recipient/applicant is living 'common law'. In fulfilling this responsibility, the following question must be answered: 'When are a woman and a man living as husband and wife [sic]?'." The document then lists the kinds of indicators which will determine whether an individual is living as a "single person" or has a spouse. The indicators are listed under the following categories: Familial; Sexual; Social; Economic. Under the sexual category the document states: "This relationship is at best difficult to prove, and for all intents and purposes is not relevant to the eligibility process''. In the other categories, the criteria are fair if the goal is to establish that the couple have the equivalent to a legal marriage. In the Familial category, for example, among the eleven criteria, along with ''the couple occupy the same premises'', are listed indicators such as ''documents such as leases are titled and signed as Mr. and Mrs.'', and ''school records of children show the couple as the parents''. Under the Social category is found ''the couple is invited and accept invitations as Mr. and Mrs. and are recognized at these social gatherings as husband and wife.'' Under the Economic category is found ''joint bank accounts and pooling of other financial resources.''

The document concludes ''All cases, where there are indications that a recipient/applicant not be living as a single person, must be referred to a supervisor.'' An investigation is conducted under the Eligibility Review Program. The Director of the Family Benefits Branch of the Ministry of Community and Social Services may order benefits to be stopped. If he/she concludes that during the period when a woman was on Family Benefits she had a man living with her for some of the time, he/she may order her future payments to be reduced until she makes up the money she illegally received. Or the case can be turned over to the Ontario Provincial Police and the woman charged with fraud. Her overpayments may still be outstanding with the Ministry even if she is sentenced to jail.

After examining the guidelines, it does seem that the Ministry's main concern is to prevent welfare cheating, given the role and responsibility of the family as we have known them, and is not concerned with sexual relationships as such.

That this is the intention was confirmed by two court cases in the 1970s. Until 1974 it was assumed that, if a man were living with a woman, he was undertaking all financial responsibility for her and her children. Therefore, if she was collecting family benefits she was defrauding society. In 1974, in *In the Matter of Ada Proc*[9], the Divisional court of the Supreme Court of Ontario held that the economic relationship rather than the sexual relationship is the key determinant of whether a couple is living together as husband and wife. In 1974, in *Re Warwick and Minister of Community and Social Services*[10], the Divisional Court confirmed the decision in the Ada Proc case that the proper test of a husband and wife relationship was economic rather than sexual. The Court found that, under the Family Benefits Act, it was valid to deny benefits to a woman living as a wife if there is an economic relationship. However, the Court added, "[we] do not accept that its [the Family Benefits Act] purpose is to deprive an applicant on moral grounds." However, this decision was overturned in the Appeal Court on the grounds that an economic relationship was only one of the factors to be taken into account in determining a spousal relationship.

These have been landmark decisions that have influenced changes in the guidelines so that sexual relationships have been downplayed. However, the overturning of the Warwick case decision by the Appeal Court has allowed the guidelines to retain that cluster of social criteria which imply a spousal relationship. Both the guidelines to welfare workers from the Ministry of Community and Social Services and the decisions of the Supreme Court of Ontario seem to indicate that sexual relationships are irrelevant in determining whether a single mother is eligible for welfare or whether she has defrauded the welfare system. In practice it does seem that sexual relationships remain an important factor in welfare fraud cases.

Two cases involving welfare fraud that received wide publicity early in 1982 are worth considering.

In one, a 37 year old mother of eight children was sentenced to a year in jail because over a period of 10 years she received a total of $588,620. in assistance, although she had sometimes lived with a truck driver. Her defense lawyer said that Mr. Myles, the truck driver, "sort of bounced around the country and had seven children with other women." The crown prosecutor had demanded an eighteen month sentence to set an example, and was determined to appeal the twelve month sentence that the judge, in his compassion, had decreed. Her three still dependent children were placed with the Children's Aid Society.[11]

In the other case, we are told by a Globe and Mail reporter that a 50 year old woman cried hysterically as she was led out of court to serve a three month jail term for a $19,373. welfare fraud.[12] Her defence counsel said that her lover had not contributed financially to her support or to that of her children, that he had lived with her off and on, but that he also had another woman friend elsewhere. The judge noted that the man "maybe took a lot and gave little." However, the judge said the courts must punish women who "are prepared to allow themselves to be used in that fashion." These are two recent examples of court judgments pronounced in a lofty moral tone, totally ignoring the economic relationships involved.

From both these newspaper accounts, it appears that the women were not being supported by men while they received welfare benefits. They needed the benefits to support themselves and their children. In neither of these cases did the woman appear to have an economic relationship with the man with whom she lived from time to time. It is hard not to come to the conclusion that these two women were condemned by the courts for daring to have sexual relationships while they were on family benefits, not because they accepted family benefits while they were at the same time being supported by men.

If anyone was cheating the Ontario Government it was surely the men. Yet they were not charged with fraud and sent to jail. In the first case, the man was actually charged with fraud, but the crown prosecutor withdrew the charge, acknowledging to the court that in welfare cases the man "often gets a free ride."[13]

Robert W. Kerr, Professor of Law at the University of Windsor, provides further evidence that sexual relationships may be the determining factor in the denial of family benefits. He examined decisions made by the Social Assistance Review Board of Ontario, the Board to which a woman denied family benefits can appeal. Although the two court decisions that we have cited state that, for a woman to be denied benefits, the woman's relationship with "a man in the house" has to be economic; and although the guidelines that we quote state that the sexual relationship is irrelevant, Professor Kerr comes to the conclusion that most of the decisions of the Review Board are ambiguous and can be interpreted as based on moral, i.e. sexual grounds.[14]

Kerr examined forty-two cases involving the "man in the house" rule on which the Board made decisions during June through August of 1977. He found it difficult to determine the Board's reasons for their decisions. The Board based its decisions on the following factors: living in common law; retention of common address; accommodation held in the man's name; paternity; sharing of expenses.

The intention behind the "man in the house" rule is equity. The two parties of a married couple cannot be considered, for welfare purposes, to be economically independent. It would be unthinkable for the wife of a doctor, say, to apply for family benefits because she wished to be independent. Similarly, the wife of a salesman or a truckdriver should not be able to claim welfare on the grounds that she has a right to independence. Therefore, in order to be fair, a man and a woman, who, though not legally married, have the same kind of relationship as a married couple, should be treated as if they were legally married. The difficulty is to determine when a couple living together has this kind of relationship.

The Family Law Reform Act (1978) has a solution that seems reasonable. Mutual support obligations are imposed on persons living together outside marriage when the couple has lived together continuously for five years, or when the two parties have a relationship of some permanence that has produced a child.

Shifting the criteria on which eligibility for welfare is based from moral to economic ones seems enlightened. But this change can also be questioned. Not only does it rob a woman of her independence, but it is also inconsistent with the way in which other relationships in which there may be an economic advantage are treated. For example, if two people live in the same house and share food expenses it would seem that they have an economic relationship. If one of them is a man with a job and other a woman on welfare, welfare fraud could be charged. However, if one of the persons is a woman with a job, even a high paying job, and the other a woman on welfare, there would be no question of fraud.

It will be interesting to monitor the application of the welfare eligibility criteria to men living as single persons, since they can now receive Family Benefits if they are raising their children on their own.

In summary, the rules governing the entitlement of women to Family Benefits in Ontario remain ambiguous and sexist despite the modifications over the years. The courts continue to confuse their attitudes towards sexual activity with their preoccupation with protecting the tax payer when making their decisions, rather than considering the evidence of an economic relationship. The Administration continues to determine an economic relationship by inference from social indicators rather than from the facts of financial transactions or even financial capability. This confusion implies that the Ministry's policy clings to assumptions about women's "rightful" dependence upon men and to assumptions about equal responsibilities in a legal marital relationship, and applies these assumptions to a common law relationship which may not be permanent and in which the man has no legal responsibilities for the children. In summary, the government's attitude leaves little or no room for divergence from the traditional concepts of the family unit, concepts which are basically sexist in structure.

Footnotes

1. See Rayna Rapp, Ellen Ross and Renate Bridenthal, "Examining Family History", *Feminist Studies,* Vol. 5, No. 8 (Spring 1979).
2. Edward Shorter, *The Making of the Modern Family* (New York: Basic Books, 1975).
3. Talcott Parsons, *The Social System* (New York: Macmillan 1964), p. 187.
4. Christopher Lasch, *Haven in a Heartless World* (New York: Basic Books, 1977), p. ix.
5. The proportion of families with children at home who have a single parent has increased in the Ottawa-Carleton region from 16 per cent at the time of the 1976 census to almost 20 per cent at the time of the 1981 census. Special calculation from Statistics Canada.

6. A review of welfare legislation appears in Linda Silver Dranoff, *Women in Canadian Law* (Toronto: Fitzhenry and Whiteside, 1977), p. 81.

7. Family Benefits Work Group, 33 Charles St. East, Toronto, M4Y 1R9, April 15, 1982.

8. Ontario Ministry of Community and Social Services, Income Maintenance Branch, Policy and Procedural Guidelines, Index 11 "Not Living as a Single Person", January, 1980.

9. (1974) 53 D.L.R. (3d) 512, 6 O.R. (2d), cited in Robert W. Kerr, "Living Together as Husband and Wife", *Low Income Law*, Vol. 1, No. 1 (November 1978).

10. (1977) 15 O.R. (2d) 682 (Div. Ct.) cited in Kerr.

11. *The Citizen,* Ottawa, editorial, January 6, 1982.

12. *The Globe and Mail,* Toronto, January 12, 1982.

13. *The Globe and Mail,* Toronto, January 5, 1982.

14. Kerr, *op. cit.*

15. *Ibid.*

Women, The Forgotten Housing Consumers

CASSIE DOYLE and JANET McCLAIN

As family and household composition have changed over the 1970s, an increasing number of women have become consumers of all forms of housing. This change in household and family composition was rarely identified in the literature which served as the basis of housing policy in Canada over the 1970s, nor were women clearly identified in the economic literature that analyzes consumer behaviour and demand for housing as a commodity. Yet, the trends revealed in almost all of our most recent national statistical data sources indicate that women have emerged as a primary group of consumers — as unattached young singles, as sole supporting heads of families, as principal wage earners in family units, as older individuals and as the principal recipients of government income assistance through transfer payments.

To date, there has been little documentation which shows how consumer demand and the needs of women are being served by public and private housing providers. This lack of documentation raises the question of whether the particular housing needs of women were ever acknowledged in the formulation of housing policies over the last ten years. Questions should also be raised as to whether the current and future demand for housing tenure, quality and utility of housing units, price ranges, location and services, and the ratio of price level to a proportion of income,[1] have been accurately assessed. For example, little is known about the status and condition of housing currently owned by women, or about women's access to government-sponsored programs such as home repair assistance loans, property tax rebates or grants for first-time buyers. Similarly, we have very little information on women as renters, except as senior citizens in subsidized housing projects. There is little information in the current literature that indicates whether market influences or price level are having an effect on women in the private sector, and little has been done to assess the increasing demand by women for subsidized housing or whether this accommodation suits their changing needs.

In the neo-classical analysis of the economics of consumption, "one of the basic assumptions underlying the theory is that consumer behaviour always involves choice."[2] Consumers will spread their choices among the goods and services which yield the most satisfaction or utility. By virtue of becoming primary consumers, women have thus assumed the classical role of being able to choose from a wide range of housing services. In home ownership, for example, this means that women have placed greater demands on the mortgage credit and insurance industries for equal treatment in lending practices, both as purchasers in their own right and as equal contributors to the basic income of their families.[3] Likewise, it is now more evident that women are active purchasers of housing in their own right, and the traditional accrual of a home as an asset through inheritance or communal property arrangements is not, as it once was, the only source of ownership attainment.[4] The ability to sustain this position as primary consumers in times of change in the labour force and inflationary pressure on the housing and mortgage markets is another issue which must be acknowledged. Still, the majority of female housing consumers are renters in the private sector.

This paper will begin by constructing a statistical profile of women, using the most recent national data sources available. The profile will include family and household composition, the income position of women by age and type of household, their labour force participation and responsibility for children, and the housing tenure status and shelter cost experience of women. Using the background information as a point of departure, this paper will demonstrate through a review of the housing and planning literature that, clearly, the current position of women as consumers and their specific housing needs were not identified in the analysis, planning and program development that preceded housing policy changes in the 1970s.

As well, universal social assumptions were made about the stratification of women. Younger single women were assumed to be temporary consumers who would not achieve any more than a marginal income level during their first years in the labour force; thus, it was thought they would pose no appreciable influence on housing demand. It was assumed that women entering the labour force as spouses would never constitute a very large group, nor was it expected that, because of health conditions or unemployment, women would emerge as the principal wage earners and economic heads of these households. These assumptions were contrary to trends which appeared earlier in the 1980s. As well, these assumptions were based on a static view of the position of women and sex bias which, to some extent, allowed the primarily male group of housing forecasters to overlook some fairly obvious facts and trends.

Population and Household Composition

The following is based on the most recent information from the Statistics Canada series, CANSIM.[5] According to the series as of June 1, 1982, the following breakdown of the Canadian population occurs. Females make up 50.4 per cent of the total population or 12,274,900. Since 1976, the female population overall has made a 0.9 per cent gain. By province, the total number of women exceeds the male population in Prince Edward Island, Nova Scotia, New Brunswick, Québec, Ontario, Manitoba and B.C. However, when one examines the age category over 55 years, the number of women exceeds men in every province, through not in the Northwest Territories and the Yukon. The female population age 55 and over has experienced a slight increase since 1976, and the ratio of males to the female population in the older age categories shows a continuing decline.

Household composition in 1976 shows that 6 per cent of families were headed by women (no spouse present) and 12.7 per cent were female non-family households. In 1981, marginal but not significant increases are shown, with 7.1 per cent of families and 14 per cent non-family households headed by women. However, the picture is not painted as clearly as it could be for individuals, unless one examines the distribution by age group. In 1976, an age breakdown within non-family households headed by women showed that 48.8 per cent were in the youngest age group 15 to 24, and 50.2 per cent from ages 25 to 64. Over age 65, there is a dramatic increase in women heading households, 74.7 per cent or nearly three-quarters of the singles and couples population at the traditional age of retirement and over. Demographic projections to the year 1991 show a slight decrease in the proportion of housholds headed by women in the younger age categories, and a shift upwards to over 80 per cent for women age 65 and over.[6] For the population over age 65 as a whole, a growth rate of 11 per cent is expected between 1976 and 1991.

The proportion of older women living alone in 1981 was 8.2 per cent at age 55, moving up to almost 15 per cent of the population between ages 65 and 69. There is a sharp increase in the population up to 45 per cent for women over age 75. In terms of family and marital status, 41 per cent of the total female population is single or part of the never-married population and 49.5 per cent are of the married population. Some 7.2 per cent of the female population are widows, with the largest proportion over age 55. Divorced women were 3 per cent of the population age 55 to 59, and it is expected that this proportion will be found to have increased in 1981. Population projections by marital status show that fewer women will remain single or never married in the older age groups.[7]

In 1976, 83 per cent of all single-parent households were headed by women, and 8.1 per cent of all families were headed by women. The overall proportion of single parents in 1981 has remained much the same, but there has been an increase in the proportion of those in the younger age groups. Of the female single parents in primary families, 40.8 per cent were under age 35, 57.2 per cent were age 35 to 64, and 2.0 per cent were over age 65.[8] By 1991, it has been projected that there will be a slight decrease in the overall proportion of female headed single-parent families (82.2%) compared to male heads, and a slight decrease in the percentage of families where the female single parent is under age 35 (32.8%) and where she is age 35 to 64 (57.6%). Thus, a smaller rate of increase in younger single-parent families headed by women is shown between 1961 and 1976 (4.4%), than was experienced in the last six years when there was a 12.4 per cent increase. However, since 1961, the proportion of young female single parents has more than doubled and is now well over one-third of all female single parents in the population.[9]

Another phenomenon worthy of some attention is the doubling up of two or more families into one household, which most recently has been associated with the so-called "blending" of the families of previously divorced single parents as they marry or live together; the formation of "supportive households" by two female single parents; and a move by single parents into relatives' homes to combine households. In 1976, only 2 per cent of all households were secondary families and this pattern is expected to continue by 1991. "However, if housing becomes more expensive and unattainable for younger persons, this proportion (of secondary families) may not show the anticipated decrease."[10]

Income Status and Age

A brief review of the 1981 preliminary estimates of income distribution show that, over all age groups, single women have lower average incomes than all individuals of both sexes. Where this is most apparent is from ages 35 to 64, and particularly ages 45 to 54, in which the average income of single women was $11,022 compared to $19,078 for all individuals. In each age group, at least 25 per cent or more of the population has an income under $5,000. Over 26 per cent of the population with an income under $3,000 falls into the under 24 age bracket and the 55 to 64 age bracket. The 35 to 44 age group has 18.3 per cent of the population that has an income over $20,000, but the average income in this age group is $12,147. However, the average income for all single women in 1981 was $9,383. This compares to the average income of single women whose principal source was wages and salaries in the following manner: $9,836 in 1980, which is slightly above the 1981 average, and $8,752 in 1979, which is slightly below the 1981 average. [11]

In comparison to the average income of single women in 1980, which was $8,242, and $10,209 for those age 35 to 44, the 1981 figures how a percentage increase of 13.8 in average income and 8 per cent in the middle age category. In a similar comparison to the 1979 figures, the average income of all women was $7,342, and $9,037 for those age 35 to 44. Thus, the percentage increase in average income to 1981 was 27.8 per cent for all single women and 22.0 per cent for those age 35 to 44, the group which has achieved highest income status.

An examination of the income statistics for families headed by women in 1980 also shows some interesting results. For all age groups, 13.6 per cent of the population has an income below $5,000, and 42.4 per cent has an income below $10,000. Women heads of families under age 34 have the highest proportion of those on low income under $5,000, 18.6 per cent, and an average income of $9,924. Those woman between the ages of 45 and 64 who head families achieve the best overall income position. Of women age 45 to 54 and 55 to 64, 27.3 per cent and 25.9 per cent respectively achieve annual incomes above $25,000. However, the average income for women in these age groups is not quite so high, $18,177 and $17,433 for each. These figures are still above the average income of $14,969 for all women heads of families. [12]

In extending our comparison further, one finds that, in 1979, the average income for all women heads of families was $13,910, and $17,040 for women in the 45 to 54 age group. Thus the percentage increases from 1979 to 1980 are not quite so dramatic as the changes in average income experienced by single women from 1979 to 1980. The increase for all women was 7.6 per cent and 6.7 per cent for those age 45 to 54. Where the most apparent income change occurs between 1979 and 1980 is for women heads of families age 25 to 34 which increases by 23.6 per cent.

A further breakdown of women heading single-parent families

through special calculations from Statistics Canada also shows some interesting results. In 1980, 16.6 per cent of single parents and, in 1979, 20.5 per cent, had incomes under $5,000. Following the same sequence of years, 52.2 per cent and 58.4 per cent had incomes under $12,000. This shows a marked difference from husband-wife families in the same time period. In 1980, 14.1 per cent had incomes below $12,000 and 17.4 per cent in 1979. Only 17.7 per cent of single-parent families had incomes over $25,000 in 1980 compared to 53.5 per cent of husband-wife families. The difference in average income was also apparent, $14,957 for single parents and $20,851 for two-parent families in which the head is the only major source of income, and $28,419 where there is more than one income. [13]

The incidence of lower income is still quite high among single-parent families despite the small gains in average income over the last few years. In 1979, the incidence of low income for single parents was 41.1 per cent, 36 per cent for all female-headed families, and 38.7 per cent for single women. In 1980, there appears to have been a shift upwards in the incidence of low income, 38.9 per cent for women heads of families, and 44 per cent for single parents among all families. There was a shift downwards to 34.7 per cent in the low-income status of single women. The 1980 poverty line for a family of three in an average urban area was $1,961.14 according to Statistics Canada calculations; revised to 1982 levels, again for the same size family, the cut-off has moved up to $15,831. The poverty line in 1980 for a one-person household was $7,152 and in 1982 this was $8,978.

Participation in The Labour Force

The growth of women in the labour force is clearly an indicator of social change of undeniable proportions. And, ''it would appear that economic pressures have considerably affected the role of women in the family . . . Although some women may have sought gainful employment outside the home for reasons of self-fulfillment, the vast majority have done so . . . to earn a decent living.''[15] Although this comment was made by Gelber in 1975, reflecting on the past ten years, it is relevant to the current context of women active in the labour force and to the necessity of them assisting their families to cope with the impact of inflation, the increasing burden of consumer debt, and the cost of providing basic support and necessities for their children.

Since 1975, the number of women in the labour force with children has increased by a little over 32 per cent. The proportion of employed women who have children under age 16 has increased to 54 per cent. As of August 1982, for example, 46.7 per cent of the female population was employed, and the highest rates of participation overall was among those age 20 to 34. Similarly, the highest rates of unemployment was experienced by those in the younger age groups, 15 to 24 years, who had a 16 to 17.8% unemployment rate.

One of the most interesting means of analyzing the labour force is by economic status, which gives a fairly clear picture of women as principal wage earners. Of the women classified as unattached individuals, 49.4 per cent participated in the labour force. As members of a family unit participating in the labour force, there were 56.4 per cent of women heads of families, 50.7 per cent of women as spouses, and a sizable porportion, 68.3 per cent, of single women heading families with children. However, as may be expected, single parents had the highest proportion of those unemployed, while the lowest unemployment rate was shown for spouses. Among those previously or currently married, there are higher rates of employment in the 20 to 44 age group. It should be noted as well that women make up nearly 74 per cent of the part-time labour force working less than 30 hours per week.[16]

In a further analysis of women by absence of spouse, the provinces with the highest rates of employment (50 per cent and over) are B.C., Ontario and the Prairie provinces. Of this group, women in Ontario and the Prairies had the largest number of children under age 16, and those in Ontario had more of their children in care arrangements. Women who were married but whose spouses were not employed participated more in the labour force in the Atlantic provinces and Québec (22.3% and 13.8%

respectively). The number of married women employed, and likely classified as secondary wage earners, is highest in Ontario and the Prairie provinces, although the largest number of school age children is shown for women in Québec and Ontario.[17]

Of all women age 45 and over who are in the labour force, Québec and Ontario also show the highest proportions of those actively employed. In 1979 and 1980, female individuals between the ages of 45 and 64 showed the highest rated average incomes. However, for women heads of families, there is a narrower range of ages 45 to 54 in which the highest level of income, and the highest average income by comparison, is achieved.[18]

Living Arrangement and Housing Tenure

Our preliminary analysis of 1980 data on housing and facilities, differentiating by household composition and housing tenure, reveals the following picture for women.

For women heads of families, 44 per cent were homeowners and 56 per cent were renters. Because there is a larger proportion (55.5%) of single women compared to women heads of families (44.5%) in the survey, most of the analysis will reflect this influence in further examination of the data. Thus, for single women, 32.7 per cent were homeowners and 67.3 per cent were renters. This is very close to the housing picture of all one-person households in the survey.[19]

Women age 35 to 54 were the highest percentage of homeowners with mortgages (over 24%). And 38.2 per cent of women over age 55 owned homes without mortgages compared to 45.2 per cent of women age 65 and over. Typically, over 50 per cent of women in these older age groups occupied single detached homes. Also, as expected, most women homeowners over age 65 occupied housing built before 1960 with mostly oil heating.

In contrast to the housing tenure status shown above, of women heads of families recorded in the consumer finances survey in 1977, 31.6 per cent were homeowners and 68.3 per cent were renters. More one-person households were renters at this time, up to 73.2 per cent, while 40.4 per cent of all families and unattached individuals were renters. By low-income status, 34.1 per cent of all families were homeowners (6.5% carrying mortgages) and 65.9 per cent were renters.[20]

Women renters typically occupy apartments, flats and row housing or duplexes. Most live in one- or two-bedroom units in housing built before 1960. The youngest group, up to age 34, and those over age 55 predominate in occupying apartment housing. They also predominate in having the lowest incomes. In April 1980, 43.7 per cent of women paid less than $250 a month for rent, 18.6 per cent paid between $250 and $550 and 37.6 per cent paid over $550 a month. A little over 59 per cent of women in the survey were paying 25% of income or below on shelter cost, while amost 30 per cent paid over 30% of their income.

In a closer look at housing expenditure and measures of affordability, women do not fare as well as one might assume. Looking at the main source of income, for example, 36.5 per cent of women renters derived their incomes from government transfer payments and retirement pensions. Of the women with mortgages, 17.5 per cent depend on these income sources. Women only achieve marginal status as homeowners with income from self-employment and investments.

Single-parent families are extremely varied in terms of housing need and life-style, but they tend to be less able to afford adequate housing than the total population.[21] Assuming an average cross-section in 1980 of the single-parent population, 63.2 per cent were renters and 36.8 per cent were homeowners. Of this latter group, 24.7 per cent, surprisingly, had mortgages. At least 43.6 per cent lived in housing built before 1960, and principally heated by oil and gas. Only 36.4 per cent lived in single detached homes, and the average number of rooms per household was a little over five. Because of the lower rated incomes of $12,000 compared to over $20,000 for all families, they inevitably pay a much higher proportion of their incomes toward shelter costs.[22]

A single parent with two children earning $11,590 per year in a clerical support position would spend over 46 per cent of her $966 monthly income to rent a two-bedroom apartment at $450 per month. If for some reason circumstances necessitated her leaving the labour force, then this mother's income could drop to $541 per month probably forcing her to move as she would be paying nearly 74 per cent of her income on rent.[23]

Finally, in examining another group that has recently gained prominence, women heads of families as "empty nesters", their problems are much more severe than for husband-wife families. At least 75 per cent of all older couples own their homes,[24] and this is not the case for older women with children about to leave home. If an older woman is in some form of subsidized housing, this will necessitate her having to relocate in a smaller housing unit when the time comes for the children to leave home, or, in some cases, her eligibility for subsidized housing may be lost altogether.

Women in Housing Policy Literature

Research and policy development in the field of housing have not addressed the needs of women in any substantive manner. To anyone who has studied the literature, this omission is readily apparent. What is not quite clear is the extent to which women are invisible. In the study of housing, as in most social research, homogeneous labels which prevent any identification of gender are employed to define the population.

To understand the extent to which the needs of women as housing consumers have been addressed in the policy literature, twenty-three documents which reflect the basic core of literature available on housing over the last 15 years in Canada were selected for examination.[25] They can be divided generally into three categories: 1) studies containing models or data which predict the trends in housing demand; 2) government policy proposals; and 3) policy analysis and commentary on trends in housing produced by research groups outside government. These documents were analyzed according to criteria which identified: 1) the methods used to assess housing demand or requirements; 2) projections of changes in household composition; 3) references to women as housing consumers; and 4) any discussion of the position of women. The following discussion is an overview of the findings.

(1) *Predictive Models*

Housing has particular characteristics which differentiate it from any other consumer good. These characteristics, most notably durability and cost, mean that the demand for housing is influenced by a range of complex factors affecting availability and supply. Any study which aims to assess future trends in the housing market is primarily centred around such supply issues as construction and land costs, mortgage interest rates, and the availability of financing. The factors affecting actual demand, largely demographic forces and income, receive much less attention.

Five major Canadian documents from the early 1970s (L.B. Smith, 1971; Dennis and Fish, 1972; Armitage and Audain, 1972; Kirkland, 1973; L.B. Smith, 1974) were reviewed with regard to their assessment of demand. The projections contained in these reports are primarily based on demographic information derived from Census data. Household requirements are analyzed according to population increases due to natural growth, immigration and migration. Age trends are taken as a primary indicator of demand. Likewise, the presence of children is used as an indicator of the number of units required. Household composition is analyzed according to the growth of the generalized "family" and "non-family" households and the results are used to determine future demand for housing. For example, Armitage and Audain include household formation in their model for estimating housing requirements. They use three general types: single adults, married couples, and single adults or married couples with children. Kirkland bases his demand projections on data from the 1971 Census with age as the primary variable, his only reference to gender being an acknowledgement that the majority of "one-parent families" are headed by females.

Following through the demand studies of the decade, the 1975 report of the Interdepartmental Study Team on Housing and Rents in British Columbia projects housing requirements for that province using data on population growth, age distribution and headship rates (the percentage of the population that are heads of households). Once again, household types are categorized as family and non-family, one-person and other.

A 1980 Canada Mortgage and Housing Corporation (CMHC) report on the long-term outlook for housing in Canada also relies on general population forecasts. The geographical distribution of the population is emphasized over an analysis of household composition, with an analysis of trends in household income included. In reference to these trends, data on the increasing number of women entering the labour market are presented. This information is used to illustrate trends regarding two-earner families. No reference is made to women living outside the traditional husband-wife, nuclear family.

The studies reviewed above are representative of the body of research used to formulate the most recent demand projections for housing in Canada. It is apparent that this sampling of research does not in any way acknowledge the sex differences in current housing demand, nor address the impact of gender on the assessment of future shelter requirements. Women housing consumers are made invisible by the typology and manner in which demographic data are classified, organized and presented. Analysis of demand is primarily focussed on the growth of "family" and "non-family" households. The underlying assumption is that housing needs will be similar within both groups. As indicated by L.B. Smith,

> The distinction between family and non-family households is significant primarily because of varying tenure preferences. It is conventionally thought that families prefer single-detached dwellings, whereas non-family households prefer multiple forms of housing, especially apartments or flats.[26]

Preference has little impact on the various dwelling types occupied, as indicated by our data.

The language of the reports systematically disguises the reality that women constitute a large proportion of housing consumers. In their seminal work on low-income housing, Dennis and Fish structure their analysis of housing need through homogeneous household labels which describe the requirements of a low-income housing consumer:

> *He* needs housing which he can afford. *He* needs a warm house in winter, with a furnace that works regularly. *He* needs decent neighbourhood services and facilities like police, garbage collection, parks, which help make *his* home a decent place in which to live. (emphasis added)[27]

(2) *Government Policy Proposals*

Utilizing the same criteria as for the demand studies, six government housing policy reports were analyzed to determine the extent to which the needs of women consumers are addressed. Once again, the primary focus of these documents is on the supply of housing stock. Priority is given to examining current programs and proposing new means to meet housing need over any detailed discussion of consumers themselves.

The first of these reports, the 1969 report of the Federal Task Force on Housing and Urban Development, highlights the need for housing assistance to low-income groups in its declaration of principles. Headed by Paul Hellyer, the Task Force was sensitive to the problems experienced by families living in high density public housing projects, but no reference is made to the household characteristics of these tenants or to the proportionate increase in female-led households which was taking place in these projects at the time. The report states that public housing is built without adequate social services or recreational facilities, but does not relate this lack of support to the particular needs of women residents.

The Ontario Report of the Advisory Task Force on Housing Policy (1973) also neglects to include a thorough analysis of housing need. The findings of the report indicate that the major housing problem in Ontario is one of affordability, with "low-income families" referred to as a homogeneous group. The report contains no specific reference to women, although other special needs groups such as the elderly are mentioned.

The 1976 CMHC Task Force on Shelter and Incomes addresses

the rising cost of housing subsidies and the adequate targeting of these subsidies to those most in need. Households are taken to be homogeneous entities, no distinction between family and non-family being made, and income is the only variable used for analysis. Women are mentioned only in a passing reference to the position of "spouse's earnings" in the calculation of household income for public housing tenants and the recipients of the Assisted Home Ownership Program.

Another CMHC report, *The Relationship Between Social Policy and Housing Policy: A Federal Perspective,* was published in 1979. Its purpose was to present current information on the housing problems experienced by Canadians and to examine the federal government's policy alternatives in housing. Household composition is broken down by "family" and "non-family", by age and family income, with no reference to the gender of the head of the household, or to women's increasing labour force participation.

In 1981, CMHC produced a *Background Document on Social Housing,* which was presented to the National All Sector Housing Conference. Aimed at outlining directions that might be taken to resolve housing problems, this document contains no anlaysis of the composition of housing consumers. A more promising study was produced the same year by CMHC and the U.S. Department of Housing and Urban Development. The purpose of this report was to develop and apply a comprehensive method of measuring housing need, and to compare its application in the two countries. Core housing need is measured by combining affordability, physical adequacy and suitability indicators. Household types were divided by families (with or without children), single parents (male or female), male or female individuals. This analysis by gender revealed that

> The most disadvantaged household type in both countries was the single parent, female-headed household of which 38% in Canada and 61% in the U.S. were in core need. Moreover, 44% of single females living alone in Canada and 51% in the U.S. were in housing need. By contrast, male single parents and male individuals living alone experienced about half the housing need of their female equivalents.[28]

Although this document does not include proposals to resolve core housing need experienced by women, it is a landmark Canadian housing policy document which gives a concrete identification of *women as housing consumers.* The progress made in this document can possibly be attributed to the influence on Canadian housing researchers produced by some exposure to American housing research and a data base which has, since 1978, separately documented the housing status of women.[29]

As can be seen in this brief review, most government policy studies have failed to analyze housing demand and need in a way that makes it possible to specifically identify women even though, in all likelihood, they have the most urgent need for government service and intervention. Age and income are the primary variables selected in the analysis of housing consumers. There is no recognition of gender as a determining influence on an individual's ability to gain access to housing in the public and private sectors or as a key factor which shaped and determined the development of social housing policy in the 1970s.

(3) *Analysis of Current Policies and Future Trends in Housing*

A third body of housing literature is contained in reports, largely produced by research institutes and social planning councils, that analyze government housing policy and recommend future directions. The reports included here for analysis are representative of the wide range of organizations involved in research on housing. The same set of criteria aimed at determining the extent to which housing policy addresses the role of women as housing consumers was applied to these reports.

The *Right To Housing* contains the proceedings of the 1968 Canadian Conference on Housing which was sponsored by the Canadian Welfare Council. These papers stress the needs of "low-income families" in relation to housing. The discussion frequently addresses the problem of poverty, with David Donnison's paper providing a comprehensive typology of the causes of poverty. However, the paper has no reference to the determining influence of gender. Generally, the labels for consumers are homogeneous, without an analysis of composition of household. Women are given just two brief mentions: in a reference to high rise apartments, concern is expressed by Marvin Lipman about the distance these housing arrangements place between a mother and her children playing; and an acknowledgement by H.N. Colburn concerning the special needs of the elderly, in which he mentions that women live longer than men.

A 1973 report by the Ontario Welfare Council provides an overall review of housing policy in Ontario, with emphasis on an evaluation of the current housing programs at the time. Although no data is presented, the report does state that welfare recipients with the highest rent-to-income ratios are mother-led families renting in the private market.

In the mid-seventies, Richard Shaffner for the C.D. Howe Research Institute (1975), the Ontario Economic Council (1976), and L.B. Smith for the Fraser Institute (1977) produced reports on housing. The major thrust of all three documents is to analyze trends in the housing market and assess the effectiveness of government housing policy. There is little discussion of the impact of household composition on housing requirements. In the Ontario Economic Council report, the question is raised, "what are the characteristics of the one-third of Canadian families that do not own homes?" The only determining variables mentioned are income and age.

The Canadian Council on Social Development reviewed Canadian social housing policy in a report published in 1977. Here, demand is assessed using the existing government data on projection targets, with additional analysis of need based on the problems of affordability and adequacy. Household types are categorized as childless single persons, childless couples, and families with children. Women as housing consumers are primarily identified in reference to the increasing proportion of mother-led families and single elderly women in public housing projects. The report states:

> One of the more unfortunate results of institutionalized sex discrimination
> in Canada, and of the current rental housing market in Canada is the fact
> that there are comparatively many more poor households headed by

women than by men and that these persons are finding it increasingly difficult to obtain housing on the private market.[30]

During this same year (1977), the Centre for Urban and Community Studies in Toronto published the proceedings of a conference on urban housing markets. Several papers discuss demand projections in relation to the need to include other variables such as wealth and housing market complexities, in future analysis. Albert Rose's paper refers to the decline of the nuclear family as the pre-eminent source of demand for housing and the growing predominance of other household forms. He mentions women as housing consumers in reference to the growing numbers of public housing applications received from female-led households.

George Fallis' study on the impact of government housing programs on income distribution in Ontario (1980) concentrates on the benefits for participants in the program. These are analyzed according to the variables of income and age, thereby making it impossible to identify the impact of gender.

Albert Rose's book, *Canadian Housing Policy: 1935-1980,* provides a comprehensive overview of housing over the past decades. In this study, without specific reference to women, there is a discussion of the changes in household composition as the two-parent, nuclear family becomes less prevalent. Once again, women are identified as the primary consumers of public housing; by the mid-seventies in Ontario, one-half to two-thirds of all applications received by housing authorities were made by women.

Novia Carter has recently also published an overview of housing in Canada. Housing demand is not analyzed to any extent in this book except in relation to the growth of the suburbs. Generally, the main reference to women is contained under the heading "Lifestyles", which discusses the impact of technology on domestic chores, the increasing participation of women in the labour force, and the child care requirements produced by the changing role of women. Unfortunately, no analysis of the specific needs of women as primary housing consumers is given.

Although references to women are scarce in these nongovernmental reports on housing, in summary, they indicate that female-headed households are the major consumers of public housing. What is missing is any analysis of why this is so. The literature contains no research on the income, labour force status, household characteristics, or age distribution of women as housing consumers. Their numbers in government subsidized rental housing are not given any significance in the analysis of social housing policy.

In reviewing all these housing policy documents, it is evident that women are generally not acknowledged as housing consumers, nor are their housing requirements addressed. Their invisibility can be attributed both to the categories used to label types of household formation and the variables selected for analysis. In the first instance, the arbitrary organization of household structures into ''family'' and ''non-family'' groupings is based on the same assumption Joan Acker[31] discusses in relation to stratification studies: the family is upheld as the unit of study. In housing it provides the single point of differentiation between two types of households.

Olivia Harris stresses the danger of applying a single, universal interpretation to the wide variations of domestic arrangements.[32] The application of general homogeneous labels to categorize patterns of co-residency distorts the manner in which women's reality is presented. Likewise, the independent variables used to analyze shelter need, primarily income and age, leave the question of gender unaddressed. Significantly, both these variables determine the housing status of women but, as gender is not inlcuded as an indicator of housing demand, these correlations are impossible to derive.

The failure of housing policy to address women as primary consumers is not an accident. As Ann Oakley and Robin Oakley show that in relation to official statistics, the conceptual scheme used to organize and present data reflects an institutionalized mode of thinking.[33] This conceptual scheme, which actually structures the data, is based in an ubiquitous ideology rooted in the patriarchal social order and sexism. Not only do the concepts employed limit the usefulness and accuracy of data, but they also serve to reinforce sexual discrimination in policy formulation and program development.

This lack of research on women as housing consumers can be attributed to deficiencies in housing policy literature, but feminist research has also failed to address the question of housing as a "women's issue". What research exists primarily analyzes housing from the perspective of environmental design and planning and domestic science. Allocation to and access by women to private and publicly-assisted housing has, unfortunately, received little consideration by researchers. This is surprising as women have clearly established themselves as primary housing consumers, as much by their more intensive use and occupancy of housing units as by their changing income and social status. They have also played a large role in tenant movements, homeowners' associations and non-profit housing organizations.

We believe that more extensive investigation of women as primary consumers would complement further development of feminist research and analysis. Housing consumption is a particularly strong indicator of the economic and social position of women. Since shelter is the largest budget item of all basic necessities, the type of housing, the community in which it is located, and access to services and to housing that is reasonably priced, are strong indicators of social status and value. Denial of access and security in the housing environment and perpetuation of circumstances of prohibitive costs are likely to continue to promote inequitable conditions for women in this decade. Emphasis and recognition of the housing status of women and the presence of inequality hold strong implications for the continuing social development for women, development which must promote fairness and equity in public policy and private sector allocation of resources.

Footnotes

1. The ratio of shelter cost to income is based on the Carver Hopwood scale for rents, now revised up to a maximum 25 per cent of income as an acceptable base proportion of income devoted to housing expenditure. This

scale was brought into effect in 1952, and has subsequently been reviewed many times in analysis of housing affordability conducted by provincial and federal governments as well as by researchers in the social welfare community. Although, this scale is still specified in most policy manuals for social housing, it may not uniformly determine the ratio of shelter cost to adjusted family income up to a maximum of 25 per cent as the means of calculation, and this level is currently subject to much debate.

2. Bennett, Peter D. and H.H. Kassarjian, *Consumer Behaviour* (Prentice-Hall, Englewood Cliffs, N.J., 1972), p. 12.

3. Frazer, Debra and Janet McClain, *Credit, A Mortgage For Life* (Canadian Council on Social Development, Ottawa, 1981), pp. 66-71.

4. McClain, Janet, "Access, Security and Power: Women are still second-class citizens in the housing market", *Status of Women News*, 6(1), Winter 1979-80, pp. 15-16.

5. Statistics Canada, *Canadian Statistical Review*, 57(9), September 1982, pp. 130-131.

6. Statistics Canada, *Household and Family Projections, 1976-2001*, Catalogue 91-522 (Ottawa, December 1981), pp. 50-51.

7. Stone, Leroy and Susan Fletcher, *Aspects of Population Aging in Canada* (Statistics Canada, Ottawa, 1981), Charts 9 and 10.

8. Statistics Canada, *Census Families in Private Households, 1981*, Catalogue 92-905 (Volume 1), p. 5-1 (Ottawa, September 1982).

9. Statistics Canada, *Household and Family Projections, op. cit.*, pp. 62-63.

10. *Ibid.*, pp. 62-64.

11. Statistics Canada, *Income Distribution by Size, Preliminary Estimates 1981*, Catalogue 13-206 (Ottawa, September 1982) and various years *Income Distributions by Size* — authors' tabular comparisons.

12. *Ibid.*

13. Statistics Canada, *Family Incomes: Census Families 1979 and 1980*, Catalogue 13-208 (Ottawa: August 1981 and 1982), and *Single Parent Families in Canada: Addendum 1979*, 1981 (off-print) — authors' comparisons.

14. Statistics Canada, *Income Distributions by Size 1979* (Ottawa, May 1981), pp. 105-107, and 125.

15. Gelber, Sylva M., "social Security and Women: A Partisan View", *International Labour Review*, 112(6), December 1975, p. 434. Also see Ralph E. Smith *et al.* (editors), *The Subtle Revolution: Women At Work* (The Urban Institute, Washington, D.C., 1979).

16. Statistics Canada, *The Labour Force*, Catalogue 71-001, August 1972, authors' comparisons. See also Judy Steed, "The Changing Voice" and "Fighting Bias at the Pay Window", *The Globe and Mail*, October 16 and 18, 1982; and Jac-André Boulet and Laval Lavallée, *Women and the Labour Market: An Analytical Framework*, Discussion Paper No. 207 (Economic Council of Canada, Ottawa, December 1981).

17. Statistics Canada, *The Labour Force* and special tables from the "1981 Survey of Child Care Arrangements", pp. 104-109, in the same volume.
18. Statistics Canada, *Income Distributions By Size,* 1979 and 1980.
19. Special tabulations from Statistics Canada, (HIFE) *Household Facilities By Income and Other Characteristics,* 1980 micro data tape, Canada Mortgage and Housing Corporation, Ottawa.
20. Statistics Canada, Consumer Income and Expenditure Division, *Home Ownership and Mortgage Debt In Canada, 1977* (Ottawa, July 1979), pp. 16-17.
21. Jordan, Elizabeth, *The Housing Needs of Female-Led One Parent Families* (Canada Mortgage and Housing Corporation (CMHC), Ottawa, November 1981), pp. 8-9.
22. Statistics Canada, HIFE, *loc. cit.*
23. McClain, Janet "Another Way of Seeing Rent Controls and the Rental Housing Market", *Urban Focus*, 10(5), May-June 1982, p. 5.
24. "Empty Nesters — a mythical market?", *From The Rooftops*, July/August 1982, p. 4.
25. The following list is the policy documents we have reviewed to determine the extent to which women are identified as housing consumers.

    (Predictive Models)

    Smith, L.B., *Housing in Canada: Market Structure and Policy Performance,* Urban Canada Problems and Prospects — Research (Monograph 2) (CMHC, Ottawa, 1971).

    Dennis, Michael and Susan Fish, *Programs in Search of a Policy* (Hakkert Press, Toronto, 1972).

    Armitage, Andrew and Michael Audain, *Housing Requirements; A Review of Recent Canadian Research* (Canadian Council on Social Development, Ottawa, 1972).

    Kirkland, John S., *Demand for Housing in Canada* (CMHC, Ottawa, 1973).

    Smith, L.B., *The Postwar Canadian Housing and Residential Mortgage Markets and the Role of Government* (University of Toronto Press, Toronto, 1974).

    British Columbia, Interdepartmental Study Team on Housing and Rents, *Housing and Rent Control in British Columbia* (Ministry of Municipal Affairs, Victoria, 1975).

    CMHC, *The Long Term Outlook for Housing in Canada, and Its Implication for Residential Construction Industry* (Ottawa, 1980).

    (Government Policy Proposals)

    Canada, *Report of the Federal Task Force on Housing and Urban Development* (Information Canada, Ottawa, 1969).

Ontario, *Report of the Advisory Task Force on Housing Policy* (Queen's Printer, Toronto, 1973).

CMHC, *Report of the Task Force on Shelter and Incomes* (Ottawa, 1976).

CMHC, *The Relationship Between Social Policy and Housing Policy: A Federal Perspective* (Unpublished, Ottawa, 1979).

CMHC, *Background Document on Social Housing* (Prepared for the All Sector Housing Conference, Ottawa, 1981).

CMHC, *Housing Affordability Problems and Housing Need in Canada and the United States: A Comparative Study* (Ottawa, 1981).

(Reports on Housing Policies and Trends)

Wheeler, Michael (editor), *The Right to Housing* (Harvest House, Montreal, 1969). Out of print.

Ontario Welfare Council, *A Study of Housing Policies in Ontario: General Report* (Toronto, 1973).

Shaffner, Richard, *Housing Policy in Canada: Learning From Recent Problems* (C.D. Howe Research Institute, Montreal, 1975).

Ontario Economic Council, *Issues and Alternatives — Housing* (Toronto, 1976).

Bourne, L.S. and J. Hitchcock, (editors), *Urban Housing Markets: Recent Directions in Research and Policy* (University of Toronto Press, Toronto, 1977).

Canadian Council on Social Development, *A Review of Canadian Social Housing Policy* (Ottawa, 1977).

Smith, L.B., *Anatomy of a Crisis: Canadian Housing Policy in the Seventies* (The Fraser Institute, Vancouver, 1977).

Fallis, George, *Housing Programs and Income Distribution in Ontario* (Ontario Economic Council, University of Toronto Press, 1980).

Fallis, George, *Housing Policy for the 1980s* (Ontario Economic Council, Discussion Paper Series, Toronto, 1981).

Rose, Albert, *Canadian Housing Policies: 1935-1980* (Butterworths, Toronto, 1980).

Carter, Novia, *Housing — Making Man's Environment Series* (Nelson, Toronto, 1981).

26. L.B. Smith (1972), p. 13.
27. Dennis and Fish, p. 37.
28. Canada Mortgage and Housing Corporation, *Housing Affordability and Housing Need* (Ottawa, 1981), p. 19.
29. See the U.S. Department of Housing and Urban Development Office of Policy Development and Research, *How Well Are We Housed?* No. 2: Female-Headed Households (Washington, D.C., U.S.G.P.O., 1978).

30. Canadian Council on Social Development, *A Review of Canadian Social Housing Policy* (Ottawa, 1977), p. 72.
31. Joan Acker, "Women and Social Stratification: A Case of Intellectual Sexism", *American Journal of Sociology,* 78(4), 1973, p. 937.
32. Olivia Harris, "Households as Natural Units", K. Young, C. Wolkowitz and R. McCullagh (editors), *Of Marriage and the Market* (CSE Books, London, 1981), pp. 49-68.
33. Ann Oakley and Robin Oakley, "Sexism in Official Statistics", J. Irvine *et al.* (editors), *Demystifying Social Statistics* (Pluto Press, London, 1979), pp. 172-189.

Male-Dominated Criminology: Implications for Women in Correctional Institutions

MAUREEN BAKER

In Canadian crime statistics, about 12% of adults and juveniles charged with property and violent criminal offences are female (Adler and Brusegard, 1980). In fact, throughout the world, women have lower rates of arrest, conviction, and incarceration, as well as lower rates of reported victimization in most crimes (Courtis, 1970). It is not surprising, then, that in the criminology literature, the criminal is usually referred to as "he", with token recognition of the female offender. This has led Smart (1976) to refer to women as the "invisible actors and victims of crime".

Although they are relatively low, women's crime rates have been steadily rising throughout the past two decades. This trend has led to increased speculation, theorizing and research on female criminality and the woman offender. For example, Adler (1975) was alarmed by the percentage increases in American women's violent crime, and concluded that a "new breed" of female criminal is developing. She suggested that women's growing assertiveness, the necessity of earning their own living, and the desire for the things which men have traditionally coveted — in short, "women's liberation" — can be blamed for women's increased criminality and rising rates of violent crime. More careful statistical studies have, however, contradicted this conclusion, and argue that violent crime is not rising among North American women (Simon, 1975; Adams, 1978), but only rates of theft, embezzlement and fraud. Others have pointed out that feminist ideology is accepted mainly by middle class

243

educated women, while poorer women, who are more likely to be arrested, are either unaware of feminism or do not accept its basic assumptions or focus (Velimesis, 1975; Jones, 1980). A more realistic connection between "women's liberation" and rising female crime rates is that they are both caused by similar social and economic changes (Fox and Hartnagel, 1979).

A second rationale for rising female crime rates is that law enforcement authorities and the courts are becoming less sexist, less protective of women, and less paternalistic in dealing with women who violate the legal system. Instead of offering chivalry to women offenders, they are now more likely to arrest them. In the past, women's crimes have often escaped detection or else they were treated more leniently by law enforcers (Pollak, 1950). What appears to be an increase in female crime is merely a trend toward equal treatment within the criminal justice system. The argument continues that surveillance and the detection of crime has become more mechanized and sophisticated, especially in the realm of shoplifting. Heavy losses have forced store managers to deal more legalistically with retail theft. This leads to a rise in arrests and convictions for theft, a crime for which a large proportion of women has always been arrested. Sociological studies of the correlates of crime rates suggest that increased efforts at crime detection and, especially, increased numbers of police personnel, lead to higher crime rates (McDonald, 1969).

Traditionally, women's criminality has been perceived as fundamentally different from that of men. While theories of men's criminality are now focussing on opportunities for learning "criminal careers", class biases in definitions of crime, and socio-economic factors affecting the labelling of deviants, theories of women's criminality have lingered on psychopathology and physiological characteristics (Smart, 1976; Smith, 1978; Ross *et al.*, 1980). Studies of women and crime have focussed on prostitution, sexual immorality, child abuse and shoplifting, and have frequently used psychoanalytic variables in explaining these activities. Theories of criminality have influenced correctional policies, as have some of the implicit assumptions about women's lifestyles and motives for behaviour. In this paper, I would like to make some of these assumptions and theories explicit, and to discuss their potential consequences for women in the criminal justice system.

Ambiguous Research Findings

In comparison to studies of male criminality, there is a paucity of research on women and crime. Several reasons have been given for this. Women's crime rates are low and their numbers in correctional institutions are small. Their crimes tend to be less violent and constitute less of a danger to the social order. While in prison, women are less likely to initiate riots, lawsuits or other disturbances which could lead to an investigation of prison conditions, rehabilitation programs or theories of criminality. And the fact that most correctional workers, police officers, lawyers, and criminologists are male may mean that women offenders are granted lower priority in treatment and research. However, in the past few years, rising rates of female crime, egalitarian ideologies, and feminist researchers have encouraged more research and evaluation of programs for women offenders.

In the literature on women and crime, research findings on the treatment of women in the criminal justice system are somewhat contradictory. Most studies argue that women are treated more leniently from initial contact with the police to the point of incarceration, so that only long term offenders ever get sent to prison. Simon (1975) reported that in the United States, only one in 6.5 arrests are women, 1 in 9 convictions are women, and one in 30 of those sent to jail is a woman. Despite changes in crime rates, Simon argues that these ratios have remained constant.

Mawby (1977) found that juvenile girls are dealt with outside the penal system more often than boys. This finding was reported earlier by Nagel and Weitzman (1971) who found that American women were less likely to have an attorney, a preliminary hearing, or a jury trial. During the pretrial period, they were less likely to remain in custody, less likely to be convicted once tried, and if they were convicted were likely to receive a milder sentence. Several studies have concluded that women "respond better" to both penal treatment and punishment, such as probation, fines, imprisonment and care in psychiatric hosptials. But this finding may merely reflect women's greater deference to authority, their docility, and their greater sensitivity to the opinions of others (Prins, 1980) or the fact that their offences and support systems differ from those of men.

Despite the fact that some studies report lenient and informal treatment for the female offender, others report heavier penalties for women in certain situations. Mawby (1977) suggested that girls are more likely than boys to be institutionalized for non-criminal reasons, such as their own protection. In contradiction to Nagel and Weitzman (1971), Mawby found that girls are more likely to be remanded in custody, even though they were eventually less likely to be sentenced to a term in prison. More severe treatment in the courts was also reported in the British study of May (1977), using a sample of juveniles.

An American study by Terry (1970) found that girls suspected of sexual offences and "incorrigibility" were far more likely to have charges brought against them than boys. Smith's study (1978) substantiated these findings by showing that offences for juvenile girls are "sexualized". Non-sexual offences are overlooked in favour of sexual misbehaviour. The delinquent girls in her study were continually referred to by correctional workers and peers as "sluts" and "prostitutes", which led to further aggression on the part of the girls. Smith discovered that these delinquent girls suffered more social ostracism from their non-delinquent peers than delinquent boys suffer, leading to extremes in female behaviour. Females tended to be either very conforming or very delinquent.

Smith stressed that delinquent girls suffer from a "double rejection". They have violated the legal norms of society and are punished for this transgression. But they have also violated the traditional norms of "feminine" behaviour. For males, delinquency often involves exaggerated "masculine" behaviour. But for females, it involves reactive "unfeminine" behaviour and females undergo a moral judgement by social workers and the criminal justice system for this reaction.

The double standard of sexuality means that activity which is acceptable for one sex is criminalized for the other. This is most apparent in the case of prostitution, where the male client is not prosecuted but the female prostitute is. However, as sexual equality becomes more widespread, policy may focus on other anti-social acts by juvenile girls which are being overlooked because of the current emphasis on "immorality".

Despite the contradictions in the research, most studies conclude that the female offender is protected from the full force of the law by paternalistic men (and occasionally women) in the criminal justice system, who see women as less capable of serious crime than men and more in need of protection rather than punishment. Criminologists have been guilty of some paternalism as well, in accepting some of the assumptions about women and crime and incorporating them into their studies. Rather than carefully analysing women's treatment, they have researched male offenders. In the next section, we will evaluate the research on women within correctional institutions to show the policy implications of some of the assumptions and theories of women's criminality.

Correctional Services for Female Offenders: Size of The Inmate Population

The small number of female inmates in Canadian jails and penitentiaries can be viewed in two different ways. First, we could argue that women are advantaged compared to male offenders, because they are sent to prison less often. The "almost nothing works" school of criminological research (Martinson, 1974; Romig, 1978) essentially argues that "rehabilitation" seldom occurs in correctional institutions, and that, in fact, prison sometimes augments antisocial and criminal behaviour. Prisons have been seen as schools of crime, which intensify hostility, and provide little deterrence from future criminal activity. Although many of these studies have been criticized for inadequate methodological controls (Ross, 1980), prisons seem to be infected with contradictory values, expectations, and programs. The guards and the social workers often disagree about the goals of institutionalization. Punishment is sometimes disguised as rehabilitation, and prisoners are subtly coerced into "voluntary rehabilitation". Inmates soon learn to give lip service to rehabilitative programs in order to get an early release. Diverting women away from institutions could be a great advantage, if other facilities were available to assist them in the community.

However, the fact that female offenders are often not sent to prison, does not necessarily mean more community services for rehabilitation. In fact halfway houses, clinics, hostels and other non-prison services are in short supply for women offenders (Ross *et al.* 1980).

Although women's prisons are smaller than those for men, with less stringent security, more privacy and more contact with the outside world (Simon, 1975), there are additional problems partially caused by their small size. In Canada, there is only one federal penitentiary for women. The Prison for Women in Kingston is in an archaic building which houses women of all ages and backgrounds. Inmates are not classified by the seriousness of their crimes or ages, as male inmates usually are. Despite the emphasis that has been placed on the continual contact with friends and kin for effective rehabilitation, many women are imprisoned thousands of miles from home (Canada, National Advisory Committee, 1977).

Occupational Training

The small numbers and relatively short sentences of women offenders have several implications for occupational training within correctional institutions. There is often not enough time for inmates to complete the programs, and if the training is tailored to fit the sentence, the quality and usefulness may be jeopardized. In other words, women are not imprisoned long enough to be rehabilitated occupationally, assuming that the programs are effective. However, we apparently cannot even make the assumption that the programs *are* effective.

A recent Canadian study concludes that there does not seem to be any relationship between occupational training within women's prisons and market needs (Ross *et al.*, 1980). Since most female prisoners have low education and poor job skills, and many have dependent children and/or have been on welfare prior to incarceration, occupational training should be a prison priority. Several government investigations and private studies have made this suggestion (Lambert & Madden, 1976; Kestenbaum, 1977; Bowker, 1978; Ross *et al.*, 1980). Inside North American prisons, women can be trained as cosmetologists, seamstresses, clerical workers, or hairdressers, but seldom in any job that could not be called a low status female job ghetto (Simon, 1975).

Vocational training is often used as a euphemism for institutional maintenance. Women are encouraged to rehabilitate themselves by learning how to do the kind of work which is consistent with the traditional concept of female sex roles and useful to institutional maintenance. But only recently have researchers questioned the value of this "training" in terms of maintaining the low status of women and saving government resources that would have to be spent if the inmates were provided with more useful skills. Female prisoners have been given little opportunity to break away from the housewife/mother role, partially because theories of women's criminality have associated criminal behaviour with a rejection of the traditional concept of the female sex role. Some "rehabilitation programs" have included the advancement of "femininity" as an ideal, such as encouraging inmates to see their future in terms of marriage and domesticity and maintaining neat appearances and feminine demeanour (Bowker, 1978; Feinman, 1979; Potter, 1978).

Although a few American institutions are beginning to offer non-traditional job training leading to skilled employment with higher pay, most programs continue to focus on dead-end, low-paying positions which reinforce conceptions of feminine dependence and service. However, research evidence shows that the prisoners themselves often regard prostitution as a more lucrative "job" than what they were trained for while incarcerated (Haft, 1974).

Preliminary research seems to indicate that job training in itself is less effective than the combination of quality training in marketable skills over an adequate length of time with some coaching in job-seeking skills, job placement and continued contact and support from employers (Walter and Mills, 1980). An American program called Wider Opportunities for Women (WOW), for example, which combined non-traditional job training with assertiveness training, feminist ideology, and concern for equal employment opportunities, was more successful in improving the placement and income of the women upon release (Kestenbaum, 1977).

Children

Although many inmates *plan* to care for their children upon release, their children have often spent considerable time in the care of relatives before and throughout the mother's incarceration. Although researchers estimate that between 60 and 80% of female inmates have dependent children (Kestenbaum, 1977; Ross *et al.*, 1980), most institutions provide neither facilities for mothers to care for their children in prison, nor special facilities for visiting children. A study of 81 federal and state prisons in the United States found that 31 institutions offered no special services or programs related to the needs of inmates' children (McGowan and Blumenthal, 1978). Although there is speculation about the effects of imprisonment on mothers and their children, there has been little systematic research to examine either the effectiveness of programs which encourage greater contact with children or the consequences of the programs to the children or the women. A Canadian study found that about two-thirds of their sample of incarcerated women had not seen their children since their imprisonment (Rogers and Carey, 1979). If the maintenance of the relationship between mothers and their children is as crucial for rehabilitation as preliminary research would suggest and as research on men has suggested (Waller, 1974), prison authorities should be creating new ways to maintain this relationship. But because child care is not a priority to male prisoners and many women's prisons have their programs modelled after men's (Bowker, 1978), policies concerning children have been neglected.

Treatment Programs

Although there is a considerable amount of North American and British research evaluating correctional programs, most research on correctional treatment has either excluded female clients or not looked at sex differences when considering outcome. The research that is available tends to be descriptive or impressionistic rather than analytical (Ross *et al.*, 1980). While the general criticism could be made that many correctional programs are not based on an adequate conceptualization of the causes of illegal behaviour, this is especially true in the case of programs for female offenders (Ross *et al.*, 1980). Ross elaborates: "The quantity and quality of research is so limited that general conclusions about whether treatment does or does not work in the case of female offenders cannot be justified." (p. iii)

A number of programs have been consistently shown to yield positive outcomes for female offenders or for mixed-sex groups. For example, programs which draw on the offender's peer group as therapeutic agents seem to be effective. Inclusion of the offender's family in the treatment also appears to be crucial. Provision of pro-social models, rather than simply punishing anti-social behaviour, is also important, as well as training in interpersonal skills. Occupational skills and job readiness training must be offered in combination with job development. Interestingly enough, there is no evidence that programs which are based on theoretical conceptions of female criminality emphasizing biological deficits or psychopathology, or which seek to foster the offender's acceptance of the feminine role, are effective. Yet many programs still emphasize traditional homemaker skills and acceptance of a dependent social role.

A number of policy decisions have been based on the Freudian assumption that many female delinquents come from unstable and impoverished backgrounds, have absent or unloving fathers, and experience problems relating to men. This assumption has led therapists and prison decision-makers to urge the appointment of male directors of detention centres for girls (Prins, 1980). Perhaps more cross-sex supervision would benefit male prisoners as well, yet there has been little effort to bring women into decision-making positions in men's institutions.

Although there is much evidence that programs for women offenders enjoy less financial support and include less diverse opportunities for training, there is some evidence in the available literature that women may need these programs more than male offenders. A smaller female prison population implies greater opportunities for experimentation. Some studies show that women are more co-operative while incarcerated (Prins, 1980) and may benefit more from counselling programs because they have better relationships with their counsellors. More incarceration distress may indicate a greater need for counselling for women. Because of sexism in sentencing, only the more serious women criminals are actually imprisoned. This means that incarcerated women have a higher than normal incidence of emotional problems (Lambert & Madden, 1976). In addition to this, women as mothers require more facilities.

However, while women prisoners may need more facilities and may benefit from them more than men do, correctional treatment for the female offender is underfunded and under-researched. Different programs for men and women offenders are justified in several ways. Resources are poured into facilities for male offenders because of their larger numbers. Female offenders tend to be more heterogeneous, which makes the administration of rehabilitation programs more difficult. Because there are so few imprisoned, they are not classified in the way that male offenders are, by age, type of offence, previous convictions, and training needs. The double standard of justice means that, in the minds of some, incerceration is enough for the female offender. It removes her from the temptation of sexual amorality or keeps her off the streets (Bowker, 1978; Ross *et al.*, 1980).

The availability and quality of the services for women

offenders depends largely on their jurisdiction. In Canada, both the federal and provincial governments are involved in corrections. Whether women are sent to an institution or into some kind of "community corrections" program may affect the nature of their treatment. The accessibility of community services and the particular type of correctional treatment may all affect the offenders' chances of rehabilitation.

What many of the programs and services lack is a broader understanding of the status of women in society and the reasons why women violate the law. Although the causes of crime are probably similar for both sexes, the treatment of offenders inside the prison must take into consideration sex differences in terms of family status, education and job training. Rehabilitation programs which have been tested for men may not work for women. Certainly in the field of criminology, we have found that sex is a crucial independent variable. Yet we know next to nothing about how criminal behaviour, court decisions, and response to treatment differ between men and women. We do not really know for what offences women are ignored and for what offences they are systematically punished. But we go on creating programs and policies to deal with women in the criminal justice system on a trial and error basis, hoping that our errors will be insignificant.

References

Adams, S.G., 1978, *The Female Offender: A Statistical Perspective*. Ottawa: Ministry of the Solicitor General.

Adler, F., 1975, *Sisters in Crime*. N.Y.: McGraw-Hill.

Adler, H.J. and D.A. Brusegard, 1980, *Perspectives Canada III*. Ottawa: Ministry of Supply and Services.

Bowker, L.H., 1978, *Women, Crime and the Criminal Justice System*. Lexington, D.C.: Heath and Co.

Canada, 1977, *National Advisory Committee on the Female Offender*, Report. Ottawa: Ministry of Solicitor General.

Courtis, M., 1970, *Attitudes to Crime and the Police in Toronto*. Toronto: Centre of Criminology, University of Toronto.

Crites, L. (ed.), 1976, *The Female Offender*. Lexington, D.C.: Heath and Co.

Datesman, S.K.; F.R. Scarpatti; and R.M. Stephenson, 1975, "Female

Delinquency: an Application of Self and Opportunity Theories''. *Journal of Research in Crime and Delinquency* 12 (2): 107-123.

Feinman, C., 1979, ''Sex Role Stereotypes and Justice for Women''. *Crime and Delinquency* (Jan.): 87-94.

Fox, J. and T. Hartnagel, 1979, ''Changing Social Roles and Female Crime in Canada: a Time Series Analysis''. *Canadian Review of Sociology and Anthropology* 16 (1): 96-104.

Haft, M.G., 1974, ''Women in Prison: Discriminatory Practices and Some Solutions''. *Clearinghouse Review* 8: 1-6.

Jones, Ann, 1980, *Women Who Kill*. N.Y.: Holt, Rinehart and Winston.

Kestenbaum, S.E., 1977, ''Women's Liberation for Women Offenders''. *Social Casework* 58: 77-83.

Lambert, L.R. and P.G. Madden, 1976, ''The Adult Female Offender: the Road from Institution to Community Life''. *Canadian Journal of Criminology and Corrections* 18 (4): 319-331.

Martinson, R., 1974, ''What Works? Questions and Answers About Prison Reform''. *The Public Interest* 35: 22-54.

Mawby, R.I., 1977, ''Sexual Discrimination and the Law''. *Probation* 24: 39-43.

May, D., 1977, ''Delinquent Girls Before the Courts''. *Medicine, Science and the Law* 17: 203-212.

McDonald, L., 1969, ''Crime and Punishment in Canada''. *Canadian Review of Sociology and Anthropology* 6 (4): 212-236.

McGowan, B.C. and K.L. Blumenthal, 1978, ''Children of Women Prisoners: a Forgotten Minority'' in Crites, L. (ed.), *op. cit.*

Nagel, S.S. and L.J. Weitzman, 1971, ''Women as Litigants''. *The Hastings Law Journal* 23 (1) Nov.: 171-198.

Parsloe, P., 1972, ''Cross-Sex Supervision in the Probation and After-Care Service''. *British Journal of Criminology* 12: 169-279.

Pollack, O., 1950, *The Criminality of Women*. Philadelphia: The University of Pennsylvania Press.

Potter, J., 1978, ''In Prison, Women are Different''. *Corrections Magazine*, December: 14-47.

Prins, Herschel, 1980, *Offenders, Deviants, or Patients?* London: Tavistock.

Rogers, S. and C. Carey, 1979, *Child Care Needs of Female Offenders*. Toronto: Ontario Ministry of Correctional Services.

Romig, D.A., 1978, *Justice for Our Children*. Lexington, D.C.: Heath & Co.

Ross, R.R.; C. Currie; and B. Krug-McKay, 1980, *The Female Offender: Treatment and Training*. Toronto: Ontario Ministry of Correctional Services.

Simon, R.J., 1975, *The Contemporary Woman and Crime*. Washington: U.S. Government Printing Office.

Smart, C., 1976, *Women, Crime and Criminology. A Feminist Critique*. London: Routledge and Kegan Paul.

Smart, C. and B. Smart (eds.), 1978, *Women, Sexuality and Social Control*. London: Routledge and Kegan Paul.

Smith, L.S., 1978, "Sexist Assumptions and Female Delinquency: An Empirical Investigation" in Smart and Smart (eds.), *op. cit.*, pp. 74-88.

Terry, R.M., 1970, "Discrimination in the Handling of Juvenile Offenders by Social Control Agencies". In P.G. Garabedian and D.C. Gibbons (eds.) *Becoming Delinquent*. New York: Aldine Press.

Velimesis, M.L., 1975, "The Female Offender". *Crime and Delinquency Literature* 7 (1): 94-112.

Waller, I., 1974, *Men Released From Prison*. Toronto: University of Toronto Press.

Walter, T.L. and Mills, C.M., 1980, "A Behavioural Employment Intervention Program for Reducing Juvenile Delinquency". In Ross, R.R. and Gendreau, P. (eds.) *Effective Correctional Treatment*. Toronto: Butterworths.

Woods, G. and H. Sim, 1981, *Highlights of Federal Initiatives in Criminal Justice:* 1966-1980. Ottawa: Solicitor General, Research Division.

Index

THE CARLETON LIBRARY SERIES

CARLETON CONTEMPORARIES

AN INDEPENDENT FOREIGN POLICY FOR CANADA? Edited by Stephen Clarkson

THE DECOLONIZATION OF QUEBEC: AN ANALYSIS OF LEFT-WING NATIONALISM by Henry Milner and Sheilagh Hodgins Milner

THE MACKENZIE PIPELINE: ARCTIC GAS AND CANADIAN ENERGY POLICY Edited by Peter H. Pearse

CONTINENTAL COMMUNITY? INDEPENDENCE AND INTEGRATION IN NORTH AMERICA Edited by W.A. Axline, J.E. Hyndman, P.V. Lyon and M.A. Molot

THE RAILWAY GAME: A STUDY IN SOCIO-TECHNOLOGICAL OBSOLESCENCE by J. Lukasiewicz

FOREMOST NATION: CANADIAN FOREIGN POLICY AND A CHANGING WORLD Edited by N. Hillmer and G. Stevenson

GENERAL LIST

1. DICCIONARIO DE REFERENCIAS DEL ''poema de mio cid'', compiled and arranged by José Jurado
2. THE POET AND THE CRITIC: A Literary Correspondence Between D. C. Scott and E. K. Brown, edited by Robert L. McDougall